Improving Project Management Skills and Techniques

M. Pete Spinner

Prentice Hall
Englewood Cliffs, New Jersey 07632

LIBRARY OF CONGRESS
Library of Congress Cataloging-in-Publication Data

Spinner, M.
    Improving project management skills and techniques / M. Pete
Spinner.
        p.   cm.
    Includes index.
    ISBN 0-13-452831-X
    1. Industrial project management.   I. Title.
T56.8.S65 1988
658.4'04--dc19   88-9689
                                                              CIP

Editorial/production supervision and
  interior design: **Kathryn Pavelec**
Manufacturing buyer: **Robert Anderson**

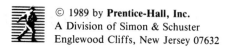 © 1989 by **Prentice-Hall, Inc.**
A Division of Simon & Schuster
Englewood Cliffs, New Jersey 07632

Printed in the United States of America

10 9 8 7 6 5 4 3 2 1

ISBN   0-13-452831-X

PRENTICE-HALL INTERNATIONAL (UK) LIMITED, *London*
PRENTICE-HALL OF AUSTRALIA PTY. LIMITED, *Sydney*
PRENTICE-HALL CANADA INC., *Toronto*
PRENTICE-HALL HISPANOAMERICANA, S.A., *Mexico*
PRENTICE-HALL OF INDIA PRIVATE LIMITED, *New Delhi*
PRENTICE-HALL OF JAPAN, INC., *Tokyo*
SIMON & SCHUSTER ASIA PTE. LTD., *Singapore*
EDITORA PRENTICE-HALL DO BRASIL, LTDA., *Rio de Janeiro*

This book is dedicated to
my mother, "a woman of valor."

"She openeth her mouth with wisdom;
and in her tongue is the law of kindness."

Contents

Part II Case Histories

Preface

Almost forty years have passed since the forerunners of project management, the critical path method (CPM) and the program evaluation and review technique (PERT), were first used. Their popularity increased through the years, and the benefits gained were published in many trade publications. At first, these benefits were publicized in construction trade magazines, then in publications relating to industrial operations, and finally, all facets of business and industry perceived applications that would increase productivity.

The project management techniques became popular tools for many engaged in research and development projects, marketing new or revised products, developing a new product, installing computer systems, and installing energy management systems as they became able to complete successful projects. There was a good growth rate in the acceptance of project management techniques. And the entrance on the scene of the personal computer allows for an improvement in project management skills.

The personal computer has permitted the concept of project management to expand phenomenally. One of the main reasons is that computer hardware and software suppliers have become aware that there is a large market for application packages whose use does not require computer graduates. Personal computers are "user friendly." As a result, the proliferation of "floppy disk" software has truly advanced the use of project management in the business and industrial world. Project timing, costs, labor/personnel, and other resources—any or all of these can now be managed more successfully with comparatively less effort and fewer "panic" situations.

In most fields it is necessary to plan and schedule projects, whether the emphasis is on timing, costs, or other resources (including personnel and labor skills).

Today's project environment is both more complex and more expansive than in the past and now requires the use of disciplined methods for proper planning and scheduling. "I can do all of this in my head" may have been a workable approach for some project managers in the past, but today's environment will not permit it.

The author's first text, *Elements of Project Management,* provided the fundamentals for arranging an effective plan and schedule for a project, as well as providing the methods for monitoring and controlling the project once it was under way. *Improving Project Management Skills and Techniques* strives to improve on the fundamentals by addressing present needs and situations through use of the computer. The ability to calculate accurately and rapidly—the ability to manipulate the data—permits more effective analysis and planning.

Manipulating data allows personnel associated with implementation of the project to become accounted for in the spirit of achieving a successful project. The current emphasis on more participative management and employee involvement (PM/EI) in business and industry is inherent in applying project management principles. This becomes immediately apparent when setting objectives, which is the initial stage of any planning process.

Much of this book, in summary form, has been used by the author to train participants in seminars and technology courses. In its complete and final form, the book will be useful in the following areas:

- Learning centers of businesses and industries that wish to offer program instruction in project management
- Vocational training centers that offer programs in construction engineering technology, industrial engineering technology, and computer programming and systems
- Basic project management seminars offered as intensive two- or three-day courses at a continuing education center
- The project management segment of a business management course in a college curriculum
- Self-training in the major elements of project management

The book is organized as follows: In Chapters 1 through 6 the fundamentals presented in *Elements of Project Management* are summarized, showing the basic steps in preparing a plan and schedule. In Chapter 7 project management software is used in calculating schedules, assigning responsibilities, updating reports, analyzing costs, and planning personnel/labor allocations. A sample project illustrates the application of project management techniques for organizing and directing it in a timely manner. Effective handling of costs and personnel/labor is also shown, culminating in a successful project.

The theme of the sample project is the installation of an energy conservation project (more specifically, an energy management system); however, the methods described have universal project management applications. Varied projects can be considered, including engineering and construction of facilities, as well as other projects in the fields of research and development, product development, marketing new products, installing computer systems, implementing manufacturing and management systems, planning and financing new business ventures, and establishing new training programs—all of these being representative of appropriate project management applications.

Chapters 8 and 9 provide case histories of two projects, the *Southfork Building Construction Project* and *Installing an Energy Management System*. The projects have different themes, but both utilize project management techniques for successful implementation. The Southfork Building Construction Project is a conventional construction project that portrays the project management skills involved in planning, scheduling, and controlling the timing, costs, and personnel/labor used to facilitate the general contractor in directing the work of the subcontractors. Also included are some features utilizing computer software, together with work experience, that makes this project valuable for teaching and for reference.

The second case history, Installing an Energy Management System, applies project management techniques to the preparation of a feasibility study. Many suppliers, engineers, finance personnel, and business planners know the value of an adequate feasibility report in obtaining project approval from management.

Using project management skills in preparing a feasibility report not only provides a uniquely effective method of obtaining project approval, but starts the process of using the project management approach in implementing the project. The uniqueness of utilizing the computer for this application could open the door for this method in future applications.

ACKNOWLEDGMENTS

This book could not have been completed without the assistance and encouragement of others. The support and cooperation of those at the Lawrence Institute of Technology and Ford Motor Company must be acknowledged. My wife, Margaret, patiently endured many boring weekends and evenings so that I could struggle through—and not forgotten are her patient efforts to keep my work areas orderly. A very special thanks to my able assistant in our seminars and other training sessions, Nan Scullin, who provided encouragement to continue. Her efforts made possible a timely and successful completion of this project.

I would also like to thank Honeywell Information Systems and International Business Machines Publications Support Services for permitting me to use excerpts from their various publications.

A very special thanks goes to Pertmaster International, Inc. (3235 Kifer Road, Santa Clara, CA 95051), for the use of their software packages, Pertmaster and Pertmaster Advance. The contributions that were offered have been very helpful in fulfilling the purpose of writing this book.

M. Pete Spinner, P.E.

Chapter 1

Introduction

In recent years the practice of project management has been structured into elements that include the management of scope, time, cost, quality, human resources, and communication. These elements may be defined as follows:

1. *Managing the scope* of the project is controlling the project based on an understanding of the aims, goals, and objectives of the sponsor of the project.
2. *Managing time* is planning, scheduling, and controlling (including monitoring) the project to achieve the time objectives proposed.
3. *Managing costs* is a term that relates to accumulating, organizing, and analyzing data for making cost-related decisions. (Cost management may be considered the *primary* function.)

   (Time management and cost management may constitute the very essence of project management.)
4. *Managing communications* concerns itself with the information flow among the members of the project team.
5. *Managing human resources* concentrates on the people in the organization.
6. *Managing the quality* of the project assures the production of a high-quality product or result upon completion of the project.

Each element is made up of any number of subelements. The intent of this book is to use these elements as they are most commonly used, thus providing the reader with the necessary basics to implement a successful project. Before proceeding with a discussion of the major topics, we shall define some additional terms related to managing projects.

DEFINITIONS

Project management is defined in business and industry as managing and directing time, material, personnel, and costs to complete a particular project in an orderly, economical manner, and to meet established objectives of time, cost, and technical results. Three major phases of a project, known as the project management cycle, are:

1. *Planning:* the initial phase of a project, where the plan of action is developed into a logical order and shown in an arrow diagram. The planning phase represents *what* work has to be done to complete the project.
2. *Scheduling:* the second phase of a project, detailing the time at which each job is to be started and completed. The times assigned for starting and completing activities are predicated on the float calculations of each of the durations of the individual project items. The scheduling phase represents *when* the work needs to be done.
3. *Controlling:* the third phase of a project, in which the progress of the project is monitored as it gets under way.

Although there is no specific definition, there are several distinguishing characteristics associated with a project: a specific starting point and a specific end point; well-defined objectives; a unique and not repetitious endeavor; cost and time schedules designed to produce a specified product or result; and many organizational and functional lines involved in achieving the objectives.

Employing project management principles in planning, scheduling, and controlling projects, when applied properly, should ensure a high degree of success in completing a project on time and within the cost and labor/personnel budgets. Among the principles that are used in projects are: network planning, management by objectives, management by exception, cost analysis, and labor/personnel allocation. Theories supporting these principles are major subjects in themselves, and numerous textbooks are available for in-depth study; only their applications are discussed in this book. Definitions and areas of application of these principles are as follows:

- *Network analysis (or planning):* graphic analysis of a project, showing the plan of action through the use of a graphic diagram (used in project planning)
- *Management by objectives:* a technique that defines objectives and arranges a disciplined procedure to measure performance against the planned objectives (used in project planning and project control)

- *Management by exception:* a technique that signals the problems for which the manager's attention is needed (used in project control)
- *Cost scheduling:* distribution of project costs over the duration of the project
- *Cost minimizing:* a technique used to reduce the time required for completing a project with the least amount of additional cost
- *Resource allocation:* assigning resources to each project activity, such as labor, personnel, costs, and equipment
- *Resource leveling:* a method of scheduling activities within their available float times so as to minimize fluctuations in day-to-day resource requirements

In another technique, *simulation,* used at times in network analysis, alternative plans, including resource leveling, are evaluated to determine the best project schedule.

Network planning and the associated project management principles are becoming increasingly popular in business. Initially, the benefits to be gained by using project management principles may have to be accepted on face value. However, it is the author's belief that the validity of these benefits will be proved when projects that use project management principles in a proper manner are seen to be completed successfully.

NETWORK PLANNING TECHNIQUES

The principle most often applied in project analysis is network planning (or network analysis). To understand network planning, one should review its history, have a knowledge of the differences between arrow diagramming and the conventional bar chart for graphical planning, and have a knowledge of the major diagramming techniques: the project evaluation review technique (PERT), the critical path method (CPM), and precedence diagramming (PCD).

Learning a diagramming technique for effective application is difficult, especially during the early stages of learning. Because of this concern, the subject is given special consideration in this book. It is the opinion of the author that the CPM approach (also known as *arrow diagramming,* or the *i,j method*) is the easiest to understand, and because of its concentration on displaying logic, this method is the diagramming technique used in this book. The other two diagramming techniques are explained briefly in Chapter 2.

In the 1950s two separate events occurred about the same time in which graphical methods were used to control the utilization of labor/personnel, time, material, costs, and facilities for project purposes. An interesting aspect was that the graphical or diagramming approach was not only used for the first time, but the two applications used the two diagramming techniques that became the most popular. The U.S. Navy's *Polaris* program used the *PERT* approach for planning and coordinating the projects associated with the development of the missile program, while DuPont adopted the *critical path* concept to improve the planning, scheduling, and controlling of their projects. The popularity of these two diagramming techniques has expanded their use to many varied projects, such as construction, design programs, model changeovers, launching a new product, and practically any other series of actions that form a complete program having a start and a finish.

The major differences between the *PERT* and *critical path* diagramming methods over the years have gradually been reduced. One reason is that the critical path concept, which is used in this book, has adopted many of the PERT features, such as highlighting milestones (or major events), and using, at times, its three-estimate approach. Included among the major differences between the PERT and critical path concepts are the following:

- PERT is "event oriented"; critical path is "activity oriented." (An event is a specific point in time, whereas an activity consumes time; therefore, PERT calculations provide starting and finishing times for the event, whereas critical path calculations provide for the starting and finishing times of the activity.)
- PERT calculates the probability of meeting a scheduled date; critical path has no provision for determining probabilities.
- PERT uses three time estimates for each activity; critical path uses one estimate.

Precedence diagramming is another form of graphic portrayal that has been popularized by the academic community and a number of hardware and software firms. The intent of this approach is to simplify, as well as clarify, the planning diagrams. This is the case for some types of projects; however, to suggest a universal change in this method would result in inefficiencies in many planning programs that have used the conventional diagramming (*i,j*) approach. The amount of improvement to be gained would not merit the retraining program that would be required.

Network diagrams overcome the deficiencies of bar chart construction, especially during the planning process, by providing the necessary information:

- Network diagrams explicitly show interrelations between jobs. A network diagram shows which jobs can be done concurrently, which ones precede, and which ones follow other jobs.
- Jobs with critical schedules are specified with their required beginning and completion dates.
- Jobs of a noncritical nature are also shown with optional beginning and end dates.

Using computer calculations based on the network diagram also permits more rapid and accurate updating of the project schedule.

In Figure 1–1 the bar chart indicates the beginning and end dates for the engineering, material procurement, construction, equipment delivery, and installation of an engineering project. For effective planning, more accurate information is required. Relationships among these jobs cannot be shown, and questions cannot be answered:

- What parts of these jobs can be done concurrently?
- What parts of each job must be completed before other parts begin?
- Must certain jobs or parts of jobs be given priority so as not to hold up scheduled completion of the project?
- Do some jobs or parts of jobs have optional starting and end dates, and what, specifically, are these optional dates?

These questions can be answered by preparing a planning (or network) diagram for the project. An example of a simple network diagram is shown in Figure 1–2. More information is required, knowledge of the technique to construct such a diagram is necessary, and additional thought and effort are essential before such a plan can be used. (Chapter 2 provides the necessary guidelines to prepare the network plan.)

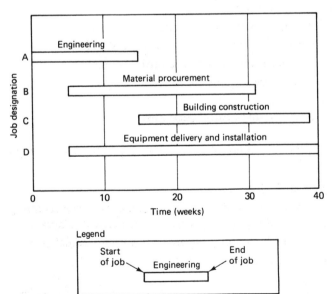

FIGURE 1-1 Bar chart for planning and scheduling a project.

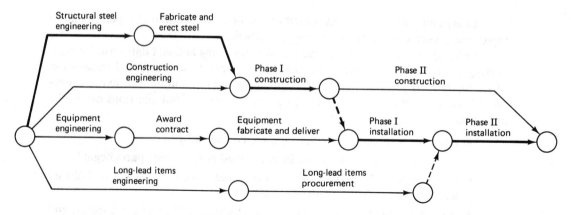

FIGURE 1-2   Network diagram for planning a project.

BENEFITS AND LIMITATIONS
OF NETWORK PLANNING

Proper planning requires effort and dedication, but the rewards make all of this worthwhile. Included among the benefits to be gained are the following:

- A disciplined basis for planning a project
- A clear picture of the scope of the project that can be read and understood easily by someone who is not familiar (but knowledgeable of the network diagramming technique) with the project
- A means of communicating what is to be done in the project
- A vehicle for use in evaluating alternative strategies and objectives
- A means of defining relationships among the project items
- A means of pinpointing those responsible for accomplishing the jobs that make up the project
- An excellent vehicle for training project personnel

There are also some limitations in network diagrams; following are the main concerns:

- The network is often difficult to interpret.
- A great deal of time is usually needed to prepare changes, often requiring a great deal of time for making modifications to the network diagram.
- A network makes it difficult to note estimated costs versus actual costs.
- Individual skills are not recognized.

These concerns are overcome through special procedures and techniques that are discussed throughout the book.

It should also be noted that while bar charts have limitations for planning purposes, they do provide an excellent communication expedient to management through their construction. Bar charts can depict, more readily than arrow diagrams, a summary of the status of the projects and are used extensively in reporting on the progress of projects.

PROJECT REPORTING

A report may be an important part of a project manager's responsibilities, as it usually is the main line of communication. Communicating with management and with other members associated with the project goes a long way toward the successful undertaking of a project. Status reports can be relatively short, and there may also be a need for a long report prepared either at the planning phase of the project (to support the objectives) or at the end of the project (as a syllabus). The key elements of a project report are as follows:

- Introduction
  - –Purpose
  - –Scope (limits)
  - –Background
- Summary (highlights of the project)
- Conclusions
- Project description
- Appendix

The *introduction* should briefly describe the *purpose* (a statement of the objective or objectives), *scope, limits* (associated with money, time, design criteria, labor, etc.), and *background* (facts behind the project).

The *summary* entitled *Highlights* or *Executive Highlights,* is made up of numbered or bullet (•) statements. Its content summarizes the completed project report. If it is a small report, it may contain decisions and judgments based on the findings given in the report.

The *conclusions* and recommendations may be combined. Each recommendation will be derived from one or more of the conclusions. The report needs to provide alternative courses of action, or options, before arriving at a conclusion or the preferred approach.

The remainder of the report, the project description and appendix, contains the detail, calculations, and reference material that support the introduction, summary, conclusions, and recommendations. The *project description* represents the "meat" of the report—*what* was done, *how* it was done, and *why* it was done. Although the description of the report contains the pertinent information, several of the key elements of the report, specifically the summary and conclusions, are more widely read, and these should be precise and comprehensive.

A long project report can be structured as shown in the following outline.

TITLE PAGE
A. Letter of transmittal
B. Table of contents
C. Introduction
D. Summary
E. Conclusions
F. Project description
   1. Plan
      a. Statement(s) of objective
      b. List of activities (with descriptions)
      c. Arrow diagram
   2. Schedule
      a. Time estimates
      b. Calendar schedule (tabulations)
      c. Bar chart schedule
   3. Project monitoring
      a. Summary bar chart
      b. Status report to management
   4. Project costs
      a. Expenditure schedule
      b. Cost control (indicated cost outcome)
      c. Cost minimizing (time/cost trade-offs)
   5. Labor plan and schedule
      a. Labor allocation (using the earliest start-time schedule)
      b. Labor leveling
G. Appendix
   1. Calculations
      a. Activity groupings
      b. Subdiagrams
      c. Earliest start times
      d. Latest finish times
      e. Critical path
      f. Total float tabulation
      g. Schedule tabulation
      h. Tabulation of required labor
      i. Schedule of required labor (bar chart approach)
      j. Load chart

  k. Tabulation of leveled labor
  l. Schedule of leveled labor (bar chart approach)
  m. Load chart
 2. Computer printouts
 3. Reference material

Plan of Action

For project management purposes a project report normally starts with the project objectives. Prior to establishing the project objectives, there usually is an approval process that contains steps like those experienced in a project where the project management approach can be applied, with project approval being the objective. In this case, the following milestones (or steps) from objectives to management approval are attained:

 1. Prepare a plan of action for the feasibility study.

 2. Gather fact-finding data on the present system.

 3. Design an improved system.

 4. Compare the cost of the improved system with that of the present system.

 5. Structure the feasibility report.

 6. Obtain management approval.

In Chapter 9, we use these steps in completing a feasibility study as an expedient toward obtaining management approval.

SUMMARY

Having project management techniques to guide and control the course of a project allows for a high degree of confidence of achieving success. Although these techniques will not replace value judgments, they do require a good amount of effort and make one *"think through"* the project in greater detail.

A plan provides data on which to base schedules that have credibility. It enables quick rescheduling of a project to meet changing or unpredictable conditions. It enables real control of projects. *And* it creates a high level of communication. *Most of all,* you need to *think!*

A plan enables more efficient use of resources, such as personnel, equipment, and money. The computer allows for even more efficient use as projects become larger and more complex.

EXERCISES

1. Define the following project management principles.
   (a) Network analysis.
   (b) Management by objectives.
   (c) Management by exception.
   (d) Cost scheduling.
   (e) Cost minimizing.
   (f) Resource allocation.
   (g) Resource leveling.
2. A project management cycle consists of three major phases. Identify them and provide a brief definition of each.
3. Prepare a table that shows the advantages and disadvantages of bar charts or Gantt charts. Do the same for the network diagramming method.
4. What are the differences between the critical path, precedence, and program evaluation review technique methods of network (planning) diagramming?
5. Define the six major elements in project management.

Chapter 2
Planning a Project

Planning is considered by many authorities to be the most important phase of project management. More time needs to be devoted to proper planning, and a disciplined approach to planning is not only desirable but essential. A common response when approached with a suggestion for the use of network diagramming for planning purposes is, "I always do it in my head." In essence, the planning diagram is a graphical presentation of the thought process in planning. A graphic analysis provides a "picture" of the scope of the project. Most important of all, preparing a plan by this method forces one to "think through" the entire project.

Three methods of diagramming are most widely used for project planning: the project evaluation review technique (PERT), precedence diagramming (PCD), and the critical path method (CPM). The CPM method of arrow diagramming for planning a project is the procedure employed in this book for providing a step-by-step approach, and tends to simplify an otherwise complicated planning "tool." There are important advantages to this method, one of the most important being that it is an excellent means of communicating *what* is to be done in the project to those that are involved. (The other two methods are explained in this chapter using the same project, the Waste Heat Recovery Project, to illustrate their individual techniques for providing a graphic display of the project plan.)

Planning a project begins with the preparation of comprehensive statements of the objectives; second, determining the activities on jobs that must be done to complete a project; and then arranging the sequence in which these jobs need to be done. Drawing the arrow diagram is the final step in this procedure. Developing the arrow diagram uses the same approach as does the plan: preparing a list of jobs required for the project, determining the relationships among the jobs, and recording these relationships on an arrow diagram.

The mechanics of making a proper arrow diagram require working knowledge of such terms as "arrows," "dummy arrows," "nodes," and "activities." An arrow is drawn for each job. The sequence of the arrows indicate the flow of work from the beginning to the end of each project. The complete diagram has one beginning point and one end point. Arrow junctions are called nodes (or events). Nodes are usually numbered, which is useful for identifying the location of the arrows in the network.

The step-by-step approach of the arrow diagramming procedure is best illustrated by going through an actual project. By using a project that will include work activities from the fields of engineering, production, sales, and advertising, the various principles of project management can best be illustrated.

PLANNING PROCEDURES

The planning phase can be the most time-consuming phase of the total project cycle; however, the time spent planning, or *what* has to be done, can also be the most rewarding. *Planning* a project will follow these steps:

1. Establish objectives.
   - State objectives. These will be derived from the requirements that motivated the project.
   - List interim objectives or *milestones*. These are significant events in meeting the main objectives.
   - Designate responsible personnel or departments. (These are the important groups whose participation in planning and scheduling are required for successful project implementation. These participating activities need to be identified early in project development.)
2. Develop a plan.
   - List *what* jobs (or activities) have to be done to complete the project.
   - Delineate the jobs by determining their relationships:
     - Determine which jobs precede and succeed every other job.
     - Determine which jobs can be accomplished concurrently.
3. Draw the arrow diagram.
   - Show the sequence in a planning (arrow) diagram. The planning process becomes complete when the graphic display in the form of a planning diagram displays the project work items and their interrelationships.

Determining *what* is to be done must be the result of a careful analysis of the project by those knowledgeable in the particular field. The network plan then makes use of an arrow diagram to display graphically the sequence and interrelations of the jobs required.

DEVELOPING A NETWORK PLANNING DIAGRAM

We use as an example the Waste Heat Recovery Project. Snyder Industries, a manufacturer of glass fibers used in industrial materials, has awarded a contract to Clawson Enterprises to design and install a "turnkey" heat recovery system. This system will recover the waste heat from the stack of a glass melting furnace, which is part of a new facility now under construction. The waste heat will be used to supplement the building heating system.

The contract provides for the project to start no later than October 4, 1982, and for the heat recovery system to be operable by April 22, 1983, a total project duration of 29 weeks. Snyder Industries has authorized a budget of $240,500 to fund this project. Another provision of the contract requires Clawson Enterprises to develop a plan of action to implement the second phase of the heat recovery system, which is scheduled to be started after the stack waste heat recovery system now under contract is operating.

Clawson Enterprises plans to utilize the necessary project management techniques to prepare an effective plan and schedule to complete the project on time and on budget. Also to be considered is the allocation of available resources to optimize the utilization of labor and personnel made available for this project.

The planning phase will follow the following procedural steps.

Step 1. Establish objectives. The initial effort in the planning phase is to establish objectives. These are shown in Figure 2–1. Dates that are to be determined are designated as TBD. Objectives concerning the expenditure budget as well as labor/personnel budget requirements are handled in the appropriate sections of the book.

Step 2. Establish the project items required. Once the objectives are established, the next step is to identify the jobs (or activities) required for accomplishing the project. At times it may be desirable to provide a description with each work activity. These are shown in Figure 2–2.

OBJECTIVES/MILESTONES	TIMING	RESPONSIBILITY
Start waste heat recovery project	October 4, 1982	Industrial relations
Complete organization	TBD	Engineering
Start equipment procurement	TBD	Engineering
Start equipment installation	TBD	Engineering
Complete waste heat recovery project	April 29, 1983	Engineering

FIGURE 2-1 Objectives for the Waste Heat Recovery Project.

ACTIVITY	DESCRIPTION
1. Design heat recovery system	Design the system to convert the stack waste heat to steam
2. Write specifications	Using designs, write specifications to instruct installation contractor
3. Research systems	Prepare optional designs to support selected systems
4. Develop organization	Determine personnel organization best suited to operate systems
5. Procure equipment	Select best proposal from equipment suppliers; award order; supervise fabrication and delivery
6. Install heat recovery system	Upon receipt of equipment, mount equipment, and make electrical and mechanical connections
7. Select operating manager	After organization is determined, select manager to supervise operations
8. Develop operating procedures	Operating manager and personnel will document the mode of operation
9. Hire operating personnel	Operating manager will select persons qualified to operate systems
10. Train operating personnel	Selected persons will receive specialized training needed to operate system
11. Select phase II project	Determine next energy conservation project that will be most feasible to install
12. Approve phase II project	Obtain management approval after submitting feasibility report
13. Prepare phase II project plan	Prepare planning diagram to graphically portray the plan of action.

FIGURE 2-2   Activities required for the Waste Heat Recovery Project.

Step 3. Divide the jobs into groups representing major sections of work. As an aid in determining the relationships between jobs, it may be desirable to group them under major categories. Known in many project management "circles" as work breakdown structure (WBS), this expedient may simplify the determination of how the jobs relate to each other. Major work sections for the Waste Heat Recovery Project are shown in Figure 2-3.

Step 4. Draw subdiagrams. Subdiagramming (Figures 2-4 and 2-5) sets up some preliminary diagrams to show the relationships of each group, which becomes

MAJOR SECTIONS OF WORK

Installation

- Research systems.
- Procure equipment.
- Install heat recovery system.

Design

- Design heat recovery system.
- Write specifications.

Personnel

- Develop organization.
- Hire operating personnel.
- Train operating personnel.

Operations

- Select operation manager.
- Develop operating procedures.

Phase II

- Select phase II project.
- Approve phase II project.
- Prepare phase II project plan.

FIGURE 2-3 Groups representing major sections of work of the Waste Heat Recovery Project.

useful in developing the network diagram. (This step is optional. An alternative approach is to expand the WBS shown in step 3.) Thoroughly prepared subdiagrams will become a valuable aid in preparing the arrow diagram. Rules associated with arrow diagramming are shown in the following section as a prelude to doing the final step.

Arrow Diagramming

1. In an arrow diagram, an arrow is used to represent a job or activity.

    a. There is no time dimension on the arrow.
    b. The work is assumed to flow in the direction in which the arrow points.

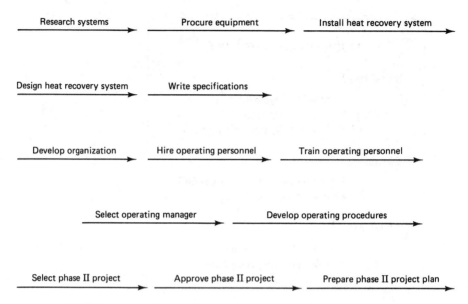

FIGURE 2–4 Subdiagram (first step) of the Waste Heat Recovery Project.

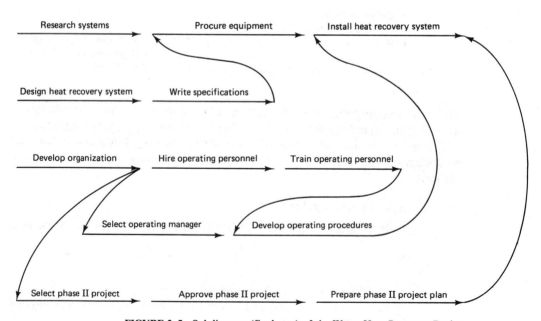

FIGURE 2–5 Subdiagram (final step) of the Waste Heat Recovery Project.

2. Job sequences are indicated by the way the arrows are interconnected. The arrow interconnections show job sequences.

   a. Job A, *design,* must be completed before job B, *fabricate,* is started.

   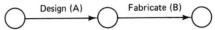

   b. Job A, *design,* can be done concurrently with job B, *write specifications.*

   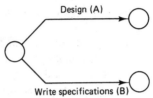

   c. Jobs A and B can be done concurrently and must be completed before job C begins.

   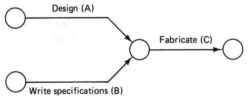

3. Two types of arrows are used in diagramming:

   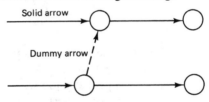

   a. *Solid* arrows represent jobs or activities.
   - The solid arrow represents a job or activity that consumes time (has a duration) and resources.
   - Work is assumed to flow in the direction in which the arrow points.
   - The length can vary (time or duration is not indicated by the length).

   b. *Dummy* arrows show special interrelations.
   - Dummy arrows are drawn as dashed lines.
   - Dummy arrows do not represent a job or activity; they have no duration and do not consume resources such as labor or dollars.
   - Dummy arrows are used as a convenience in drawing the network.
   - Dummy arrows are used to maintain identification of activities.

4. The beginning and end of each arrow is called a *node*. A node has the same reference as an event. For example, node 1 can be noted as *start* design: node 2, *complete* design or *start* fabricate.

   a. The circles with numbers 1, 2, 3, and 4 are nodes.

   b. Job A can also be identified as job 1,2; job B as job 2,3; job C as job 3,4.

   c. Each arrow (job or activity) is identified by two nodes: the *i* node at the beginning of the arrow and the *j* node at the end of the arrow. *i* and *j* references are used in a number of computer programs developed on project management.

   d. A node has the same reference as an event.

   e. A node or event is a point in time and has no duration.

5. Effective planning of the jobs or activities in a project requires that certain techniques be adhered to in diagramming the network. For example, note the following diagram:

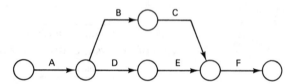

Job B in the diagram has the following positions in the project:

   a. Job B follows job A.

   b. Job B precedes job C.

   c. Job B can be performed concurrently with job D.

   d. Jobs B and D may start as soon as job A is completed.

6. When two or more arrows begin at the same node, this does not necessarily mean that the work they represent will be scheduled to start at the same time.

7. Two or more arrows that end at the same node do not necessarily have an identical "finish date."

Step 5. Develop the arrow diagram. Finally, the arrow diagram is developed to show the relationships of the groups (Figures 2–6 and 2–7). There may be several intermediate steps in drawing the arrow diagram when planning longer and more complex projects. But the work will be less involved and cumbersome if all the previous steps in the planning process are thoroughly prepared.

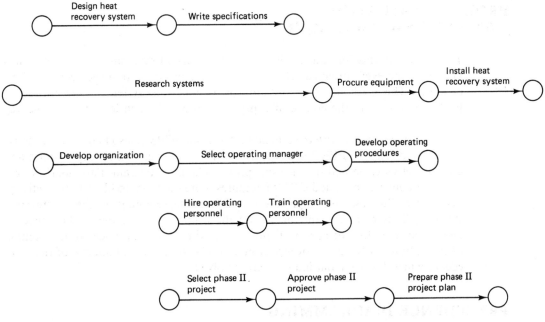

FIGURE 2-6 Planning diagram (first step) of the Waste Heat Recovery Project.

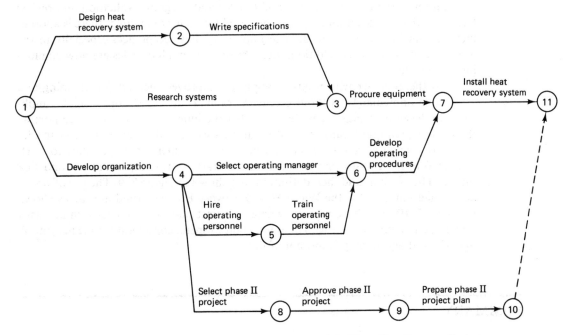

FIGURE 2-7 Planning diagram (final step) of the Waste Heat Recovery Project.

PROJECT EVALUATION
AND REVIEW TECHNIQUE

The project evaluation and review technique (PERT) diagramming method, also known as the event-oriented scheme, shows descriptions within the event symbols or nodes. This method is an adaptation of the milestone system, where milestones being key points in the course of a project can also be considered to be the key events.

When compared with the critical path method (CPM), also known as the activity-oriented scheme, PERT is unwieldy, as there are considerably more nodes and dummy activities needed for the same project planning diagram. Particularly where activities converge on a node, PERT requires more dummies to identify the activity. Figure 2–8 illustrates the application of PERT diagramming on the Waste Heat Recovery System project, and this should allow the reader to recognize the efficiency and the articulation, or lack of it, involved in the PERT approach. In the opinion of the author, PERT does not represent a good choice for the majority of the projects in which business and industry are involved.

PRECEDENCE DIAGRAMMING

In addition to the critical path method (CPM) and program evaluation and review technique (PERT) diagramming methods used for project planning, there is another method that has gained considerable popularity and acceptance, especially in the academic community. In addition, many businesses and industries are now employing this technique.

To the beginner who needs to apply an improved method for planning and scheduling immediately, without extensive training, the PDM approach is complicated to develop. It must be understood that the immediate objective is to portray the project plan graphically, so that it can be used. PDM requires the user to diagram work activities and their relationships with an understanding of start-to-start, start-to-finish, finish-to-finish, and finish-to-start relationships, and lag and link timing. The symbols and their definitions are shown in Figure 2–9. The use of precedence diagramming for the Waste Heat Recovery Project would appear as shown in Figure 2–10. For those projects where a project plan is to be drawn in an easily understood manner by one who does not want to spend considerable time in symbology, CPM diagramming is more useful.

SUMMARY

The initial step in developing a project plan is to establish the objectives. The project plan is then developed by transforming the interconnecting activities of the project

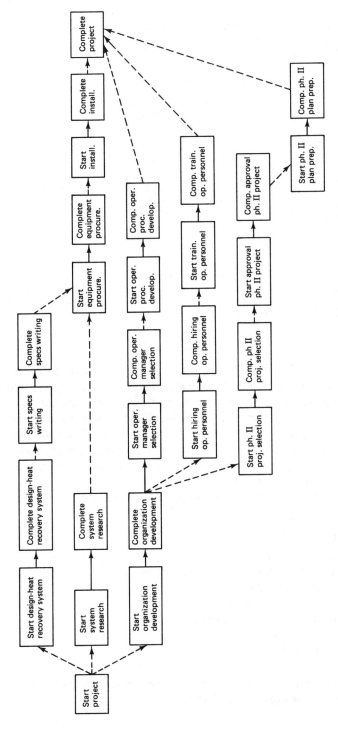

FIGURE 2-8 Project evaluation review technique diagram of the Waste Heat Recovery Project.

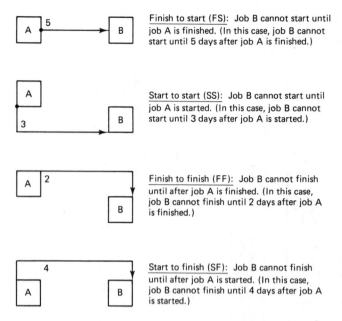

Finish to start (FS): Job B cannot start until job A is finished. (In this case, job B cannot start until 5 days after job A is finished.)

Start to start (SS): Job B cannot start until job A is started. (In this case, job B cannot start until 3 days after job A is started.)

Finish to finish (FF): Job B cannot finish until after job A is finished. (In this case, job B cannot finish until 2 days after job A is finished.)

Start to finish (SF): Job B cannot finish until after job A is started. (In this case, job B cannot finish until 4 days after job A is started.)

FIGURE 2–9 Symbols used to show precedence diagramming relationships.

into a network diagram. The diagram was constructed in accordance with the rules so that the network would be accurate and allow for consistent interpretations.

The main advantage of developing a project plan by the arrow diagramming technique is that you must "think through" the project. Even though this approach is time consuming, it is extremely rewarding. Your efforts will become noticeable especially when problems arise and quick responses and solutions are made possible through the background knowledge set up by the experience gained during development of the planning process.

Planning can also be summarized as follows:

1. Establish objectives.
2. Identify:
   a. Work items
   b. Interrelationships of work items
   c. Responsibilities
   d. Timing requirements
   e. Resource requirements
      • Personnel/labor
      • Costs

Although part of the planning process, resource requirements will be discussed in more detail in subsequent chapters.

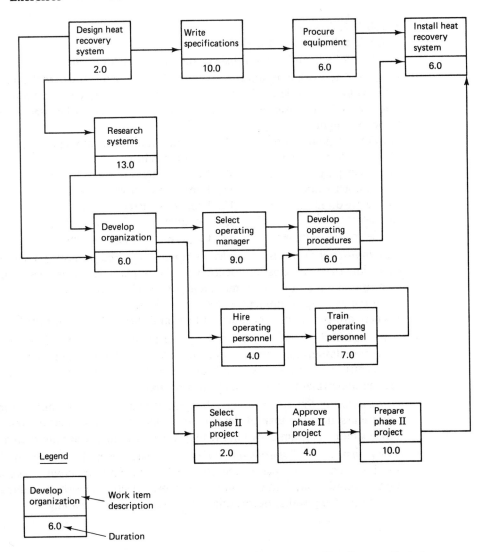

FIGURE 2-10 Precedence diagramming for the Waste Heat Recovery Project.

EXERCISES

1. Draw a diagram for the following:
   - Project consists of five jobs: A, B, C, D, and E.
   - At project start, jobs A and B can begin.
   - Job C follows job A (only).

- Job D follows A and B.
- Job E follows jobs B and C.
- When jobs D and E are finished, the project is complete.

2. Develop a network diagram for a theater planning project, where the major project jobs have been defined. The activities are listed below in a random fashion. There may be differences of opinion on the sequence to be used to arrive at "opening night."

  1. Form organization.
  2. Complete financing.
  3. Select play.
  4. Contact stars.
  5. Select director.
  6. Select cast.
  7. Select set designer.
  8. Conduct publicity campaign.
  9. Conduct rehearsals.
  10. Conduct dress rehearsals.
  11. Book out-of-town shows.
  12. Procure scenery.
  13. Conduct out-of-town shows.
  14. Prepare for opening night.

3. (*For Industrial Supervision students*) You are required to move your production operation from the existing location to a new plant 25 miles away. Develop a plan to make the move with minimum lost production time.
   - All the existing equipment will be reinstalled.
   - There are two similar production lines and they will be reinstalled.

4. (*For Engineering students*) Your architectural engineering firm has been chosen to prepare designs and specifications for a large building project. Develop a plan for identifying the responsibilities of the civil, electrical, and mechanical engineering departments to implement this project.

5. (*For Computer Systems students*) As systems manager of a manufacturing firm, you are assigned the task of developing a plan for an information system. Prepare a simple diagram showing the major activities in developing such a system.

6. (*For Construction Supervision students*) Prepare a sample network of 10 to 15 jobs involved in constructing a house. (Include such major activities as constructing the foundation, framing, siding, millwork, electrical work, plumbing, building and painting walls, decorating the interior, and landscaping.)

Chapter 3

Developing the Project Schedule

Before beginning the scheduling of a project, it will be necessary to estimate the time required to complete each activity. This information normally needs to be furnished by experienced persons who can establish the amount of time the job will require under specified conditions. Where there are estimates that appear biased, the three-estimate approach—optimistic, pessimistic, and most likely—may be used to offset the bias.

Simple knowledge of addition and subtraction is all that is needed with the manual method. The initial scheduling calculations can usually be done expeditiously by noting them directly on an arrow diagram. In this chapter earliest starting and latest finishing times of each project work item are explained.

Initially, computation of the earliest start times produces the project duration, which is checked against project objectives. If project timing objectives are not met, changes will be necessary. However, before specific duration times can be changed, it will be necessary to complete the latest finish times. In this chapter we explain how to develop the total float and identify the critical items. To meet project objectives, it may be necessary that the duration be compressed by expediting some of the critical items on the project. The earliest start and latest finish times make it possible to identify readily the critical items located on the critical path.

Although this chapter emphasizes manual schedule calculations, the use of computer calculations, explained in a subsequent chapter, may be more appropriate for use in most projects now that microcomputers have become popular. However, the manual approach does provide the background and an analysis of the major scheduling factors noted above, and therefore should be understood before alternative scheduling methods are used.

The principal benefits derived from timing calculations developed by this method are as follows:

- Establishing the project duration
- Identifying the critical project activities
- Identifying the project activities where there is scheduling flexibility without lengthening project duration

SCHEDULING PROCEDURE

In the scheduling phase we are concerned with the timing aspects; that is, how much time each job is expected to require for completion, and *when* each job will be scheduled to begin and end. Scheduling a project will follow this procedure:

1. After the sequence of jobs has been planned and laid out in a network diagram, the timing can be established.
   a. Estimate the time required to complete each project item.
   b. Calculate the scheduled times of each project item.
   c. Compare the required time (time estimate) with the available time to complete each job.
   d. Identify the critical jobs.
   e. Determine the float times of the noncritical jobs.
2. If the project duration time that is calculated initially is not acceptable, make adjustments to the plan so as to meet the project deadline that is acceptable.
3. Establish a time schedule. (Using a bar chart will show the schedule effectively)

TIMING ESTIMATES

After completing the initial arrow diagram, a time estimate is obtained for each job in the project, and shown on the arrow diagram. When shown on the diagram, certain rules for uniformity and clarity are applied:

- Place time estimates (the work time durations) on the bottom side of the arrow.
- Show time units (as a general statement or with each of the job time estimates).
- Use whole numbers for simplifying manual calculations. (However, most computer programs will accept decimals, that is, parts of a day, month, etc.)

Planning estimates are the initial estimates that are obtained and are based on how much time the job should actually take if everything proceeds on a normal basis. It is desirable that persons familiar with the work to be performed make the time estimates based on their best judgment. Since these persons may be held responsible for their estimates, there is a tendency for them to pad the estimates to provide a cushion for contingencies.

After the project duration has been calculated (assuming normal conditions), if it does not meet objectives, attention needs to be directed to the time estimates given those jobs that have critical timing. The timing of several of these jobs may need to be adjusted, so the scheduling calculation process begins again. Negotiating the shortening of time estimates with the parties responsible requires some diplomacy, as there may be a reluctance to make the job more difficult.

Three-Time-Estimate Approach

Persons familiar with the project who are supplying the estimates may be influenced by previous experiences, creating a bias in their opinions. To offset this bias, a method using three time estimates can be adopted. The three time estimates—optimistic, normal, and pessimistic—for each activity are used to offset the bias that may be present in a one-time estimate:

$$\text{expected time} = \frac{(\text{optimistic time}) + 4(\text{normal time}) + (\text{pessimistic time})}{6}$$

Optimistic time is the shortest possible time required for completing an activity. Everything goes as planned: deliveries are on time, machines and equipment operate without breakdowns, personnel work within the standards. *Normal time* is the time most frequently required if the activity were repeated many times under similar conditions. (This is the estimate that should be used in the arrow diagram, as there is no contingency added.) *Pessimistic time* is the maximum possible time required to complete an activity. About everything goes wrong: delivery difficulties, work delays, accidents.

When using the three estimates, the expected time will be biased toward the pessimistic time. The one-time-estimate approach usually has a contingency built in which tends to have the same estimated value as the three-time-estimate approach. This approach is used when there may be some uncertainty as to the scheduled timing estimates. Note on the project network diagram (Figure 3–1) the optimistic, scheduled, and pessimistic times for the critical project items in the waste heat recovery project.

With the three time estimates, the statisticians have provided formulas for calculating the probability of meeting the project duration or even meeting the scheduled finish date of an activity.

The basic factors used in the three time estimates can be translated into a distribution curve (Figure 3–2). The example used is the activity *develop organization*. The location of the time estimates on the time scale determines the type of

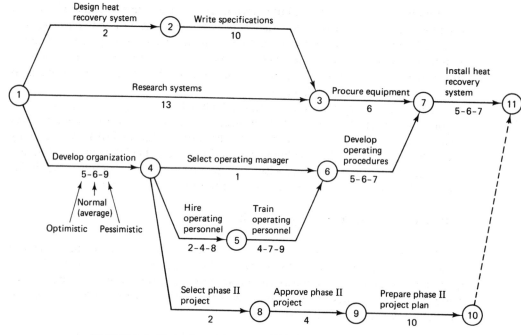

FIGURE 3-1   Three time estimates applied to the Waste Heat Recovery Project System.

curve that might represent the distribution: the spread of *a* (optimistic time) and *c* (pessimistic time), and the location of *b* (most likely time). It is assumed that the curve has only one peak—the most likely time for completion. The *b* at this peak represents the completion date that has the greatest probability of occurring, while the low points, *a* and *c*, indicate dates that have a small chance of being realized.

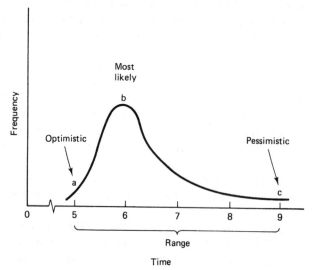

FIGURE 3-2   Distribution curve for activity *develop organization*.

The expected time to complete the activity *develop organization* is calculated as follows:

> Optimistic time: 5 weeks
> Pessimistic time: 9 weeks
> Most likely time: 6 weeks

$$\text{expected time, } t_e = \frac{5 + 4 \times 6 + 9}{6} = 6.3 \text{ weeks}$$

The method of estimating the probability that a schedule date can be derived is first, to determine the expected time (t_e) for each activity.

ACTIVITY	TIME (WEEKS)			
	Optimistic	Most likely, t_s	Pessimistic	Expected, t_e
Develop organization	5	6	9	6.3
Hire operating personnel	2	4	8	4.3
Train operating personnel	4	7	9	6.8
Develop operating procedures	5	6	7	6.0
Install heat recovery system	5	6	7	6.0
		29		29.4

From the table, the sum of the critical items equals the project duration. The two project duration values to be used are

> scheduled time, t_s = 29 weeks
> expected time, t_e = 29.4 weeks

The method for calculating the variance of the activity *develop organization* follows these steps. *Variance* is a term that describes the uncertainty associated with how much time will be required to complete the activity. If the variances are large (which indicates that the optimistic and pessimistic estimates are far apart), there is great uncertainty as to when the project will be completed. On the other hand, a small variance indicates very little uncertainty.

The *standard deviation* (σ) is a measure of the spread of a distribution. It is the root mean square of the deviations of the various items for their average. For our purposes, the standard deviation can be approximated as being equal to one-sixth of the range.

> Range: $9 - 5 = 4$
>
> Standard deviation: $\frac{4}{6} = 0.67$

In statistical terms the variance is equal to the standard deviation squared.

$$\text{variance} = \sigma^2$$

$$\sigma^2 = \left(\begin{array}{c}\text{standard}\\\text{deviation}\end{array}\right)^2 = 0.44$$

Calculating the variance for the total project is shown in the following table.

Activity (Critical)	Range	Standard Deviation	Variance
Develop organization	4	0.67	0.44
Hire operating personnel	6	1.00	1.0
Train operating personnel	5	0.83	0.69
Develop operating procedures	2	0.33	0.11
Install heat recovery system	2	0.33	0.11

$$\text{Project variance: } \Sigma\sigma^2 = 2.36$$

$$\sqrt{2.36} = 1.53$$

The square root of the sum of the critical project activity variances are used in the calculation for determining the probability of meeting the scheduled duration date.

The formula used by statisticians to provide the probability estimate is

$$Z = \frac{t_s - t_e}{\sigma} = \frac{29 - 29.4}{1.53} = \frac{-0.4}{1.53} = -0.26$$

where Z = measure related to the probability of meeting the scheduled data
t_s = scheduled time for the activity
t_e = expected time for the activity
σ^e = standard deviation—the square root of the sum of the variances of the activities (critical activities)

Using a table such as that shown in Figure 3-3, we find that for a value of $Z = -0.26$, the probability is 0.397. This means that there is a *39.7%* chance of meeting the scheduled date of *29 weeks* for the project.

It should be noted that the probability feature is not as widely used as it has been in the past because of the overly pessimistic times biasing the project completion time toward the pessimistic side. The validity of the probability calculations themselves has been questioned.

Z	PROBABILITY	Z	PROBABILITY
0.0	0.5000	−3	0.0013
0.1	0.5398	−2.9	0.0019
0.2	0.5793	−2.8	0.0026
0.3	0.6179	−2.7	0.0035
0.4	0.6554	−2.6	0.0047
0.5	0.6915	−2.5	0.0062
0.6	0.7257	−2.4	0.0082
0.7	0.7580	−2.3	0.0107
0.8	0.7881	−2.2	0.0139
0.9	0.8159	−2.1	0.0179
1.0	0.8413	−2.0	0.0228
1.1	0.8643	−1.9	0.0287
1.2	0.8849	−1.8	0.0359
1.3	0.9032	−1.7	0.0446
1.4	0.9192	−1.6	0.0548
1.5	0.9332	−1.5	0.0668
1.6	0.9452	−1.4	0.0808
1.7	0.9554	−1.3	0.0968
1.8	0.9641	−1.2	0.1151
1.9	0.9713	−1.1	0.1357
2.0	0.9772	−1.0	0.1587
2.1	0.9821	−0.9	0.1841
2.2	0.9861	−0.8	0.2119
2.3	0.9893	−0.7	0.2420
2.4	0.9918	−0.6	0.2743
2.5	0.9938	−0.5	0.3085
2.6	0.9953	−0.4	0.3446
2.7	0.9965	−0.3	0.3821
2.8	0.9974		
2.9	0.9981	−0.2	0.4207
		−0.1	0.4602
3.0	0.9987	−0.0	

FIGURE 3-3 Probability table.

MANUAL TIMING CALCULATIONS

Once time estimates are obtained, the next step is to calculate the timing of each activity. For calculating manually the earliest start and finish times, the network diagram is used and the time estimates are placed on the diagram.

Calculating the Earliest Start Time

The earliest possible time an activity can begin without interfering with the completion of any of the preceding activities is termed the *earliest start time*. These guides should be remembered in calculating the earliest start times for a project:

- The calculation of earliest start times commences with the beginning mode of the arrow diagram (time 0), and continues.
- If only one arrow leads into a node, the earliest start time for jobs starting at the node is determined by adding the earliest start time for the preceding job to the time estimate for the preceding job. The earliest start time at node 8 in the following drawing is the sum of the earliest start time at node 4, (6), and the time estimate for job 4,8, (2).

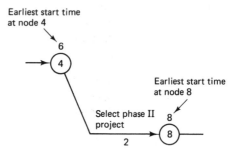

- If more than one arrow leads into a node, the earliest start time calculation is made through each of the arrows as noted in the following drawing. The largest total is the earliest start time for the node.

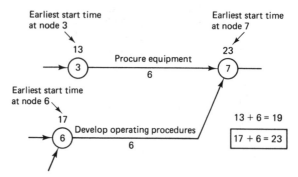

By using this approach to calculate earliest start times for all the nodes, the earliest start times for all nodes are calculated and are noted on Figure 3-4.

Calculating the Project Duration

The jobs on the longest path in the diagram (the critical path) total 29 weeks for completion. This is the minimum project duration for this particular plan with these

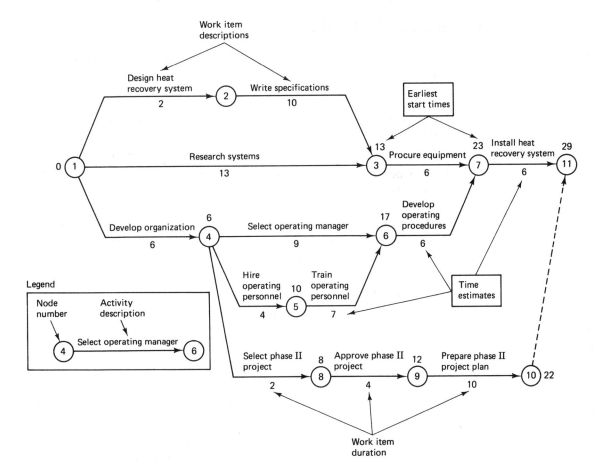

FIGURE 3-4 Network diagram: time estimates and earliest start times for the Waste Heat Recovery Project.

time estimates. The project duration can also be expressed as the earliest start time of the end node of the project. (It is at this point that a check should be made as to whether the timing objectives are met. If the start of the project timing was October 4, 1982, the completion time of 29 weeks is April 25, 1983, meeting one of the main objectives. Other milestones whose schedules were met are as follows:

ACTIVITY	WEEKS AFTER TIME 0	SCHEDULED DATE
Complete organization	6	11/15/82
Start equipment procurement	13	01/03/83
Start equipment installation	23	03/14/83

Calculating the Latest Finish Time

The latest time an activity must be completed without delaying the end of the project is termed the *latest finish time*. These guides should be applied in determining the latest finish times for a project:

- The project duration must first be determined by calculating the early start times.
- The project duration is the latest finish time of the end node of the project.
- The calculation of latest finish times involves working from the end node back through each node to the first node in the project.

If more than one arrow originates at a node, the calculation of latest finish time is made via each arrow and the *smallest* result is through each node to the end of the diagram.

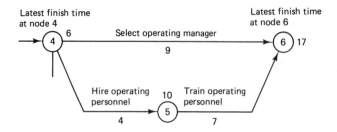

Job 4,6:   17   Latest finish time at node 6
                 − 9   Time estimate for job 4,6
                 ───
                   8

Job 4,5:   10   Latest finish time at node 5

                 − 4   Time estimate for job 4,5
                 ───
                   6

The latest finish time at node 4 is 6 days, the smaller of the two results. Were the latest finish time for jobs coming into node 4 set at 8 days, there would not be enough time remaining to complete job 4,5 by its required latest finish time of 10. By using this approach to calculate the latest finish times for all the nodes, the latest finish times are calculated and are noted on Figure 3–5.

As in the case of the earliest start times, at this time the major milestone finish dates of the early start schedule can be either compared with the objectives or used for objectives to be met. (Use time 0, 10/04/82, as the base data to determine the calendar dates.)

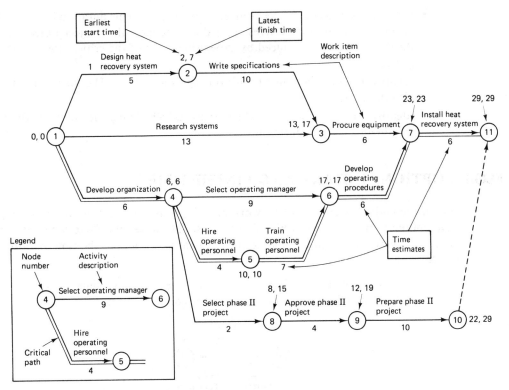

FIGURE 3–5 Network diagram: time estimates, earliest start times, latest finish times, and critical path for the Waste Heat Recovery Project.

Activity	Completion Date
Select operating manager	01/31/83
Equipment procurement	03/14/83
Equipment installation	04/25/83

As the plan thus far suggests that timing objectives can be met, we can continue without making any changes at this time. If timing objectives are not met, proceed with the remaining timing calculations, then examine critical items for possible timing adjustment to satisfy timing objectives.

With the calculation of the total float, which uses the earliest start and latest finish values, each job can be identified as critical, meaning no schedule flexibility, or having float time that allows for optional starting and finishing times. The benefits to be gained from these calculations are:

- Establishment of the project duration of the plan. This duration is checked against the project objectives. If it does not meet the project objectives, the duration can be reduced by expediting some of the critical jobs on the project.
- Identification of the longest path through the project. The longest path is also the critical path.
- Identification of jobs for which there is scheduling flexibility without lengthening project duration.

FLOAT: OPTIONAL START AND FINISH TIMES

One of the major advantages of network planning is that it identifies the jobs that have optional starting and finishing dates. These jobs have total float, which is the difference between the time *available* for performing a job and the time *required* for doing it.

available time = latest finish time − earliest start time
required time = time estimate for completing job

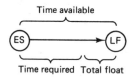

Another way to express total float can be seen in Figure 3–6. The time available for job 4,6 is the difference between the latest finish time and the earliest start

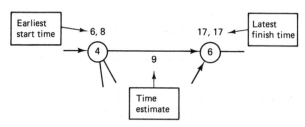

Calculating total float

Activity (node number)	Latest finish time	(−)	Earliest start time	(−)	Time estimate for completing job	=	Total float
4, 6	17	(−)	6	(−)	9	=	2

FIGURE 3-6 Calculating total float for the Waste Heat Recovery Project.

time. The time estimate for job 4,6 is subtracted from the time available to determine the total float.

The total float figures (Figure 3-7) are vital in scheduling a project. Where jobs have no (or 0) float, they cannot be delayed without extending the length of the project. Jobs with float permit leeway in scheduling. Total float figures indicate all the places where float is available and may indicate the same float at more than one place. This is apparent on the chain of activities along the same path.

The benefits to be derived from the timing calculations are principally

- Establishment of the project duration for the plan
- Identification of the longest path (critical path) through the project
- Identification of jobs for which there is scheduling flexibility without lengthening project duration

TABULATING THE SCHEDULE

The schedule tabulated the optional starting and finishing times of the project jobs as well as the total and free floats of the project jobs (Figure 3-8). The following

Activity (Node Numbers)	Latest Finish Time	(−)	Earliest Start Time	(−)	Time Estimate for Completing Job	=	Total Float
1,2	7	(−)	0	(−)	2	=	5
1,3	17		0		13		4
1,4	6		0		6		0*
2,3	17		2		10		5
3,7	23		13		6		4
4,6	17		6		9		2
4,5	10		6		4		0*
5,6	17		10		7		0*
6,7	23		17		6		0*
4,8	15		6		2		7
8,9	19		8		4		7
9,10	29		12		10		7
7,11	29		23		6		0*
10,11†	29		22		0		7

*Critical path.
†Dummy—has no time duration.

FIGURE 3-7 Computation of total float for the Waste Heat Recovery Project.

i,j	DESCRIPTION	TIME (WEEKS)	EARLIEST		LATEST		FLOAT TOTAL
			Start	Finish	Start	Finish	
1,2	Design heat recovery system	2	0	2	5	7	5
1,3	Research systems	13	0	13	4	17	4
1,4	Develop organization	6	0	6	0	6	0
2,3	Write specifications	10	2	12	7	17	5
3,7	Procure equipment	6	13	19	17	23	4
4,5	Hire operating personnel	4	6	10	6	10	0
4,6	Select operating manager	9	6	15	8	17	2
4,8	Select phase II project	2	6	8	13	15	7
5,6	Train operating personnel	7	10	17	10	17	0
6,7	Develop operating procedures	6	17	23	17	23	0
7,11	Install heat recovery system	6	23	29	23	29	0
8,9	Approve phase II project	4	8	12	15	19	7
9,10	Prepare phase II project plan	10	12	22	19	29	7
10,11	Dummy	0	22	22	29	29	7

FIGURE 3-8 Schedule tabulation for the Waste Heat Recovery Project.

formulas can be used to complete the calculations of the optional starting and finishing times:

$$\text{latest start} = \text{earliest start} + \text{total float}$$
$$\text{earliest finish} = \text{latest finish} - \text{total float}$$

SETTING UP THE CALENDAR SCHEDULE

The tabulated schedule can be converted into a calendar schedule, which will make it more presentable for reporting and more convenient in monitoring the project. The calendar schedule will be helpful in preparing the bar chart schedule that can be used by project personnel. Based on a start date of October 4, 1982, the calendar schedule for the Waste Heat Recovery Project is as shown in Figure 3–9.

CONSTRUCTING THE BAR CHART
TIME SCHEDULE

Although the network diagram is excellent for laying out and planning a job, the bar chart is more readable for depicting a schedule. Other advantages of using a bar chart time schedule are as follows:

- Programs are displayed effectively.
- Jobs behind schedule are readily shown on a bar chart.
- Completion dates are specifically noted.

The bar chart time schedule (Figure 3–10) can be plotted or laid out after the schedule is calculated. The procedure for constructing this bar chart is as follows:

1. Use the earliest start time for each project activity.
2. The length of each bar is the duration of each activity.
3. Plot one activity per line. (In some cases it may be advantageous to plot a number of activities on one line. If the critical path items are shown on one line, a change in the planned schedule of each item and the effect on the project duration can be noted immediately.)

Bar charts used by planners as "working" bar charts may include the float times on these charts to help show the complete float picture. The computer graphics will also show total float times.

SUMMARY

Scheduling a project will follow this sequence:

- Time estimates
- Timing calculations
- Job scheduling

Time estimates, an important part of the project scheduling, involve getting a time estimate for each job in the project. The time estimate represents the amount of time an experienced person thinks the job will require under specified conditions. The first set of time estimates is generally made on the assumption that the project

i,j	Description	Time (Weeks)	Earliest Start	Earliest Finish	Latest Start	Latest Finish	Float Total
1,2	Design heat recovery system	2	10/4/82	10/18/82	11/8/82	11/22/82	5
1,3	Research systems	13	10/4/82	1/3/83	11/1/82	1/31/83	4
1,4	Develop organization	6	10/4/82	11/15/82	10/4/82	11/15/82	0
2,3	Write specifications	10	10/18/82	12/27/82	11/22/82	1/31/83	5
3,7	Procure equipment	6	1/3/83	2/14/83	1/31/83	3/14/83	4
4,5	Hire operating personnel	4	11/15/82	12/13/82	11/15/82	12/13/82	0
4,6	Select operating manager	9	11/15/82	1/17/83	11/29/82	1/31/83	2
4,8	Select phase II project	2	11/15/82	11/29/82	1/3/83	1/17/83	7
5,6	Train operating personnel	7	12/13/82	1/31/83	12/13/82	1/31/83	0
6,7	Develop operating procedure	6	1/31/83	3/14/83	1/31/83	3/14/83	0
7,11	Install heat recovery system	6	3/14/83	4/25/83	3/15/83	4/25/83	0
8,9	Approve phase II project	4	11/29/82	12/27/82	1/17/83	2/14/83	0
9,10	Prepare phase II project plan	10	12/27/82	3/7/83	2/14/83	4/25/83	7

FIGURE 3-9 Calendar schedule for the Waste Heat Recovery Project.

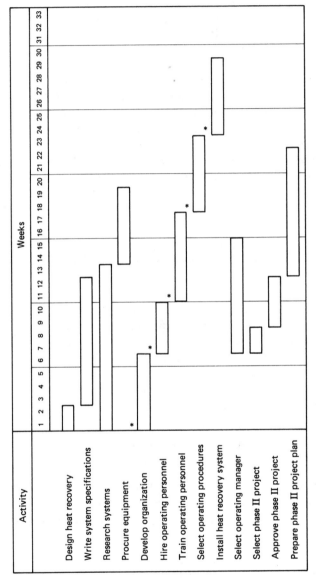

FIGURE 3-10 Bar chart time schedule for the Waste Heat Recovery Project.

*Critical path activities

will be accomplished on a normal basis (employing readily available resources and using a minimum of overtime and other special measures).

Where there may be uncertainties about the estimates employed, the use of three time estimates—optimistic, normal, and pessimistic—can bring the uncertainties into a clear focus. The timing calculations provide information to schedule a project effectively. For small projects, calculations can be made manually; for larger projects, a computer is used. In the first series of calculations, the earliest start times and latest finish times of each activity are determined.

Computation of the earliest start times also yields the project duration. This duration is checked against project objectives. If it does not meet project objectives, the duration must be compressed by expediting some of the critical jobs on the project. With earliest start times and latest finish times, the float values are derived, which makes it possible to identify jobs that have optional starting and finishing dates. The float values also permit identification of the longest path (or "critical path") through the project, that is, the critical items that have no float.

With the planning diagram, the list of critical activities, and the remainder of the jobs with their available float, the project can now be scheduled. The technique for developing a job schedule is the use of the bar chart time schedule.

EXERCISES

1. Given the following diagrams, compute the earliest start and latest finish times, and total float. Locate the critical path on the planning diagrams.
   (a) Theater planning (page 45).
   (b) New equipment installation (page 43).
   (c) Computer installation (page 44).
   For the Computer installation project prepare a schedule for each of the following responsible departments:

   > PE—Plant Engineering
   > IR—Industrial Relations
   > CS—Computer Systems Department

   The schedule should include the earliest and latest start dates, earliest and latest finish dates, and available float for each work item.

2. For each of the projects in Problem 1, complete a work sheet showing schedule information as follows:

   - Job
   - Description
   - Duration
   - Earliest start time
   - Earliest finish time

   - Latest start time
   - Latest finish time
   - Total float
   - Free float
   - Independent float

NEW EQUIPMENT INSTALLATION

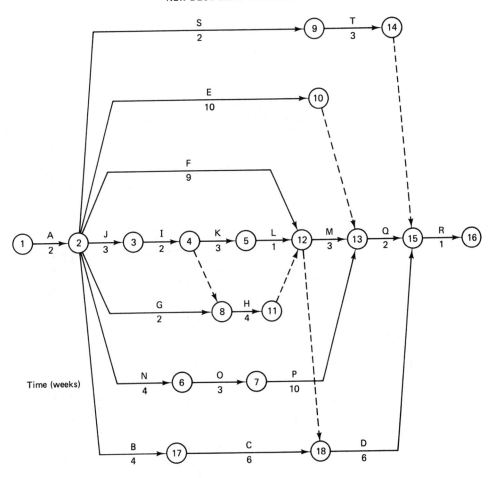

Time (weeks)

A	1, 2	Design equipment	K	4, 5	Fabricate equipment (shop)
B	2, 17	Design building	L	5, 12	Assemble equipment (shop)
C	17, 18	Construct building — phase I	M	12, 13	Install — phase I
D	18, 15	Construct building — phase II	N	2, 6	Design controls
E	2, 10	Procure long-lead equipment items	O	6, 7	Select controls supplier
F	2, 12	Procure ancillary equipment	P	7, 13	Fabricate and assemble controls
G	2, 8	Remove existing equipment	Q	13,. 15	Install — phase II
H	8, 11	Prepare site	R	15, 16	Debug equipment
I	3, 4	Design equipment installation	S	2, 9	Develop operating procedures
J	2, 3	Detail equipment	T	9, 14	Select and train personnel

COMPUTER INSTALLATION

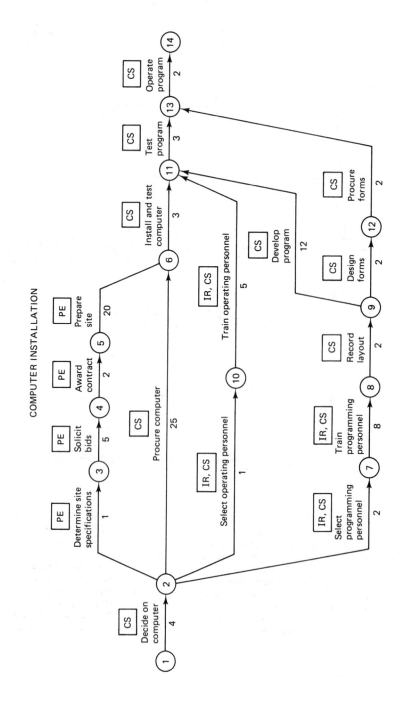

3. The following activities must be accomplished to complete an office remodeling project:

	Estimated
Activity	Duration (days)
Procure paint	2
Procure new carpet	5
Procure new furniture	7
Remove old furniture	1
Remove old carpet	1
Scrub walls	1
Paint walls	2
Lay new carpet	1
Move in new furniture	1

(a) Draw an arrow diagram for this project.
(b) When can the new furniture be moved in?
(c) What is the project duration?

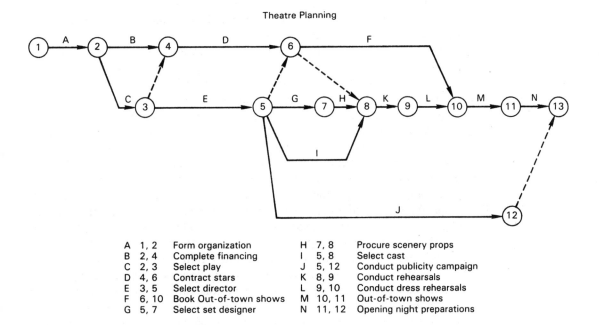

Theatre Planning

A	1, 2	Form organization	H	7, 8	Procure scenery props
B	2, 4	Complete financing	I	5, 8	Select cast
C	2, 3	Select play	J	5, 12	Conduct publicity campaign
D	4, 6	Contract stars	K	8, 9	Conduct rehearsals
E	3, 5	Select director	L	9, 10	Conduct dress rehearsals
F	6, 10	Book Out-of-town shows	M	10, 11	Out-of-town shows
G	5, 7	Select set designer	N	11, 12	Opening night preparations

Chapter 4

Monitoring and Controlling the Project

Project control, the third phase of the project management cycle, generally consists of monitoring the progress of each project item, assessing its effects on the total project, and taking the necessary action on the critical items to keep the project on the planned schedule. The bar chart is one of the best expedients to keep track of job progress; and a summary bar chart is prepared for management review, depicting progress on a weekly or monthly basis.

In the previous two phases we were concerned with planning, which featured preparation of the planning diagram, and scheduling, featuring the scheduling calculations. We now use the planning and scheduling information to develop a bar chart time schedule, then to develop a summary bar chart as a communication aid in a project status report, and finally, to prepare a project status report.

The project status report informs management of project performance. By examining the status reports, the managers can make an appraisal of the project. The report highlights critical areas, and through applying the principle of management by exception, management can objectively evaluate the problem areas.

The status report may include three documents: cover letter, executive highlights, and the project summary. The cover letter contains brief statements of the overall progress of the project; executive highlights, in bullet (•) form, highlight the status of the most important aspects of the project; and the project summary contains a summary bar chart as well as commentary emphasizing critical items.

Project status reporting revolving around milestones is an effective application of the management-by-exception principle. Milestones are events that are of a major importance toward achieving objectives. The milestone approach isolates the behind-schedule activities so that corrective action can be taken early in the project.

46

CONSTRUCTING THE PROGRESS SCHEDULE

In addition to its use in depicting schedules, the bar chart excels in keeping track of the progress of a job. Actions taken on a daily, weekly, or monthly basis can be shown on the same bar chart as that drawn for the time schedule. Charts of this type are called *progress schedules*. Usually, each item is shown separately and its accumulative progress is noted on the progress schedule.

There are several rules that should be followed that will allow uniform interpretation in reading the progress schedule:

1. The rectangular bars (▭) represent the project items in a timing sequence to meet the projected completed date. The portion that is completed is filled in (▬).

2. Critical project event dates, or milestones (▽), are left hollow until that event is completed, and then filled in (▼).

3. The planned program completion milestone (▽) is shown in the upper right of the chart. If the completion milestone requires a time change because of changes in scope, technical problems, late deliveries, and so on, the updated completion milestone will be noted by a dashed line (▽).

Several other expedients may also be shown, depending on the manner in which you want to interpret progress. For example, extending the rectangular bar with a dashed bar may depict a completion delay for a specific project item. (If the bar chart depicts float times on appropriate activities, it can readily be determined if delays in these activities will affect the project completion date.)

To illustrate a progress schedule, let us assume that we are reviewing the status at the end of week 12 (Figure 4–1). The following activities have deviated from their planned schedule:

ACTIVITY	STATUS
Write specifications	Behind 2 weeks
Research systems	Behind 3 weeks
Hire operating personnel	Behind 2 weeks
Approve phase II project	Behind 4 weeks

All the other activities have progressed, are progressing, or are planned to progress according to their planned schedule.

CONSTRUCTING THE SUMMARY BAR CHART

A summary bar chart is an excellent communication device to inform management of the status of the project. How it is summarized from the bar chart schedule, the manner in which the current status is described, and how off-schedule items are

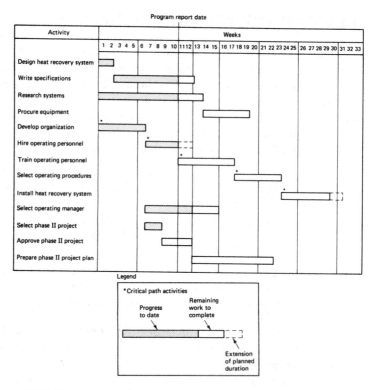

FIGURE 4-1   Progress schedule for the Waste Heat Recovery Project.

handled to maintain progress schedules will determine how effective it is as a management tool.

The basic elements in constructing a summary bar chart are somewhat similar to those of a status schedule. The main difference is that the items in the status schedule are grouped to represent major sections of the project items. For example, in the Waste Heat Recovery Project, the major sections would be as follows:

- *Design.* Design heat recovery system; write specifications.
- *Install.* Research system; procure equipment; develop operating procedures; install heat recovery system.
- *Personnel.* Develop organization; hire operating personnel; train operating personnel.
- *Phase II program.* Select phase II project; approve phase II project; prepare phase II project plan.

The summary chart uses the latest start schedule. In contrast to the progress schedule that normally uses the earliest start schedule for implementing the project, the latest start schedule is more appropriate for the summary bar chart to be submitted to management.

Providing late start dates to those responsible for implementation of the project allows for no margin when there may be delays. However, this timing approach is useful, after the fact, for reporting to management on the overall project.

To illustrate, at the end of week 12, the project is 2 weeks behind schedule. The primary reason is that the critical group item, *personnel,* is presently 2 weeks behind. There are other trend factors that, shortly, could also begin to contribute to the project being behind schedule. All these trend factors can be shown on the summary bar chart. (Showing the available float for these items is an option, to be used if the reader is knowledgeable in the use of this technique.)

The project duration is extended 2 weeks because the project activity *hire operating personnel,* a critical item, is behind 2 weeks. This is noted on the progress schedule in two locations: The rectangular bar for *hire operating personnel* is shown to be extended by the 2 weeks with a dashed bar, and the dashed updated completion milestone is shown to the right of the chart.

To illustrate a summary bar chart (Figure 4–2), let us assume that we are preparing a management report on the status of the work activities at the end of week 12, highlighting the behind-schedule items, as follows:

Activity	Based on Earliest Start Time	Total Float (Weeks)
Design	Behind 2 weeks	5
Research systems	Behind 3 weeks	4
Hire and train operating personnel	Behind 2 weeks	0
Phase II program	Behind 4 weeks	7

Based on earliest start times and the available total float, the present status of the work activity group *hiring and training operating personnel* is the main project item that affects the completion date at the present rate of progress. Unless there are alternative plans to expedite work in this group, this project will be completed 2 weeks later than planned.

CONSTRUCTING THE PROJECT STATUS REPORT

A project status report is prepared on a regularly scheduled basis (usually monthly) and reflects program content in a summary form. The main features of a project status report are as follows:

- Status of key project items
- Assessment of key project items
- Resolution of "troubled" areas

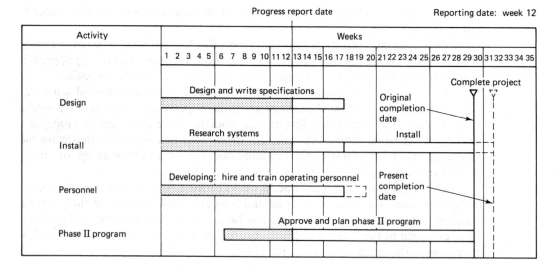

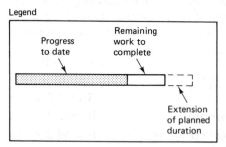

FIGURE 4-2 Summary bar chart for the Waste Heat Recovery Project.

This report usually contains the following documents:

- Cover letter
- Executive highlights
- Project summary
  - Bar chart
  - Project status
  - Milestone report

Cover Letter

The cover letter (Figure 4-3) is addressed to the management personnel whose activity is participating or has an interest in the particular project. It explains briefly the program of the job, anticipated completion dates of major events, the status of critical items, and potential solutions to possible problems.

Messrs.

SUBJECT: STATUS OF WASTE HEAT RECOVERY

At this time the waste heat recovery
system will be completed on May 10, 1983,
two weeks later than the original plan.
Problems in acquiring qualified operating
personnel were the main reasons for the
delay. However, plans are now underway
to change the training schedule so that
the original introduction date can be met.

A review with the equipment suppliers
indicated that equipment will be delivered
on a timely basis that will permit installation to start January 31. While December
trials were not completed and were incon-
clusive, the mechanical difficulties that
contributed to the trial malfunctions have
been corrected and are ready for the January trials.

The Phase II program plans have been
revised to bring the program back on schedule.

For further status details, please review the program status highlights that are
attached.

M. Spinner
Program Analysis

FIGURE 4-3   Cover letter showing status of the Waste Heat Recovery Project.

Executive Highlights

The executive highlights (Figure 4–4) focus on the status of the important aspects of the project. Highlights can be in the form of a bullet (•) listing; they should consist of only a brief sentence or two, without going into much detail. In brief, progress status reports and executive highlights may sometimes be incorporated in the cover letter.

Project Summary

The project summary (Figure 4–5) includes a bar chart that combines the work activities in a graphic form in such a manner that management can review the overall project and be spared the countless details associated with day-to-day activity. It applies the management-by-exception principle, which allows more attention to the critical items.

STATUS REPORTING USING THE MILESTONE APPROACH

Milestones are selected events that are of a major importance toward achieving objectives. They are key events usually showing the completion date of a major phase of the project, the delivery date of a major equipment item, or the date of a key management decision to make the project maintain its successful completion. These events may or may not be on the critical path.

The milestone approach is an excellent "tool" for reporting project status in a summary form to higher management, as it summarizes the status of the major

---

- Fabrication of process equipment is over 75% completed, and about 60% of the assembly is completed. "Debugging" at Tech Center, prior to shipment, is expected to begin early January.
- Equipment tryout will start January 15; and by February 1, the supplier expects to confirm his ability to make system operable.
- Delivery of equipment is expected to be completed by March 14.
- Installation is expected to begin March 14.
- Employment agencies are behind about 2 weeks in supplying qualified operating personnel to train. The training course is to be accelerated by 2 weeks.
- The phase II program is being extended to coincide with the launching date. This has allowed for improvement in travel schedules and outside consultant participation.

FIGURE 4-4   Executive highlights for the Waste Heat Recovery Project.

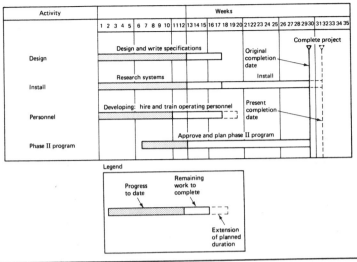

Design. All work is on schedule and essentially complete.

Progress to date. General note: There has been little development progress in the past 6 weeks. Most of the trial malfunctions have been caused by mechanical difficulties, which are being corrected for the scheduled January trials.

- *Install*—Fabrication about 75% complete, is planned to be ready for "debugging" by January 15 at the Tech Center prior to shipment. Required for debugging: the air control panel, which is now being fabricated, and the electrical control panel order, which was awarded December 1. Both panels are expected to be completed and shipped to the Tech Center in December.

- *Organization*—Employment agencies are lagging behind in providing qualified operating personnel. Hiring is not expected to be complete until December 27, 2 weeks behind schedule. Plans to reduce by 2 weeks the length of the training sessions are now being discussed and will be described in the next report. The training activity is a critical item and needs to be started on schedule to avoid delaying the entire project.

- *Phase II program*—Planning the phase II program is not expected to be completed until January 24, 4 weeks later than initially planned. Decisions on equipment selection and method of operation were resolved in mid-December. No timing problem is anticipated and at the time of this report there appears to be ample time to complete the phase II plan.

Milestone Report. Schedules remain essentially the same as in the last report. Operating the waste heat recovery system is now scheduled to start May 10, 1983, 2 weeks later than the original planned schedule. Alternative plans are now being developed to reduce the time planned to train operating personnel, a critical project item that was set to be completed by January 31, 1983, but is now 2 weeks behind schedule.

FIGURE 4-5 Project summary: bar chart, project status, and milestone report for the Waste Heat Recovery Project.

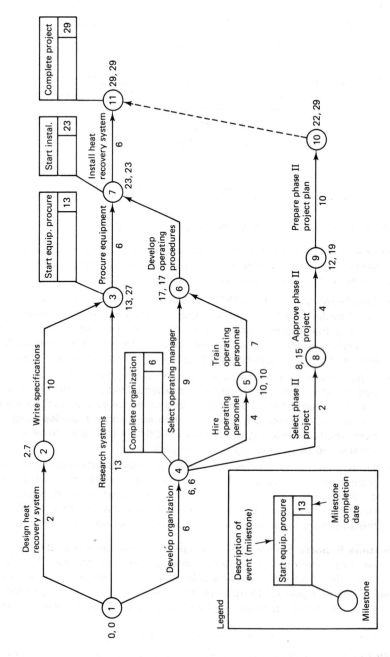

FIGURE 4-6 Network diagram: milestone report for the Waste Heat Recovery Project.

events. Milestones noted on a network diagram represent the key starting and/or completion dates of major events (Figure 4–6). Use of a computer may be necessary for any meaningful analysis.

The computer-oriented milestone technique provides a condensed version or summary of the project (Figure 4–7). It offers a number of advantages, such as:

- The computer printout milestone listing provides a precise form for use in program monitoring.
- The computer program can sort a milestone listing of behind-schedule activities, highlighting the items that must be expedited.
- Additional milestones can be added during the course of the project.

```
PROJECT MANAGEMENT                              WASTE HEAT RECOVERY                              DETROIT, MICHIGAN
          REPORT TYPE :MILESTONE                                        PRINTING SEQUENCE  :Earliest Activities First
                                                                        SELECTION CRITERIA :MILESTONE
          PLAN I.D.   :WHR      VERSION  5                              TIME NOW DATE      : 4/OCT/82
============================================================================================================
          MILESTONE                           EARLIEST EVENT              LATEST EVENT
          DESCRIPTION                             TIME                       TIME
============================================================================================================
   1-  1 START PROJECT                          4/OCT/82                    4/OCT/82
   4-  4 START PERSONNEL PROCUREMENT           15/NOV/82                   15/NOV/82
   3-  3 START EQUIPMENT PROCUREMENT            3/JAN/83                   31/JAN/83
   7-  7 START EQUIPMENT INSTALLATION          14/MAR/83                   14/MAR/83
   -------------------------------------------------------------------------------------------------------
  11- 11 COMPLETE PROJECT                      25/APR/83                   25/APR/83
============================================================================================================
```

FIGURE 4–7 Computer printout of milestone for the Waste Heat Recovery Project.

SUMMARY

The third phase of the project management cycle is a project control step which consists of monitoring the progress of the project activities, comparing them with the plan, and taking the required action when there are deviations from the plan. An effective expedient used to inform management of project performance is the project status report. This report is designed in such a manner that management, when examining the status report, should be able to make a sound performance apprisal of the project. The status report highlights the critical areas, and through applying the principle of management by exception, management can objectively evaluate the problem areas.

EXERCISES

1. Draw a bar chart time schedule for the following projects whose schedules were developed in Chapter 3.
   (a) Computer installation.
   (b) New equipment installation.

2. Show the status on the bar chart time schedule of the *New equipment installation* project in its 12th week, reflecting the following progress of the work activities:

	BEHIND (WEEKS)
Prepare detail equipment	2
Prepare site	4
Fabricate equipment (in shop)	2
Assemble equipment (in shop)	2
All other work activities are progressing as planned	

Does present status indicate an extension of the present project duration? If so, show on bar chart.

3. Show the status on the bar chart time schedule of the *Computer installation project* in its 10th week, reflecting the following progress of the work activities:

	BEHIND (WEEKS)
Procure computer	2
Select programming personnel	3
Select operating personnel	6
Solicit bids	2
All other work activities are progressing as planned	

4. Prepare a summary bar chart for a management report for the following:
  (a) Computer installation
  (b) New equipment installation

Chapter 5

Scheduling and Controlling Project Costs

Another major project management responsibility is the effective management of costs. Planning, scheduling, and controlling costs for accomplishing a successful project are essential and are very important to develop. On many projects, costs may be considered more important than the timing considerations. In this section several important aspects of project costs are considered:

- Preparing a *project cost schedule*
- *Controlling project costs* by predicting final cost outcome at selected periods during the course of the project
- Reducing project duration at minimum additional cost—*cost minimizing* (sometimes referred to as time/cost trade-offs)

Cost estimates for the project activities are provided by experienced personnel. Analogous to time estimates, they need to be reviewed to avoid bias. The importance of the cost estimates is apparent, as the sum total of the project costs relates back to these costs. Usually, the costs associated with the activities on the network diagram are *variable* costs. In many instances there may be fixed costs that need to be included when total project cost reviews are made.

DEVELOPING THE PROJECT COST SCHEDULE

Prerequisite to developing a *project cost schedule* is a completed bar chart timing schedule. Costs relate to time, and applying costs to the time schedule for determining cost status is a prudent requirement for managers of projects. Once the bar chart time schedule is completed, the next step in developing a cost schedule is to prepare the cost slope for each job. The cost slope is defined as the cost incurred in performing a job over a time unit.

After the cost slope is calculated, the next step is to determine the amount of project expenditures over a specific period. A planned distribution of costs using these time periods is constructed, and if required, can be used to compare with actual costs at selected time periods throughout the course of the project.

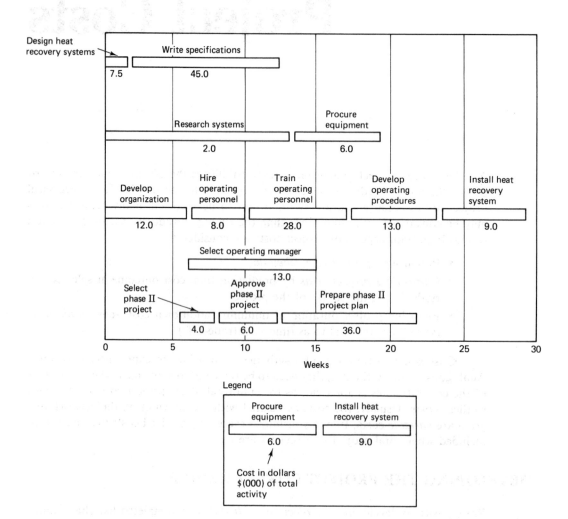

FIGURE 5-1   Bar chart cost schedule for the Waste Heat Recovery Project.

The following steps are taken to develop a cost schedule:

1. Complete the bar chart time schedule and add the cost value of each activity to its corresponding bar.
2. Calculate the cost slope (cost per unit of time); doing so will identify the time increment that is necessary for the unit costs to be determined.
3. Tabulate the cost schedule.
4. Plot the cost distribution graph.

Preparing the Bar Chart Cost Schedule

The bar chart cost schedule (Figure 5-1) is simply the costs of the activity applied to the bar chart time schedule. These costs are placed at the bottom of the bars of their corresponding activities.

Calculating the Cost Slope

The cost slope is the cost of each project activity over a unit length of time. Once the time unit is selected, a simple format, such as that illustrated in Figure 5-2, facilitates the development of the cost slope.

PROJECT ACTIVITY	COST (DOLLARS)	DURATION (WEEKS)	COST SLOPE (DOLLARS/WEEK)
Design heat recovery system	$ 7,500	2	$ 3,750
Research systems	2,000	13	154
Develop organization	12,000	6	2,000
Write specifications	45,000	10	4,500
Procure equipment	6,000	6	1,000
Hire operating personnel	8,000	4	2,000
Select operating manager	13,000	9	1,444
Select phase II project	4,000	2	2,000
Train operating personnel	28,000	7	4,000
Develop operating procedures	64,000	6	10,666
Install heat recovery system	9,000	6	1,500
Approve phase II project	6,000	4	1,500
Prepare phase II project plan	36,000	10	3,600
Total	$240,500		

FIGURE 5-2   Calculating the cost slope (cost per week) for the Waste Heat Recovery Project.

Follow the specific instructions below to develop the format shown in the figure.

COLUMN	INSTRUCTIONS
Project activity	Enter the description of the project activity
Cost	Enter the total cost in dollars of performing the project activity
Duration	Enter the total duration time of the project activity
Cost slope	Enter the result of dividing the *cost* column by the *duration* column

Tabulating the Cost Schedule

A cost schedule tabulation in an important base document used for preparing periodic project expenditures. A suggested format is shown in Figure 5–3. Follow the specific instructions below to develop the format shown in the figure.

COLUMN	INSTRUCTIONS
Period	Enter the period of time that is desired to determine the expenditures
Activity	Enter the description of the project activity
Activity time	Enter the time units that the activity performs within the time period.
Cost slope	Enter the cost slope that was developed previously
Expenditures	Enter the result of multiplying the *activity time* column by the *cost slope* column.

Constructing the Cost Distribution Graph

The cost distribution graph (Figure 5–4) can be used to develop a graphic portrayal of the project costs for each time period.

MONITORING PROJECT COSTS

An expedient in project cost control is the *indicated cost outcome* report. This is a management-by-exception application that can predict overspending (or cost overruns) of significant project items, allowing time and thought for cost corrections.

PERIOD	ACTIVITY	ACTIVITY TIME (WEEKS)	COST SLOPE (DOLLARS/WEEK)	TOTAL ACTIVITY EXPENDITURES (DOLLARS)
0–5	Design heat recovery system	2	$ 3,750	$ 7,500
	Research systems	5	154	770
	Write specifications	3	4,500	13,500
	Develop organization	5	2,000	10,000
	Total 0–5			$31,770
6–10	Research systems	5	154	774
	Write specifications	5	4,500	22,500
	Develop organization	1	2,000	2,000
	Hire operating personnel	4	2,000	8,000
	Select operating manager	4	1,444	5,776
	Select phase II project	2	2,000	4,000
	Approve phase II project	2	1,500	3,000
	Total 6–10			$46,050
11–15	Research systems	3	154	464
	Write specifications	2	4,500	9,000
	Procure equipment	2	1,000	2,000
	Train operating personnel	5	4,000	20,000
	Select operating manager	5	1,444	7,220
	Approve phase II project	2	1,500	3,000
	Prepare phase II project	3	3,600	10,800
	Total 11–15			$52,484
16–20	Procure equipment	4	1,000	4,000
	Train operating personnel	2	4,000	8,000
	Develop operating procedures	3	10,666	31,998
	Prepare phase II project plan	5	3,600	18,000
	Total 16–20			$61,998
21–25	Develop operation procedures	3	10,666	31,998
	Install heat recovery system	2	1,500	3,000
	Prepare phase II project plan	2	3,600	7,200
	Total 21–25			$42,198
26–29	Develop operating procedures	4	1,500	6,000
	Total project costs			$240,500

FIGURE 5-3 Calculating the cost schedule for the Waste Heat Recovery Project.

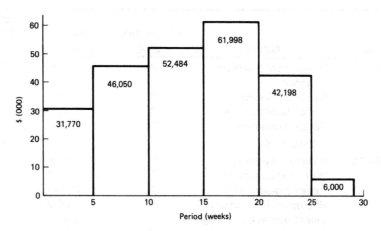

FIGURE 5-4   Cost distribution graph for the Waste Heat Recovery Project.

One of the main features of this report is detecting "early warning signs" on project overspending.

Indicated cost outcome reports are usually prepared monthly; however, the method is flexible so as to consider critical cost conditions that may require cost status reports at more frequent intervals. Use the format shown in Figure 5-5 to develop the indicated cost outcome. Follow the specific instructions below to develop the indicated cost outcome format shown in the figure.

COLUMN	INSTRUCTIONS
Project item	Enter the description of each project job activity
Authorized (budgeted)	Enter the estimated dollar amount that has been developed and approved for completing the project activity item
Committed to date	Enter for each activity the amount that has been spent and/or ordered as of the date of the report
Future commitments	Enter the additional costs that will be needed to complete the activity (these projections are usually estimated)
Indicated outcome	Enter the sum of the *committed to date* column by the *future commitments* column for each activity; this figure is compared to the authorized (or budgeted) amount to determine the cost performance of each item
Variance (over) or under	Enter the difference between the *authorized* column and the *indicated outcome* column
Percent (over) or under	Enter the result of dividing the difference between *authorized* column and *indicated outcome* column, divided by *authorized* column amount (multiply by 100 to arrive at percentages)

Project Item	Authorized (Budgeted)	Committed to Date	Future Commitments	Indicated Outcome	Variance (Over) or Under	Percent (Over) or Under
				Reporting date:	Week 15	
				Start date:	0	
				Completion date:	Week 29	
Design heat recovery system	$ 7,500	$ 8,000	$ —	$ 8,000	$ (500)	(6.7)
Research system	2,000	2,000	—	2,000	—	—
Develop organization	12,000	10,500	—	10,500	1,500	8.3
Write specifications	45,000	50,000	—	50,000	(5,000)	(11.1)
Procure equipment	6,000	1,500	3,000	4,500	1,500	25.0
Hire operating personnel	8,000	4,000	3,500	7,500	500	6.3
Select operating manager	13,000	12,000	—	12,000	1,000	7.7
Select phase II project	4,000	2,000	—	2,000	2,000	50.0
Train operating personnel	28,000	25,000	7,000	32,000	(4,000)	(14.3)
Develop operating procedures	64,000	1,000	63,000	64,000	—	—
Install heat recovery system	9,000	—	9,000	9,000	—	—
Approve phase II project	6,000	5,500	—	5,500	500	8.3
Prepare phase II project plan	36,000	10,000	36,000	46,000	(10,000)	(27.7)
	$240,500	$131,500	$121,500	$253,000	$(12,500)	(5.2)

FIGURE 5-5 Indicated cost outcome report (week 15) for the Waste Heat Recovery Project.

Reporting date: Week 15

- Project expenditures are 5.2% over budget.
- Commitments to date: 55% of total authorized.
- Project is 50% complete.
- Outstanding items that indicate high overruns:
  a. Train operating personnel (14.3%)
  b. Approve phase II project (27.7%)

Recommendations to reduce overruns:

a. Train operating personnel—projected expenditures, $7,000; total indicated cost, $32,000; variance, $4,000 over authorized amount.

   Recommendation: Modify training program to permit operating personnel complete course earlier. Reducing time of training program could reduce project costs by $3,000.

b. Prepare phase II project plan—projected expenditures, $36,000; total indicated cost, $36,000; variance, $20,000 over authorized amount.

   Recommendation: Reduce travel time to supplier's plant; reduce presentation aids for an $8,000 saving.

Detailed report on reducing overrun will be included in the next report.

FIGURE 5-6   Indicated cost outcome highlights for the Waste Heat Recovery Project.

Recommendations to bring project costs back to planned costs are shown in Figure 5-6.

Preparing the Accumulative Cost Report

The accumulative cost report provides a graphic picture of the actual costs compared to the plan, as well as showing the indicated cost outcome. This chart (Figure 5-7) is useful in the analysis of projected cost expenditures, and shows project cost status. The accumulative cost report can also be calculated on most project management software packages. Sometimes called the "cash flow curve," an example is shown on Figure 5-8 (cost accumulation through end of 3/MAR/83).

COST MINIMIZING: TIME/COST TRADE-OFFS

The *cost minimizing technique* permits reducing the project duration at minimum additional cost. Option schedules are derived from this approach. Reducing duration time considers the additional costs associated with overtime, extra personnel,

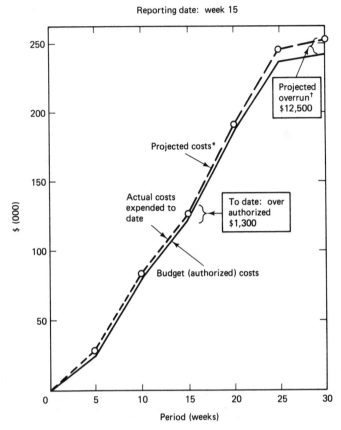

Reporting date: week 15

*Projected costs — total funds needed to complete project.
†Projected overrun — additional funds required to complete project.

Legend

Period	Budgeted costs	
(weeks)	Cost	Accumulated cost
0–5	$31,770	$ —
6–10	46,050	77,820
11–15	52,484	130,304
16–20	61,998	192,302
21–25	42,198	234,500
26–29	8,000	240,500

FIGURE 5-7 Accumulative cost report for the Waste Heat Recovery Project.

and additional equipment. On the other hand, reduced duration time also considers the indirect costs associated with overhead, insurance, and interest on capital loans. These costs are reduced as project duration time is reduced.

Termed also time/cost trade-offs or "crash" programs, cost minimizing uses the network plan as a basis to develop the alternative schedules. Once the plan with

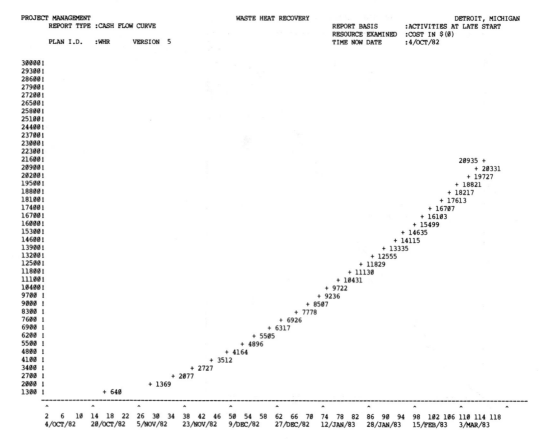

FIGURE 5-8 Sample computer-generated cash flow curve for the Waste Heat Recovery Project.

normal times and costs are established, the next required step is determining the time each job can be reduced by "crashing" each job, and the costs for accelerating each job. From these data the extra cost incurred for reduced project duration times can be calculated. The main consideration is to reduce the project duration with those critical jobs whose time estimates can be reduced with minimal cost.

Cost minimizing is concerned with determining how to reduce the time required for completing a project with the least amount of added costs. If the initial project duration, as developed by the network planning technique, does not satisfy planned timing objectives, the cost minimizing method can develop alternative schedules. From these options the best job schedule, in terms of minimum additional costs, can be determined.

To illustrate this procedure, we will apply the cost minimizing technique to the Waste Heat Recovery Project, where we intend to accelerate the date for the completion of the project. The network diagram shown in Figure 5-9a and the time schedule shown in Figure 5-9b note the project time to be 29 weeks.

If the time duration is not acceptable, the following steps can be taken to obtain optional times:

1. Obtain normal time, normal cost, crash time, and crash cost for the direct labor costs of each job (Figure 5-10). From these data, calculate the cost slope. (The cost slope gives the increase in cost for a decrease in time.)

   a. *Normal time:* job time estimate which assumes the use of normal personnel, equipment, and so on

   b. *Normal cost:* estimated cost for performing the project within the normal time

   c. *Crash time:* minimum estimated time in which a job could be completed if the job is accelerated

   d. *Crash cost:* normal cost plus the extra cost involved in accelerating a job

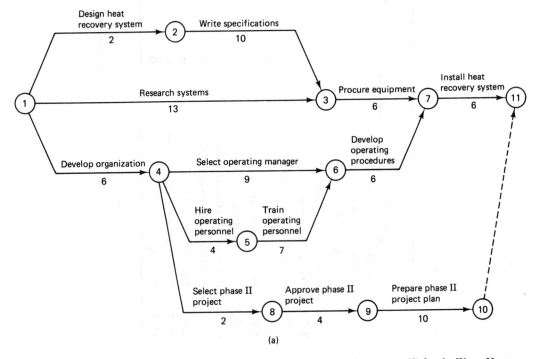

(a)

FIGURE 5-9 (a) Network diagram and (b) timing schedule (on page 68) for the Waste Heat Recovery Project.

i,j	Description	Time (weeks)	Earliest Start	Earliest Finish	Latest Start	Latest Finish	Float Total
1,2	Design heat recovery system	2	0	2	5	7	5
1,3	Research systems	13	0	13	4	17	4
1,4	Develop organization	6	0	6	0	6	0
2,3	Write specifications	10	2	12	7	17	5
3,7	Procure equipment	6	13	19	17	23	4
4,5	Hire operating personnel	4	6	10	6	10	0
4,6	Select operating manager	9	6	15	8	17	2
4,8	Select phase II project	2	6	8	13	15	7
5,6	Train operating personnel	7	10	17	10	17	0
6,7	Develop operating procedures	6	17	23	17	23	0
7,11	Install heat recovery system	6	23	29	23	29	0
8,9	Approve phase II project	4	8	12	15	19	7
9,10	Prepare phase II project plan	10	12	22	19	29	7
10,11	Dummy	0	22	22	29	29	7

FIGURE 5-9 (b)

i,j	PROJECT ACTIVITY DESCRIPTION	NORMAL		CRASH		Cost Slope (dollars/week)
		Duration (weeks)	Cost (dollars)	Duration (weeks)	Cost (dollars)	
1,2	Design package	2	$ 7,500	2	$ 7,500	$ –
1,13	Order stock	13	2,000	9	4,000	500
1,4*	Organize sales office	6	12,000	4	14,000	1,000
2,3	Set up packaging facility	10	45,000	7	52,500	2,500
3,7	Package stock	6	6,000	5	8,000	2,000
4,5*	Hire sales personnel	4	8,000	3	10,000	2,000
4,6	Select distributors	9	13,000	6	22,000	3,000
4,8	Select advertising agency	2	4,000	1	5,500	1,500
5,6*	Train sales personnel	7	28,000	5	3,400	3,000
6,7*	Sell to distributors	6	64,000	4	69,000	2,500
7,11*	Ship stock to distributors	6	9,000	4	11,800	1,400
8,9	Plan advertising campaign	4	6,000	3	8,000	2,000
9,10	Conduct advertising campaign	10	36,000	6	52,000	4,000
			$240,500			

*Critical path activities.

FIGURE 5-10 Normal/crash data for the Waste Heat Recovery Project.

2. Determine the minimum additional cost for reducing the project duration by 2 weeks. Use the project activities on the critical path, and start with those with the least cost slope.

In Figure 5-11 the least cost slope exists with job 1,4, where a 2-week reduction can be effected at an additional cost of $1,000 per week. Since job 7,11 can be reduced in duration by 2 weeks at a cost of $1,400 per day, this job would be the next one to compress. The last job on the critical path is job 5,6, and it can be crashed 1 week at a cost of $3,000, so that the project can be crashed for a total of 9 weeks. However, at this point job 4,6 also becomes critical and a reduction of 1 week for this item at an additional cost of 3,000 for a total cost of $6,000 to maintain the project to be crashed the full 9 weeks. By completing this process, the proj-

Project Duration (Weeks)	Normal Cost	Job Code	Reduced Time (Weeks)	Additional Cost	Normal and Crash Costs
29	$240,600				$240,500
27		1,4	2	$2,000	242,500
25		7,11	2	2,800	245,300
23		4,5	1	2,000	
		6,7	<u>1</u>	<u>2,500</u>	
			2	4,500	249,800
21		6,7	1	2,500	
		5,6	<u>1</u>	<u>3,000</u>	
			2	5,500	254,300
20		5,6	1	3,000	
		4,6	<u>1</u>	<u>3,000</u>	
			2	6,000	260,300

FIGURE 5-11 Calculations of direct costs and crash costs for the Waste Heat Recovery Project.

ect duration has been reduced to its minimum time of 20 weeks at a total cost of $260,300, a reduction of 9 weeks at an additional cost of $19,800.

As total project costs are comprised of both direct and indirect costs, the next step is applying the same cost minimizing approach to indirect costs. Indirect costs are such items as overhead office expenses, insurance, interest on loans to finance the project, and so on. Indirect costs have a tendency to decrease with the decrease in project time. Tabulations of indirect costs are shown in Figure 5-12.

As the cost slope of the indirect costs ($2,000 per week) is greater than the weighted average of cost slopes of the direct costs (ranging from $1,000 to $3,000 per week), the total cost of this project is reduced as the duration time is reduced. (This condition should be investigated on projects, as it may have an impact on planning, overtime, additional equipment, etc.)

The project duration can be crashed from 29 weeks to 23 weeks to reach the minimum cost, the lowest total project cost of $306,800. If time is a premium, the project can be crashed to its minimum duration time of 20 weeks for $312,300. The total cost curve for the 20- to 29-week period as noted in Figure 5-13 shows the alternate project costs (the sum of the direct and indirect costs), the normal time, and crash times.

PROJECT DURATION (WEEKS)	DIRECT COSTS	INDIRECT COSTS Normal	INDIRECT COSTS Crash	INDIRECT COSTS: NORMAL AND CRASH	TOTAL COST: DIRECT AND INDIRECT
29	$240,500	$70,000		$70,000	$310,500
27	242,500		$(4,000)	66,000	308,500
25	245,300		(4,000)	62,000	307,300
23	249,800		(4,000)	58,000	307,800
21	254,300		(4,000)	54,000	308,300
20	260,300		(4,000)	52,000	312,300

FIGURE 5–12 Calculations of additional indirect costs and total costs to crash the Waste Heat Recovery Project.

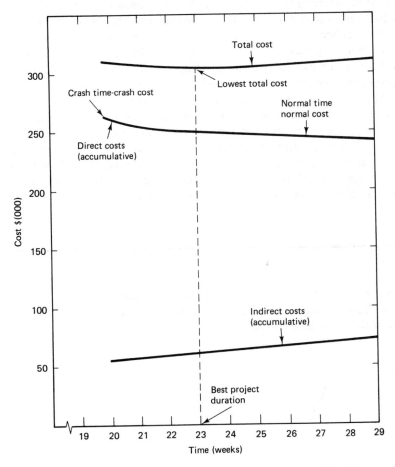

FIGURE 5–13 Graphic illustration of crashing the Waste Heat Recovery Project.

SUMMARY

Scheduling and controlling costs are an essential part of project management. Comparing actual costs with budgeted or planned costs during the life of the project is an important part of project management as the aspects of timing, and in many projects, expenditures beyond those authorized may cause the project to be terminated before its planned duration.

Project cost schedules follow closely time schedules, and they are prepared through the use of graphic timing charts. The charting of actual expenditures against planned expenditures is as noticeable in status reports as are the time schedule data.

Once cost estimates are established, similar to the development of time estimates, arranging these costs in a periodic display will provide the project cost schedule. Controlling costs through the indicated cost outcome method is done to ensure that project spending is contained within the planned (or budgeted) amounts. The indicated cost outcome report reviews and evaluates the spending status of the project, what has been spent, and what is planned to be spent. The report provides an early warning to project personnel if there are evidences of excessive spending. An item that may indicate an overrun trend approaching more than 10% by the end of the project will be targeted and remedial action will need to be taken.

The cost minimizing technique is used to determine the optimum completion time of a project or to accelerate the completion of a project at minimum additional cost. The information that is derived is of great value to management in the planning phase, as well as determining the effect of schedule changes during project implementation. The technique is used in conjunction with the network planning method. It can be applied with manual calculations for small projects, and with the aid of computer software for large and/or complex projects.

EXERCISES

1. Prepare a cost schedule and accumulated cost curve for the Computer Installation Project using both manual and computer calculations (use early start schedule with a start date of October 4, 1982).

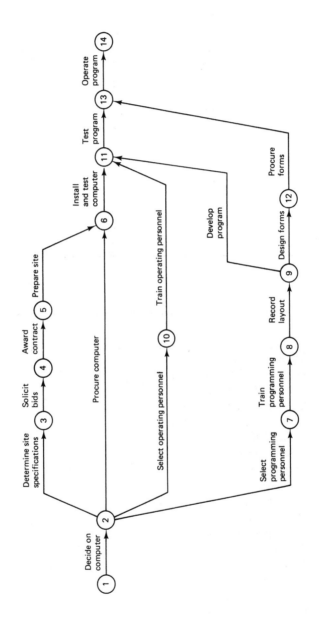

TOTAL FLOAT CALCULATION—COMPUTER INSTALLATION

ACTIVITY	LATEST FINISH	EARLIEST START	DURATION	TOTAL FLOAT
1,2	4	0	4	0*
2,3	5	4	1	0*
2,6	32	4	25	3
6,11	35	32	3	0*
3,4	10	5	5	0*
4,5	12	10	2	0*
5,6	32	12	20	0*
2,10	30	4	1	25
10,11	35	14	5	16
11,13	38	35	3	0*
2,7	17	4	4	9
7,8	25	6	8	11
8,9	27	14	2	11
9,11	35	16	12	7
9,12	36	16	2	18
12,13	38	18	2	18
13,14	40	38	2	0*

*Critical Path

PROJECT ACTIVITY	COST (DOLLARS)
Decide on Computer	$ 3,200
Determine Site Specifications	800
Procure Computer	100,000
Select Programming Personnel	1,600
Select Operating Personnel	800
Solicit Bids	2,000
Award Contract	800
Prepare Site	66,000
Install & Test Computer	9,000
Train Programming Personnel	8,000
Record Layout	2,000
Develop Program	24,000
Design Forms	2,000
Train Operating Personnel	8,000
Test Program	5,400
Procure Forms	2,000
Program Operational	2,400
TOTAL	$238,000

2. (Assume start date: October 4, 1982). Prepare a cost schedule and accumulated cost curve for the New Equipment Installation Project (p. 43) using both manual and computer calculations (consider both early start and late start schedules).

Job	Earliest Start	Latest Finish	Job	Earliest Start	Latest Finish
A	0	2	K	5	11
B	2	7	L	8	16
C	6	13	M	12	19
D	12	19	N	2	6
E	2	19	O	6	9
F	2	16	P	9	19
G	4	14	Q	19	21
H	6	16	R	21	22
I	2	8	S	2	18
J	2	8	T	4	12

New Equipment Installation

Project Activity	Cost (Dollars)
Design equipment	$ 2.0
Prepare equipment design detail	5.4
Prepare equipment installation drawings	1.0
Remove existing equipment	5.0
Prepare site	20.0
Design building	20.0
Construct building—phase I	150.0
Construct building—phase II	85.0
Fabricate equipment (in shop)	15.0
Procure ancillary equipment	54.0
Procure long-lead equipment items	60.0
Assemble equipment (in shop)	10.0
Install equipment—phase I	12.0
Install equipment—phase II	8.0
Develop operating procedures	2.0
Select and train personnel	3.0
Debug equipment	3.0
Develop and design automatic controls	1.6
Select controls supplier	1.2
Fabricate and assemble controls package	25.0
Total	$483.2

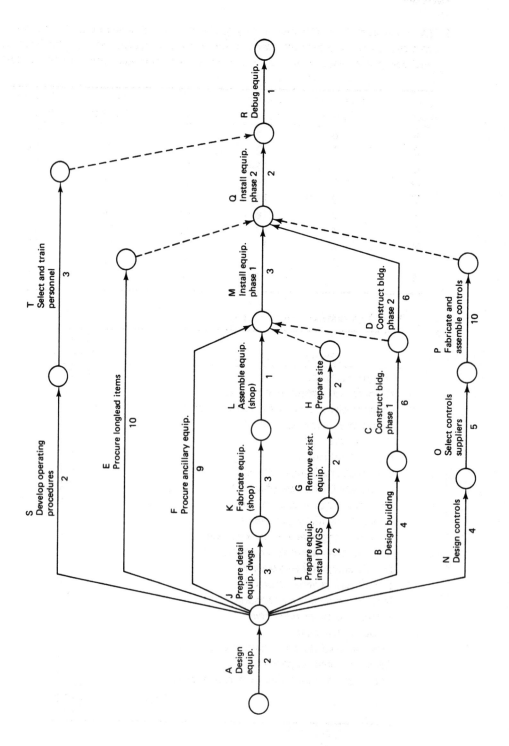

EQUIPMENT INSTALLATION: TOTAL FLOAT

JOB	DESCRIPTION	LATEST FINISH TIME	EARLIEST START TIME	DURATION	TOTAL FLOAT
1,2	Design equipment	2	0	2	0*
2,3	Develop operating procedures	18	2	2	14
3,4	Select & train personnel	21	4	3	14
2,5	Develop & design automatic controls	6	2	4	0*
5,6	Select controls supplier	9	6	3	0*
6,7	Fabricate & assemble controls package	19	9	10	0*
2,8	Procure long lead equipment	18	2	10	6
2,15	Procure ancillary equipment	16	2	9	5
2,11	Prepare equipment installation drawings	12	2	2	8
11,16	Remove existing equipment	14	4	2	8
16,17	Prepare site	16	6	2	8
2,9	Design building	7	2	4	1
9,18	Construct building: Phase I	13	6	6	1
18,19	Construct building: Phase II	19	12	6	1
2,12	Prepare equipment detail drawings	8	2	3	3
12,13	Fabricate equipment	11	5	3	3
13,15	Assemble equipment (in shop)	16	8	1	7
15,19	Install equipment: Phase I	19	12	3	4
19,20	Install equipment: Phase II	21	19	2	0*
20,21	Debug equipment	22	21	1	0*

*Critical path

(a) Compare the total costs of the manual and computer approach after the 5th week of the project (November 8, 1982).

(b) Calculate the total costs as of November 8, 1982 using the accumulative cost curve (cash flow curve) for both the early start and late start schedules.

From the above results, what schedule should be used if cash flow is a problem for this project and further financing will not be available until the 5th week of the project (November 8, 1982)? Provide reason(s) for your choice. Are there any other alternatives?

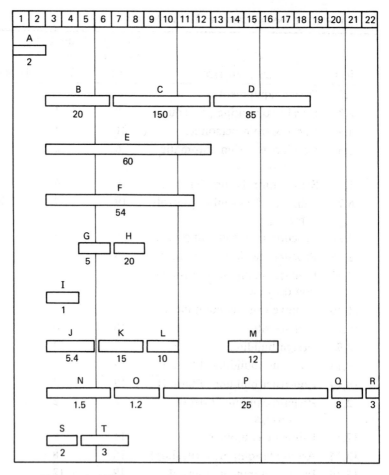

· Figures are in $(000)

· Figures are cost for complete activity. (See cost slope tabulation for cost/week.)

LEGEND

A	Design equipment	K	Fabricate equipment (in shop)
B	Design building	L	Assemble equipment (in shop)
C	Construct building phase I	M	Install equipment phase I
D	Construct building phase II	N	Develop and design auto controls
E	Procure long lead equipment	O	Select controls supplier
F	Procure ancillary equipment	P	Fabricate and assemble controls pkg.
G	Remove existing equipment	Q	Install equipment phase II
H	Prepare site	R	Debug equipment
I	Prepare equipment installation drawings	S	Develop operating procedures
J	Prepare equipment design detail drawings	T	Select and train personnel

Chapter 6

Planning Personnel/Labor Requirements

NEED FOR PLANNING PERSONNEL/LABOR

Resources in a project can refer to money, personnel, equipment, material, and skills. Assuming that personnel and labor make up the main resources of a project, this chapter is devoted to allocating personnel and labor requirements and then leveling their requirements within the prescribed project time limits. Effective leveling will reduce peaks and valleys in demands, minimize crew sizes, and avoid, or at least minimize, idle time or downtime. For a successful project, an organization needs to achieve these goals. There are advantages for an organization to strive to balance the overall requirements over reasonable periods of time. A business or industrial firm should be hiring an employee to work the life of the project, making one feel that once hired there is reasonable assurance of consistent employment. A firm's efficiency is reduced through layoffs and rehires. Meeting peak demands can provide problems that can possibly be avoided with effective leveling procedures. All sorts of intuitive methods for leveling (or normalizing) labor for project purposes have been tried with partial success. Satisfactory results are obtained when intuitive methods, supported by a disciplined approach, are used.

To establish a base it will be necessary to establish arbitrary available personnel/labor levels. Consequently, when scheduling personnel/labor, the first adjustments are made with the noncritical jobs, that is, those with the most float times. Next, adjustment is made with jobs almost on the critical list; and finally, if leveling is not achieved, then adjusting the highest-priority jobs, those on the critical path, may be necessary to satisfy the leveling process. Adjusting jobs on the critical path, in most cases, means lengthening the duration of the project. The resource leveling program is a valuable tool for the project planner and is used together with the cost and timing factors to arrive at the desirable project plan.

PLANNING PERSONNEL REQUIREMENTS

The Waste Heat Recovery Project is used to illustrate, by manual methods, the planning approach for personnel requirements planning, that is, normalizing the number of personnel required for the project. The project objectives are:

1. Complete the project in 29 weeks.
2. Maintain a constant crew size of four engineers and six management team members.

EARLY START SCHEDULING

From the network planning diagram and the total float tabulations, the critical and noncritical jobs are determined. These are shown on Figures 6–1 and 6–2, respectively.

After constructing the diagram and calculating the total float, initial leveling efforts can follow. Draw a bar chart showing each job at its earliest start time and

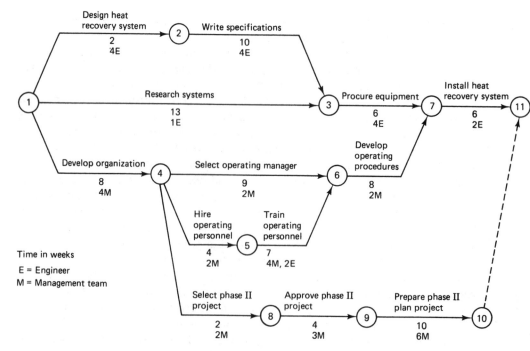

FIGURE 6–1 Network diagram for the Waste Heat Recovery Project.

Activity (Node Numbers)	Latest Finish Time	(−)	Earliest Start Time	(−)	Time Estimate for Completing Job	=	Total Float
1,2	7		0		2		5
1,3	17		0		13		4
1,4	6		0		6		0*
2,3	17		2		10		5
3,7	23		13		6		4
4,6	17		6		9		2
4,5	10		6		4		0*
5,6	17		10		7		0*
6,7	23		17		6		0*
4,8	15		6		2		7
8,9	19		8		4		7
9,10	29		12		10		7
7,11	29		23		6		0*
10,11†	29		22		0		7

*Critical path.
†Dummy—has no time duration.

FIGURE 6-2   Total float tabulation for the Waste Heat Recovery Project.

continuing for its assigned duration. Show the weekly crew below each activity bar on the bar chart. Figure 6–3a shows this arrangement. Total the crew requirements for each period, which can either be shown with the bar chart or tabulated as shown in Figure 6–3b.

If the earliest start schedule is used, the requirements for engineers will range from two to seven and the management team will range from two to twelve over the project duration of 29 weeks. The graphic load chart portrays these requirements rather effectively, as shown in Figure 6–4. From the graphic load chart the peaks and valleys of the personnel requirements reveal poor work continuity; therefore, additional leveling efforts are necessary to effect a more normal distribution.

LATE START SCHEDULING

As shown in Figure 6–5a, adjusting the time schedule to show the noncritical jobs starting at their latest start and continuing for its assigned duration provides another labor distribution arrangement. As handled previously with the earliest start sched-

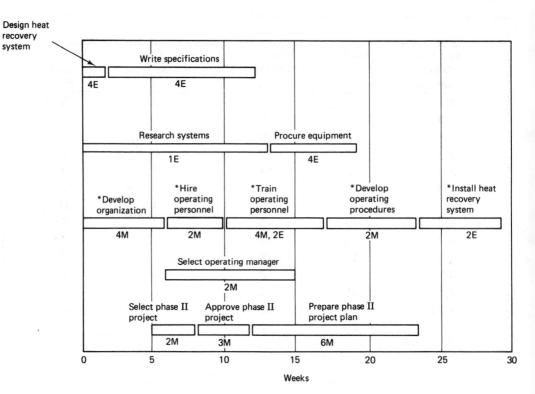

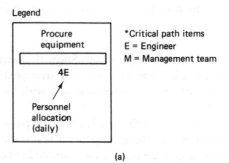

(a)

		WEEK																
	0	1–6	7	8	9	10	11	12	13	14	15	16	17	18	19	20–22	23	24–29
Engineers	—	5	5	5	5	5	7	7	3	6	6	4	4	4	4	—	—	2
Management team	—	4	6	6	7	7	9	9	12	12	12	10	10	8	8	8	2	—

(b)

FIGURE 6–3   Labor leveling for the Waste Heat Recovery Project: (a) bar chart time schedule (earliest start time) with labor allocation; (b) labor distribution tabulation using the earliest start schedule.

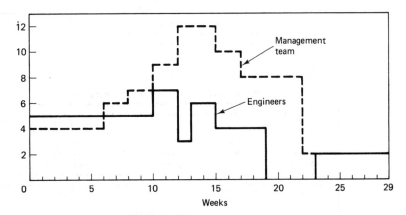

FIGURE 6-4 Graphic load chart of labor allocation (earliest start time) for the Waste Heat Recovery Project.

ule, the weekly crew is totaled and the work force is checked for continuity. Figure 6–5b shows the tabulation of the personnel requirements for each time period.

With the jobs starting at their latest start times, there is still poor work continuity; actually, the same personnel conditions exist as when all the jobs were starting at their earliest start. From the latest start schedule, the requirements for engineers range from two to seven (with one exception, no engineers are used the first week of the project). The management team requirements range from two to eight over the length of the project. Further leveling efforts need to be considered, using the jobs having float times that can be adjusted, if the project objectives of using four engineers and six management team members are to be met. Figure 6–6 is a graphic load chart portraying the personnel requirements when the project is scheduled with all of the activities starting at their latest start.

The personnel distribution chart suggests that trying to achieve the personnel objective within the planned project duration of 29 weeks may not be possible. Considering alternatives such as extending the project 2 weeks, and possibly longer, may be necessary if it is not possible to acquire additional engineers and management team members for this project.

To continue with the manual procedure as described, on a trial-and-error basis, will be time consuming and complex. Although manual efforts can be used for relatively small projects, the personnel-leveling process for this project is too complex for manual resolution. Use of the computer for assisting in resolving resource-leveling situations is discussed in Chapter 7.

Most project management computer programs have a resource allocation feature. The computer program, basically a trial-and-error process, is similar to the manual approach. There are printed resource charts showing the skills required by time period, and there are printouts available for the earliest start schedule, latest

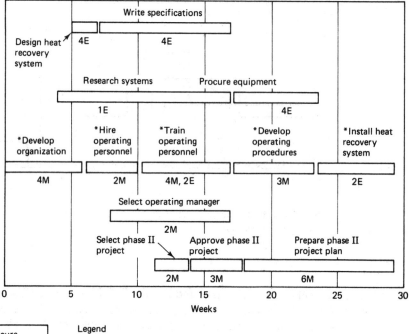

(a)

	WEEK																			
	0	1	2	3	4	5	6	7	8	9	10	11	12	13	14	15	16	17	18	19–23	24–29
Engineers:	—	—	4	4	4	5	5	5	5	5	5	7	7	7	3	3	3	3	4	4	2
Management team:	—	4	4	4	4	4	4	2	2	4	4	6	6	8	8	8	9	9	3	8	6

(b)

FIGURE 6-5 Personnel leveling for the Waste Heat Recovery Project: (a) bar chart time schedule (latest start time) with labor allocation; (b) personnel leveling using the latest start schedule.

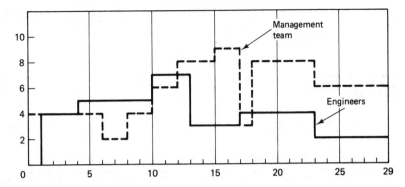

FIGURE 6–6 Graphic load chart of personnel allocation (latest start time) for the Waste Heat Recovery Project.

start schedule, and various adjusted time schedules that provide different leveling arrangements to suit the needs of the project.

SUMMARY

A complete planning process needs to include not only time and cost factors which have to be satisfactorily related in the project schedule, but an additional factor must be considered: the resources available to do the jobs, such as labor, personnel, equipment, space, and funds.

The resource-leveling program, by a manual approach if the project is small, or using a computer program for larger or complex projects, allocates the resources available to a project such that period-to-period changes in the levels of resources will be minimized. The resource-leveling program can also be used to determine the minimum project duration when given a limited quantity of resources.

The resource-leveling approach follows these steps:

1. Specify the number of each skill or resource required for each activity or job.
2. Specify by time period the number of each skill or resource using the earliest start schedule.
3. Knowing the availability of each resource, schedule the jobs within the framework of the planning network so that specified availabilities are not exceeded and requirements are "leveled."
4. If leveling and keeping within the available resources are not possible, the program must either be extended or overtime must be considered for those

skills that exceed what is available. (A computer program is necessary to accomplish these tasks.)

EXERCISES

1. Given below are the labor data for the new equipment installation project:

LABOR ALLOCATION*

JOB DESCRIPTION	PERSONNEL (DAILY AVERAGE)					
	DR	DE	EN	EL	PF	LA
Design equipment		4				
Prepare equipment design detail	6					
Prepare equipment installation drawings		2				
Remove existing equipment			1			6
Prepare site			1	2	4	
Design building	6	4				
Construct building—Phase I			1	4	4	8
Construct building—Phase II			1	6	6	4
Fabricate equipment (in shop)		1				
Procure ancillary equipment		2				
Procure long-lead equipment items		2				
Assemble equipment (in shop)		1				
Install equipment—Phase I			1	2	4	
Install equipment—Phase II			1	2	4	
Develop operating procedures			2			
Select and train personnel			2			
Debug equipment			1	2	4	
Develop and design automatic controls			1			
Select controls supplier			1			
Fabricate and assemble controls package			1			

*DR, draftsman; DE, designer; EN, engineer; EL, electrician; PF, pipe fitter; LA, laborer.

(a) The daily requirements for each skilled trade (or personnel) for the new equipment installation project for both the *earliest start schedule* and the *latest start schedule.*

(b) The *available* skilled trades/personnel are as follows:

	No. Available/day
Designers	4
Draftsmen	6
Engineers	4
Pipefitters	6
Electricians	6
Laborers	8

Determine the better schedule (early start or late start) if skilled trades/personnel availability is critical. (One approach is to determine overtime costs of each skilled trade/personnel for each schedule—one of the factors to determine the better schedule.)

(c) Using the better schedule what are the overtime requirements per week for each skilled trade/personnel?

2. The labor allocation for the Theater Planning Project is noted on the screen print as follows:

PROJECT ITEMS, DURATION (DAYS)

```
FROM    TO    DURATION    DESCRIPTION


1    -> 2        20        FORM ORGANIZATION
2    -> 3        10        SELECT PLAY
     -> 4        20        COMPLETE FINANCING
3    -> 4        0         DUMMY
     -> 5        20        SELECT DIRECTOR
4    -> 6        40        CONTRACT STARS
5    -> 6        0         DUMMY
     -> 7        10        SELECT SET DESIGNER
     -> 8        10        SELECT CAST
     -> 12       70        CONDUCT PUBLICITY CAMPAIGN
6    -> 8        0         DUMMY
     -> 10       20        BOOK OUT-OF-TOWN SHOWS
7    -> 8        40        PROCURE SCENERY PROPS
```

(continued on next page)

FROM	TO	DURATION	DESCRIPTION
8 -> 9		30	CONDUCT REHEARSALS
9 -> 10		10	CONDUCT DRESS REHEARSALS
10 -> 11		50	OUT-OF-TOWN SHOWS
11 -> 13		10	OPENING NIGHT PREPARATIONS

FROM   TO   RESOURCES ALLOCATED PER UNIT TIME

```
1   -> 2    PA3 $P.40 DP.40
2   -> 3    PA4 $P.75 DP.75
    -> 4    PA2 $P3.50 DP3.50
3   -> 5    PA2 $P2.00 DP2.00
4   -> 6    PA8 $P1.50 DP1.50
5   -> 7    PA3 $P4.75 DP4.75
    -> 8    PA10 $P4.00 DP4.00
    -> 12   PA4 $P3.75 DP3.75          LEGEND
6   -> 10   PA2 $P8.50 DP8.50 SA4
7   -> 8    PA2 SA4 $P4.29 DP4.29      PA    PRODUCTION ASSISTANTS
8   -> 9    PA4 SA6 $P3.33 DP3.33
9   -> 10   PA4 SA8 $P1.00 DP1.00      SA    STAGE ASSISTANTS
10  -> 11   PA4 SA8 $P4.00 DP4.00
11  -> 13   PA2 SA2 $P3.00 DP3.00      DP,$P EXPENSES
```

(a) Find the total weekly requirements (daily average) for Production Assistants and Stage Assistants for both the earliest start schedule and the latest start schedule.

(b) There are available 12 Production Assistants, and 6 Stage Assistants.

　　(1) What schedule allows for the least amount of overtime for Stage Assistants? Production Assistants?

　　(2) If overtime rate for Stage Assistants is $18.00/hr. and Production Assistants is $14.00/hr. and the schedule is an eight-hour day, what is the total *overtime cost* for Stage Assistants? Production Assistants?

(c) From your findings, which schedule—earliest start or latest start—would you select for use for the Theater Planning Project? Why?

Chapter 7

Role of the Computer

In previous chapters, manual methods were discussed for use in developing time schedules, analyzing costs, and determining labor/personnel requirements. Although manual methods for preparing computations are feasible for small or simple projects, most projects require the use of computers (especially microcomputers) because of their many advantages. The growing popularity and use of the computer in so many fields has also brought into its "fold" project management efforts. The computer has become as necessary a tool to project management activity as the tools used in any of the trades.

Specifically, project personnel have found that the use of a computer makes it possible to:

- Handle very *rapidly* large projects that would require many labor-hours if calculations were made manually.
- Handle *accurately* a complex project in which manual calculations would inevitably be vulnerable to errors.
- Make updating runs as often as desired without excessive expenditure of personnel.
- Print the results of the analysis in a useful and readable format.
- Undertake time/cost trade-off and resource-leveling analysis, which is difficult and extremely time consuming when done manually.

Proper application of computers can be a distinct aid in effective planning; however, it should be emphasized that a computer cannot *plan* or *analyze* a project.

SOFTWARE PACKAGES

Deciding on the proper computer software to be used is of major concern to the user, as the dynamic nature of projects requires quick and accurate response to questions that arise during their implementation. Normally, people involved in project management have comparatively little knowledge of the merits of the physical elements (or hardware) of the computer and the methods of instruction (or software) that are used to direct the computer. But they know what information they expect from reports that are generated from the computer. When computer software firms realize that the user is not familiar with software preparation, their selling success is based on convincing the user that their package will suit the needs of the user, and is "friendly"; that is, the user needs to know little more than the planning data that he or she needs to enter to produce reports.

Mainframe and microcomputers use on-line interactive systems. Data can be accepted from either precedence diagramming or arrow diagramming (the technique used in this book). Input data can be from activity-oriented work items (arrow diagramming) or the start-to-start, start-to-finish, finish-to-start, and finish-to-finish relationships with time delay and lag that typify precedence diagramming. Most computer programs allow for multiple-activity starts at the beginning of a project and multiple-activity finishes at the completion of the project. Also, almost every software package will have an error-detection feature.

Generally, the main features of a software package are:

- *Network generation:* processes input data, builds the needed internal files, performs all necessary calculations, writes the network onto a master file when requested, and prints any selected output reports.
- *Update:* updates an existing network by changing the network structure and data associated with work items and relationships among them, reports any progress against any work items in process, and writes the updated results onto the master file. Any requested output reports are also printed.
- *Maintenance:* recomputes dates of work items based on current or revised data entered in this run, but does not alter the network's structure.
- *Detailed reports:* should be targeted to users, such as project analysts, first-line supervision, or financial personnel. Selected information should be obtained easily, such as work occurring during a certain time segment or related to a given resource. An important part of the total project control phase is the fact that report data need to be printed in sequence by *organizations.* Other sequence sorts are required for start or finish dates, and by major work activities.

Preparing Input Data

Especially for the inexperienced, preparing computer input data from the instructions in the user's manual provided by the software supplier can be difficult. (The author's observations of user's manuals, in general, is that they give little consideration to those with a limited computer background.)

In negotiating acquisition of a project management program, the user should request that a representative of the supplier be available to instruct the user through at least one complete project that the user is interested in implementing. At the present time almost all project management software packages use the interactive method of processing project input data.

Interactive Input

Interactive input capability allows the user to enter data in free-form, interactive question-and-response sequences, all of which are described in the user's guide that is provided. An advantage of the interactive input capability is that it simplifies the preparation of input data for project management systems and facilitates the examination of output results. A feature is its end-user-oriented procedures, which enable project management people with limited computer experience to work directly with the capabilities of an on-line interactive system.

The on-line interactive system functions through a keyboard remote terminal and the main computer's on-line, time-sharing mode. During a question–response sequence, the user is prompted with questions that request specific input data items. The user responds with answers and data entries that request desired actions to be taken. If the user makes a detectable error in a response, a diagnostic message is displayed to advise the user of corrective action that can be taken immediately.

The on-line interactive input system includes three communication modes and allows the user to choose between the second two for entry of the bulk of all input data.

1. *Question mode.* Input data requested from the user are part of a specific question.

2. *Descriptor mode.* Logical abbreviations are used for data which allow for multiple entries on each line.

3. *Menu mode.* This mode provides for direct data entry based on a prescribed data sequence.

Interactive input features on-line, conversational means of entering input data and requesting output reports containing the processed results, and prompts users with questions to guide them through data input to either generate a new network or update an existing network. It offers users a choice of detail in questions. A new user can receive the complete question forms that explain the exact user responses, while an experienced user can receive very brief questions for more rapid progress.

Types of Output Reports

Software packages provide basic information on the latest status of the user's project. Of main concern to the user is that the reports are designed in formats or graphics that are suited for all levels of management to understand and for use in any analysis that project conditions may require.

- *Milestone report:* lists all milestones in a network and their various calculated, actual, and scheduled dates.
- *Schedule report:* lists all specified work items, with various key dates, floats, durations, and calendar information.
- *Weekly bar chart:* shows graphically the duration and relative time frame of all specified work items using a weekly scale.
- *Scheduled earnings report:* lists the cost status for all specified work items, showing estimated cost, projected cost, actual cost to date, and earned cost.
- *Resource utilization report:* shows graphically the weekly resource utilization for all specified work items.
- *Resource schedule report:* lists all specified work items with various key resource scheduling dates and floats.

There may be as many as 30 output reports that can be provided for basic information on the latest project status. Reports are designed in various project formats suited for various levels of project management or project analysts, and with cost reports similarly designed toward use by various financial groups.

Representative Suppliers and Packages

The intent of providing the list of representative suppliers is a guidance expedient only. The needs of the project in achieving successful completion, using the computer application as one of the tools, should determine the software program to be used. On many occasions the computer mainframe hardware configuration that is available for use will limit the project management programs that can be considered. On most occasions a computer mainframe or minicomputer configuration is not available for use for project management purposes, and may be just too large to use.

The personal computer is not as limited as the mainframe computer in meeting the requirements of project management applications, and there is a possibility that a person involved in a specific project can write a program or have another person in the firm do it. However, the proliferation of microcomputer software suppliers does not make this approach feasible.

There exist various software packages that do what is needed, or close to it, and can be timesavers. Listed below are a representative group of software suppliers that have project management software and the brands of computer (or operating systems) on which their software is claimed to run. Many of the programs may run on more than one type of computer and will also be available in a variety of formats. Some of these packages will require particular setups, and the amount of memory required will also vary.

Some of these programs are part of a general-purpose or even an integrated software package. A presentation package can create charts and graphs; a spreadsheet program can compare project cost and timing data; database managers can keep track of project data; and processors can be used for writing reports.

As personal computers with the accompanying software are still in a dynamic phase, there will be more and improved software available, as well as greater variety, as programs are written for the newer more powerful microcomputer and operating systems. The designated project management packages for personal computer (PC) or microcomputers are intended for guidance only. There is extensive literature on project management software, and with a reasonable review, one can select the proper "package."

The representative list of personal computer software that follows is for guidance only. The specific needs of the project should determine selection.

	OPERATING SYSTEMS	INTERFACE WITH OTHER PC APPLICATIONS
PROJECT MANAGER WORKBENCH Applied Business Technology 365 Broadway New York, NY 10013	MSDOS	dBASE III Lotus 1-2-3
MicroGANTT Earth Data Corporation P.O. Box 13169 Richmond, VA 23225	CP/M 80 MSDOS PCDOS	ASCII programs
HARVARD TOTAL PROJECT MANAGER Harvard Software Inc. 521 Great Road Littleton, MA 01460	PCDOS	DIF programs
ARTEMIS 200 Metier Management Systems 5884 Point West Drive Houston, TX 77036	MSDOS	
PRIMAVERA PROJECT PLANNER Primavera Systems Inc. Two Bala Plaza Suite 925 Bala Cynwyd, PA 19004	MSDOS	ASCII programs
QUICKNET Project Software and Development Inc. 14 Story Street Cambridge, MA 02138	MSDOS	ASCII programs

(continued on next page)

	OPERATING SYSTEMS	INTERFACE WITH OTHER PC APPLICATIONS
SUPERPROJECT Sorcim/IUS 2195 Fortune Drive San Jose, CA 95131	PCDOS	dBASE Lotus 1-2-3
MICROTRAX Softrak Systems P.O. Box 22156 AMF 1977 West North Temple Salt Lake City, UT 84122	CP/M MSDOS UNIX XENDO	ASCII programs
PROMIS Strategic Software Planning 222 Third Street Cambridge, MA 02142	MSDOS	ASCII programs
PERTMASTER ADVANCE PERTMASTER IN CONTROL Westminster Software Inc. 2570 El Camino Real Mountain View, CA 94040	CP/M MSDOS PCDOS	ASCII database programs

All of the microcomputer software packages listed will handle between 200 and 10,000 activities, depending on the specific package. And there are other vendors not listed who may have a package more suitable for your needs. There are trade periodicals that will have advertisements or articles on available software that will be more up to date than will most other sources.

Features such as number of projects that the package can handle, number of resources, resource leveling and allocation, report generation, and link to mainframe capability are included in selective software packages. Vendors' promotional material will describe the features available.

Personal computers use two types of software. Systems software includes operating systems and programming languages, and application programs. Operating systems link hardware and applications software to a specific microprocessor. They are critical to the operation of any computer because they determine which programming language and applications programs can be used. The operating system package typically contains a number of utility programs for formatting disk, copying data or program files from one disk to another, displaying a list of programs or data on a disk, and editing programs and data. Included among the existing program packages are these operating systems:

- *Apple DOS:* proprietary disk operating system written for the Apple computer. Apple DOS, TRS-DOS, and MS-DOS are not compatible.
- *CP/M (Control Program for Microprocessors):* developed by Digital Research Corp., Pacific Grove, CA. It has become the standard operating system for 8-bit microcomputers.
- *MS-DOS:* distributed by Microsoft Corp., Bellvue, WA. Because of the large amount of software written for it, this operating system is considered by some to be the standard for 16-bit microcomputers. Its popularity is associated with PC-DOS, a version of MS-DOS for the IBM PC microcomputer.
- *PC-DOS:* version of MC-DOS for the IBM PC microcomputer.
- *TRS-DOS:* proprietary disk operating system for Tandy/Radio Shack 8-bit microcomputers. TRS-DOS, Apple DOS, and MS-DOS are not compatible.
- *UNIX:* developed by Bell Laboratories in 1960 for use on minicomputers, such as the DEC PDP-11; allows certain application programs written on minicomputers to be transferred to larger microcomputers with minimal changes. It runs on Intel 8086, Motorola MC68000, and Zilog Z8000 microprocessors and allows more than one user to run several programs simultaneously. Several versions are available.

Included among the more popular programming languages used to develop microcomputer software are the following:

- *APL (A Programming Language):* a general-purpose language that is self-teaching and interactive, requiring relatively fewer instructions for complex operations.
- *BASIC (Beginners' All-Purpose Symbolic Instruction Code):* the most popular language for microcomputer programming. It is a fairly easy language for nonprogrammers to learn and remember because many of the commands are English words. It can be used for a variety of engineering applications.
- *COBOL (Common Business-Oriented Language):* uses natural words and phrases that can be recognized by nontechnical users. It offers limited mathematical capabilities but works well for manipulating text and data.
- *FORTRAN (FORmula TRANslator):* one of the more widely used languages for engineering work because such a large number of engineering programs have been written in it. FORTRAN is large-computer oriented, but versions are available for the large microcomputers.
- *PASCAL:* designed to speed the writing of large complex programs. It is a highly readable language that encourages structured programming and is often used in education and research.

FEATURES OF A PROJECT MANAGEMENT PACKAGE

A typical personal computer project management package is considered to be a relatively sophisticated tool, and is an easier package to learn and use effectively than is a mainframe software program. A personal computer software package will usually perform the following functions:

- Assign resources to activities
- Print bar chart schedules
- Provide flexibility in report design
- Identify milestones
- Print resource histograms
- Identify slippage by negative float
- Provide search/sort functions for reports

A software supplier will claim that:

- The program is user friendly.
- Help functions will display on the screen.
- Software documentation is available.
- The program is compatible with other software packages.
- The program will plot the network (a plotter needs to be available).

Software packages for microcomputers are being improved so that resource leveling and allocation features are now available. Data entry can be entered using entry screens, system prompts, and interactive query language (or question and answer). As an example, a computer software package presently available contains these salient functions:

- *Housekeeping:* calendar data, abbreviation dictionaries, system details, etc.
- *Scheduling:* schedule, resource data, milestone
- *Reports:* standard schedule listing, bar charts, resources, cost, personnel summary
- *Resources:* cost, personnel histograms

Housekeeping

This project management program requires a calendar from which the start and finish dates of activities are calculated, and an abbreviation file which is used for resource scheduling and for categorizing activities (sorts). When a program is started up, the main menu (list of user options) will appear as follows:

```
                              PERTMASTER



Do You Want To :-

        1 : Produce an Up-to-Date Plan ?
        2 : Get Reports From an Up-to-Date Plan ?
        3 : Do Some Housekeeping ?
        4 : End this Session ?

PRESS THE NUMBER OF YOUR CHOICE [   ] or ? for HELP
```

Calendar File. To generate a calendar file, enter "Do some housekeeping." The screen will change to

```
                            V V V V V V V
                            < PERTMASTER >
                            Λ Λ Λ Λ Λ Λ Λ

Do You Want To :-

        1 : Work with Calendars ?
        2 : Work with Abbreviation Dictionaries ?
        3 : Change Printer Details ?
        4 : Change other System Details ?
        5 : Delete old Plans from a Disk ?
        6 : Copy Plans from One Disk to Another Disk ?
        7 : Merge Plans Together ?
        8 : Do None of These ?

PRESS THE NUMBER OF YOUR CHOICE [   ] or ? for HELP
```

Enter "Work with calendars." The screen will display another menu, which will allow you to work with the calendars:

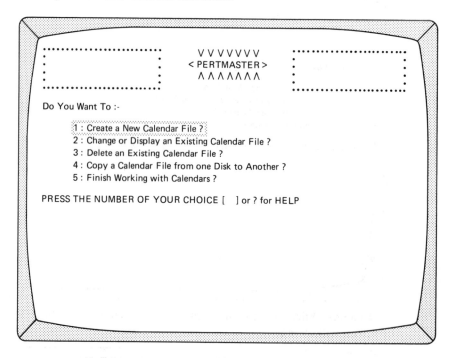

```
                           V V V V V V
                          < PERTMASTER >
                           ∧ ∧ ∧ ∧ ∧ ∧

Do You Want To :-

        1 : Create a New Calendar File ?
        2 : Change or Display an Existing Calendar File ?
        3 : Delete an Existing Calendar File ?
        4 : Copy a Calendar File from one Disk to Another ?
        5 : Finish Working with Calendars ?

PRESS THE NUMBER OF YOUR CHOICE [    ] or ? for HELP
```

After the user has indicated that a calendar file is to be created, a calendar code name is selected. There are a series of screens that allow the user such calendar options as the following:

- Listing the time frame of the project
- Specifying which days of the week are working or nonworking
- Specifying nonworking holidays
- Specifying time periods that are continuously working or nonworking

Once the user's choices are completed, the calendar can be shown on the screen or printout. A calendar printout will be especially useful when the user needs to select specific milestone dates that must be met to ensure timely completion of the project.

Once the user has selected all the desired calendar options, the original calendar menu will appear that has shown not only the available options, but the opportunity to finish working with calendars:

```
                    V V V V V V V
                    < PERTMASTER >
                    ∧ ∧ ∧ ∧ ∧ ∧ ∧


Do You Want To :-

        1 : Create a New Calendar File ?
        2 : Change or Display an Existing Calendar File ?
        3 : Delete an Existing Calendar File ?
        4 : Copy a Calendar File from one Disk to Another ?
        5 : Finish Working with Calendars ?

PRESS THE NUMBER OF YOUR CHOICE [   ] or ? for HELP
```

Abbreviations File. The abbreviations file is useful for keeping a record of all the labor, personnel, costs, equipment, and material by listing their codes or abbreviations that are used first in entering input data, and then in the resources and sorting reports.

```
                    V V V V V V V
                    < PERTMASTER >
                    ∧ ∧ ∧ ∧ ∧ ∧ ∧


Do You Want To :-

        1 : Create a New Abbreviations File ?
        2 : Change or Display an Abbreviations File ?
        3 : Delete an Old Abbreviations File ?
        4 : Copy a File from Disk to Disk ?
        5 : Finish Working with Abbreviation Files ?

PRESS THE NUMBER OF YOUR CHOICE [   ] or ? for HELP
```

After entering the number to create a new abbreviations file, there would be a series of menus that request the user to provide the following:

- Code name for the abbreviations file
- (Two letters) abbreviations and full descriptions for the resources and responsible persons or functions

When all the abbreviations and full descriptions have been entered, the main abbreviations menu will appear on the screen.

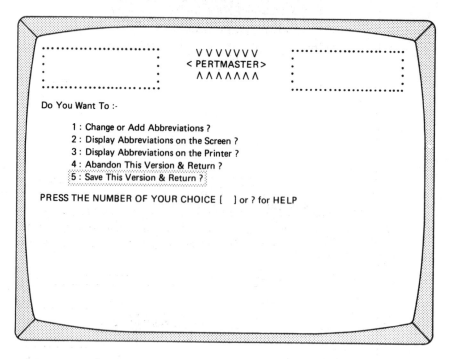

```
. . . . . . . . . . . . . . . . . . . .     V V V V V V     . . . . . . . . . . . . . . . . . . . .
.                                  .     < PERTMASTER >     .                                  .
.                                  .     ∧ ∧ ∧ ∧ ∧ ∧     .                                  .
. . . . . . . . . . . . . . . . . . . .                     . . . . . . . . . . . . . . . . . . . .

Do You Want To :-

            1 : Change or Add Abbreviations ?
            2 : Display Abbreviations on the Screen ?
            3 : Display Abbreviations on the Printer ?
            4 : Abandon This Version & Return ?
            5 : Save This Version & Return ?

PRESS THE NUMBER OF YOUR CHOICE [    ] or ? for HELP
```

After saving the abbreviations file, the main menu will appear, and the user is now ready to input the project data.

Input Plan Data

The user will work with a new plan (or consider updating an existing project plan or file). A screen offering this choice will appear.

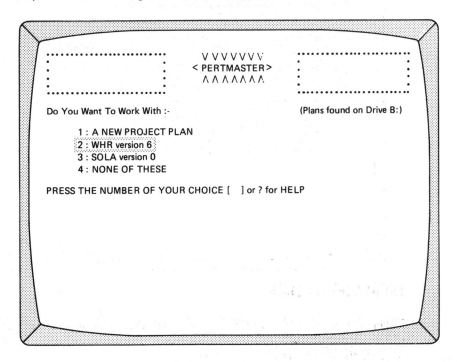

The next screen requires the user to list information that will show as titles (or headings) on the report and will include such additional information as calendar and abbreviations file code names, and arrow or precedence type of diagramming. Using the text sample project, Waste Heat Recovery Project, the completed screen would appear as follows:

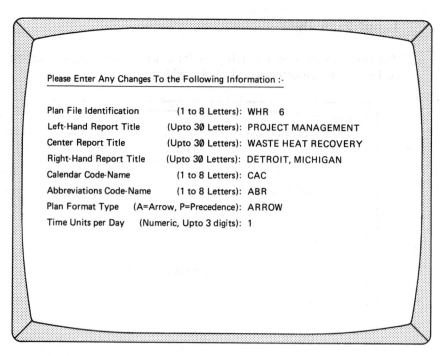

Please Enter Any Changes To the Following Information :-

Plan File Identification   (1 to 8 Letters): WHR   6
Left-Hand Report Title   (Upto 30 Letters): PROJECT MANAGEMENT
Center Report Title   (Upto 30 Letters): WASTE HEAT RECOVERY
Right-Hand Report Title   (Upto 30 Letters): DETROIT, MICHIGAN
Calendar Code-Name   (1 to 8 Letters): CAC
Abbreviations Code-Name   (1 to 8 Letters): ABR
Plan Format Type   (A=Arrow, P=Precedence): ARROW
Time Units per Day   (Numeric, Upto 3 digits): 1

Input Timing Data

Depending on the software that is to be used, there will be a series of screens with menus to denote that data for a new project are to be entered. The next screen requests the timing data:

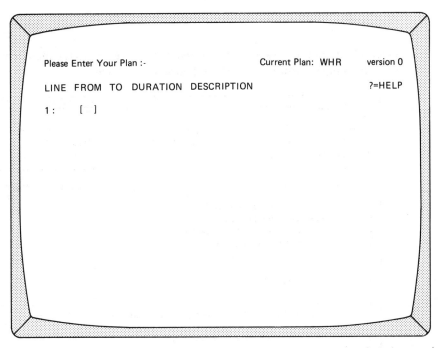

```
Please Enter Your Plan :-              Current Plan: WHR    version 0

LINE  FROM  TO  DURATION  DESCRIPTION                    ?=HELP

 1 :    [  ]
```

The return key moves from heading to heading, the user entering the required information: *FROM* and *TO,* or *i* and *j* nodes, respectively, for each activity, together with its duration (time in days) and description. A typical completed screen of the Waste Heat Recovery Project appears like this:

```
COMMAND?  Ø    Ø                  Current Plan: WHR    version 6

LINE  FROM      TO      DURATION  DESCRIPTION              ?=HELP
 1 :  START->   1                 NOT BEFORE DAY 2
 2 :    1     <>MILESTONE         START PROJECT
 3 :          ->  2         10    DESIGN HEAT RECOVERY SYSTEM: EG
 4 :          ->  3         65    RESEARCH SYSTEMS: EG
 5 :          ->  4         30    DEVELOP ORGANIZATION: IR
 6 :    2     ->  3         50    WRITE SPECIFICATIONS: EG
 7 :    3     <>MILESTONE         START EQUIPMENT PROCUREMENT
 8 :          ->  7         30    PROCURE EQUIPMENT: EG
 9 :    4     <>MILESTONE         START PERSONNEL PROCUREMENT
10:           ->  5         20    HIRE OPERATING PERSONNEL: IR
11:           ->  6         45    SELECT OPERATING MANAGER: IR
12:           ->  8         10    SELECT PHASE II PROJECT: FP
13:    5      ->  6         35    TRAIN OPERATING PERSONNEL: IR
14:    6      ->  7         30    DEVELOP OPERATING PROCEDURES: EG
15:    7     <>MILESTONE          START EQUIPMENT INSTALLATION
16:           ->  11        30    INSTALL HEAT RECOVERY SYSTEM: EG
17:    8      ->  9         20    APPROVE PHASE II PROJECT: FP
18:    9      ->  10        50    PREPARE PHASE II PROJECT: FP
19:    10     ->  11         Ø    DUMMY
```

Reports

Once all the timing data are entered, the user can return to the main menu and "call up" the report menu screen, which appears as follows:

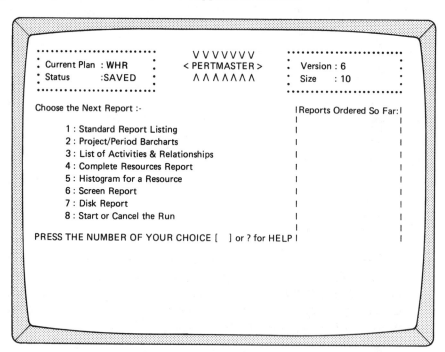

Choosing the standard report listing can provide a tabulated schedule for all or selected activity timing with optional start and finish dates; project/period bar charts provide graphic representation of the timing tabulations.

Timing reports in the form of a scheduling sequence or critical activities are available:

```
.......................          V V V V V V V        .........................
: Current Plan :WHR    :        < PERTMASTER >       :  Version : 0          :
: Status       :SAVED  :        ∧ ∧ ∧ ∧ ∧ ∧ ∧        :  Size    : 10         :
.......................                              .........................

Do You Want This Report to Have :-

        1 : The Earliest Activities First ?
        2 : The Output in Alphabetical Sequence ?
        3 : The Most Critical Activities First ?

PRESS THE NUMBER OF YOUR CHOICE [   ] or ? for HELP
```

Reports sorted by responsible activities, the work breakdown structure (WBS), and milestones can be chosen with this screen:

```
.......................          V V V V V V V        .........................
: Current Plan :WHR     :        < PERTMASTER >       :  Version : 6          :
: Status    :ANALYSED   :        ∧ ∧ ∧ ∧ ∧ ∧ ∧        :  Size    : 21         :
.......................                              .........................

SELECTIVE REPORTING FACILITY — STANDARD REPORT

Enter the KEY on which to Select Activities & Its Location:-

(1) Selection Key    : Ø                               Ø

(2) Starting Location :

TYPE 'MILESTONE' if you would like a Milestone report
Press RETURN if you would like all activities to be printed        ? = HELP
```

The user may also "order" a bar chart that covers the entire project time frame that is copied on one page—an appropriate size for attaching to a project status report.

When the timing reports have been generated, the user can return to the main menu to continue updating, receive additional reports, or simply end this session. The type of reports that are generated include the following:

- Work schedule report (early start schedule)
- Bar chart schedule (early start)

There are other types of timing reports available for specific concerns. These are shown in later chapters describing specific projects where there is a need to carry out effective planning and control of the projects. There are times, as the user is adding input to the plan, that other actions are required.

Milestones

Once the plan has been entered and saved, the user can update the plan by adding the input data to obtain a milestone report. There are other features, such as fixing milestone dates and scheduling project start and completion dates, that provide a more complete timing plan.

Resources

One option may be to continue updating the plan by adding resources to all or any of the activities. The procedure for adding resources starts by calling up the screen that displays the input for the Waste Heat Recovery Project:

```
COMMAND?  Ø   Ø               Current Plan: WHR           version 7

LINE     FROM      TO      RESOURCES ALLOCATED PER UNIT TIME     ?=HELP
 1 :      1      ->  2      EN4 $C75 TC75
 2 :             ->  3      EN1 $C3 TC3
 3 :             ->  4      MT4 $C40 TC40
 4 :      2      ->  3      EN4 $C90 TC90
 5 :      3      ->  7      EN4 $C20 TC20
 6 :      4      ->  5      MT2 $C40 TC40
 7 :             ->  6      MT2 $C30 TC30
 8 :             ->  8      MT2 $C40 TC40
 9 :      5      ->  6      MT4 EN2 $C80 TC80
10:      6      ->  7      MT2 $C210 TC210
11:      7      -> 11      EN2 $C30 TC30
12:      8      ->  9      MT3 $C30 TC30
13:      9      -> 10      MT6 $C72 TC72
```

The resources required by this activity are entered: Engineer (*code* EN) and Management Team Members (*code* MT) as required, with appropriate cost input (*code* TC and *code* $C). Once all the resources data have been entered, there are several reports that the user will find useful.

Complete Resource Report. The series of questions and answers for the Resource report input is similar to those pertaining to the timing reports. There is an added feature of acquiring a late start schedule in addition to the early start schedule. Daily or weekly resource requirements (user choice) are printed out for a "quick" review of total resources required for the project.

Histogram Reports

These graphics are available through a series of screens by entering the two-letter abbreviations that were entered in the project input.

Report Printouts

Figures 7-1 to 7-6 are examples of printed reports that provide the user (whether the person is a project manager, project engineer, or project coordinator) with a powerful tool to use in planning as will as controlling the project. Using the Waste Heat Recovery System as the example project, selected reports, with accompanying analyses, show the reader the information to be gained from these reports.

PROJECT MANAGEMENT   WASTE HEAT RECOVERY   DETROIT, MICHIGAN
      REPORT TYPE :STANDARD LISTING   PRINTING SEQUENCE :Earliest Activities First
                                                                                SELECTION CRITERIA :ALL
      PLAN I.D.   :WHR   VERSION 4   TIME NOW DATE   : 4/OCT/82

ACTIVITY DESCRIPTION	EARLIEST START	EARLIEST FINISH	LATEST START	LATEST FINISH	DURATION	FLOAT
1- 4 DEVELOP ORGANIZATION .IR	4/OCT/82	12/NOV/82	4/OCT/82	12/NOV/82	30	0 *
1- 3 RESEARCH SYSTEMS .EG	4/OCT/82	31/DEC/82	1/NOV/82	28/JAN/83	65	20
1- 2 DESIGN HEAT RECOVERY SYSTEM .EG	4/OCT/82	15/OCT/82	8/NOV/82	19/NOV/82	10	25
2- 3 WRITE SPECIFICATIONS .EG	18/OCT/82	24/DEC/82	22/NOV/82	28/JAN/83	50	25
4- 5 HIRE OPERATING PERSONNEL .IR	15/NOV/82	10/DEC/82	15/NOV/82	10/DEC/82	20	0 *
4- 6 SELECT OPERATING MANAGER .IR	15/NOV/82	14/JAN/83	29/NOV/82	28/JAN/83	45	10
4- 8 SELECT PHASE 2 PROJECT .FP	15/NOV/82	26/NOV/82	3/JAN/83	14/JAN/83	10	35
8- 9 APPROVE PHASE 2 PROJECT .FP	29/NOV/82	24/DEC/82	17/JAN/83	11/FEB/83	20	35
5- 6 TRAIN OPERATING PERSONNEL .IR	13/DEC/82	28/JAN/83	13/DEC/82	28/JAN/83	35	0 *
9- 10 PREPARE PHASE 2 PROJECT .FP	27/DEC/82	4/MAR/83	14/FEB/83	22/APR/83	50	35
3- 7 PROCURE EQUIPMENT .EG	3/JAN/83	11/FEB/83	31/JAN/83	11/MAR/83	30	20
6- 7 DEVELOP OPERATING PROCEDURES .EG	31/JAN/83	11/MAR/83	31/JAN/83	11/MAR/83	30	0 *
7- 11 INSTALL HEAT RECOVERY SYSTEM .EG	14/MAR/83	22/APR/83	14/MAR/83	22/APR/83	30	0 *

- This report was run on October 4, 1982, when the project was planned to start.

- *Develop organization* must start on October 4, 1982, as this activity's timing is critical. 0* in the total float column signifies that the activity has no float and is on the critical path.

- *Design heat recovery system* can start on October 4 (the start date of this activity can be delayed until its late start of November 8, the extent of its float time).

- *Research systems* can start on October 4 (optional late start date is November 1).

- April 22, 1983, is the late finish date or *install heat recovery system,* the last activity in the project.

- The critical activities, those on the critical path and listed as "none" in the *total float* column, are the following:

	Must Start by:	Must Complete by:
Develop organization	10/4/82	11/12/82
Hire operating personnel	11/15/82	12/10/82
Train operating personnel	12/13/82	1/28/83
Develop operating procedures	1/31/83	3/11/83
Install heat recovery system	3/14/83	4/22/83

FIGURE 7-1 Work schedule report (early start schedule) for the Waste Heat Recovery Project.

```
PROJECT MANAGEMENT                          WASTE HEAT RECOVERY                          DETROIT, MICHIGAN
        REPORT TYPE :COMPRESSED PERIOD BARCHART              PRINTING SEQUENCE :Earliest Activities First
                                                             SELECTION CRITERIA :ALL
        PLAN I.D.   :WHR      VERSION  4                     TIME NOW DATE     : 4/OCT/82
================================================1982==================1983=================================
    PERIOD COMMENCING DATE          14    !1    !6    !3    !7    !7    !4    !
    MONTH                           !OCT  !NOV  !DEC  !JAN  !FEB  !MAR  !APR  !
    PERIOD COMMENCING TIME UNIT     !2    !22   !47   !67   !92   !112  !132  !
=========================================================================================================
   1-  4 DEVELOP ORGANIZATION .IR   !CCCCCC!CCCC  !     !     !     !     !     !
   1-  3 RESEARCH SYSTEMS .EG       !=====!========!=====!=......  !     !     !     !
   1-  2 DESIGN HEAT RECOVERY SYSTEM .E !====..!......  !     !     !     !     !     !
   2-  3 WRITE SPECIFICATIONS .EG   !   ===!=======!=====.!........  !     !     !     !
  ------------------------------------------------------------------------------------------------
   4-  5 HIRE OPERATING PERSONNEL .IR  !     !  CCCCC!CC   !     !     !     !     !
   4-  6 SELECT OPERATING MANAGER .IR  !     !=====!=====!=====....  !     !     !     !
   4-  8 SELECT PHASE 2 PROJECT .FP    !     !====!=.....  !     !     !     !     !
   8-  9 APPROVE PHASE 2 PROJECT .FP   !     !==!=====.!.........!..   !     !     !     !
  ------------------------------------------------------------------------------------------------
   5-  6 TRAIN OPERATING PERSONNEL .IR !     ! CCCCC!CCCCCCCCC !     !     !     !
   9- 10 PREPARE PHASE 2 PROJECT .FP   !     !   =!========!=====!=......!......  !
   3-  7 PROCURE EQUIPMENT .EG         !     !   !=========!==....!..   !     !
   6-  7 DEVELOP OPERATING PROCEDURES . !     !     !    !CC!CCCCCC!CCC   !     !
  ------------------------------------------------------------------------------------------------
   7- 11 INSTALL HEAT RECOVERY SYSTEM . !     !     !     !     ! CCCCC!CCCCCC !
=========================================================================================================
Barchart Key:- CCC :Critical Activities  === :Non Critical Activities   NNN :Activity with neg float  ... :Float
```

- The project is planned to start with *develop organization* on October 4, 1982.
- The project is planned to complete with *install heat recovery system* on April 22, 1983.

FIGURE 7-2 Project bar chart (early start schedule) for the Waste Heat Recovery Project.

```
PROJECT MANAGEMENT                          WASTE HEAT RECOVERY                          DETROIT, MICHIGAN
        REPORT TYPE :PERIOD BARCHART                         PRINTING SEQUENCE :Earliest Activities First
                                                             SELECTION CRITERIA :ALL
        PLAN I.D.   :WHR      VERSION  5                     TIME NOW DATE     : 4/OCT/82
================================================1982===============================================1983=======
    PERIOD COMMENCING DATE       14   !11  !18  !25  !1   !8   !15  !22  !29  !6   !13  !20  !27  !3   !
    MONTH                        !OCT !    !    !    !NOV !    !    !    !    !DEC !    !    !    !JAN !
    PERIOD COMMENCING TIME UNIT  !2   !7   !12  !17  !22  !27  !32  !37  !42  !47  !52  !57  !62  !67  !
=============================================================================================================
   1-  4 DEVELOP ORGANIZATION (IR   !CCCCC!CCCCC!CCCCC!CCCCC!CCCCC!CCCCC!     !     !     !     !     !     !     !
   1-  3 RESEARCH SYSTEMS (EG)      !=====!=====!=====!=====!=====!=====!=====!=====!=====!=====!=====!=====!=====!.....!>
   1-  2 DESIGN HEAT RECOVERY SYSTEM (E !=====!=====!.....!.....!.....!.....!     !     !     !     !     !     !     !
   2-  3 WRITE SPECIFICATIONS (EG)  !    !    !=====!=====!=====!=====!=====!=====!=====!=====!=====!=====!.....!.....!>
  -----------------------------------------------------------------------------------------------------------
   4-  5 HIRE OPERATING PERSONNEL (IR) !    !    !    !    !    !CCCCC!CCCCC!CCCCC!CCCCC!     !     !     !
   4-  6 SELECT OPERATING MANAGER (IR) !    !    !    !    !    !=====!=====!=====!=====!=====!=====!=====!>
   4-  8 SELECT PHASE 2 PROJECT (FP)   !    !    !    !    !    !=====!=====!.....!.....!.....!     !     !     !
   8-  9 APPROVE PHASE 2 PROJECT (FP)  !    !    !    !    !    !    !    !=====!=====!=====!=====!.....!.....!>
  -----------------------------------------------------------------------------------------------------------
   5-  6 TRAIN OPERATING PERSONNEL (IR) !    !    !    !    !    !    !    !    !    !CCCCC!CCCCC!CCCCC!CCCCC!>
   9- 10 PREPARE PHASE 2 PROJECT (FP)   !    !    !    !    !    !    !    !    !    !    !    !=====!>
   3-  7 PROCURE EQUIPMENT (EG)         !    !    !    !    !    !    !    !    !    !    !    ! =====!>
=============================================================================================================
Barchart Key:- CCC :Critical Activities  === :Non Critical Activities   NNN :Activity with neg float  ... :Float
```

- This bar chart is used to show the weekly or daily status of completed work.
- Whereas the project bar chart (Figure 7-2) is used to show status for management reporting, this bar chart is used for operating personnel to develop status.

FIGURE 7-3 Weekly bar chart (early start schedule) for the Waste Heat Recovery Project.

109

```
PROJECT MANAGEMENT                        WASTE HEAT RECOVERY                              DETROIT, MICHIGAN
      REPORT TYPE :STANDARD LISTING                                  PRINTING SEQUENCE  :Earliest Activities First
                                                                    SELECTION CRITERIA : (EG)
      PLAN I.D.   :WHR      VERSION  5                               TIME NOW DATE       : 4/OCT/82
```

ACTIVITY DESCRIPTION	EARLIEST START	EARLIEST FINISH	LATEST START	LATEST FINISH	DURATION	FLOAT
1- 3 RESEARCH SYSTEMS (EG)	4/OCT/82	31/DEC/82	1/NOV/82	28/JAN/83	65	20
1- 2 DESIGN HEAT RECOVERY SYSTEM (EG)	4/OCT/82	15/OCT/82	8/NOV/82	19/NOV/82	10	25
2- 3 WRITE SPECIFICATIONS (EG)	18/OCT/82	24/DEC/82	22/NOV/82	28/JAN/83	50	25
3- 7 PROCURE EQUIPMENT (EG)	3/JAN/83	11/FEB/83	31/JAN/83	11/MAR/83	30	20
6- 7 DEVELOP OPERATING PROCEDURES (EG)	31/JAN/83	11/MAR/83	31/JAN/83	11/MAR/83	30	0 *
7- 11 INSTALL HEAT RECOVERY SYSTEM (EG)	14/MAR/83	22/APR/83	14/MAR/83	22/APR/83	30	0 *

- Selection criteria (EG) represent the engineering department's responsibility to prepare designs and specifications, procure equipment, and develop operating procedures.
- The engineering department will concentrate on developing the operating procedures, the sole critical item under their responsibility.
- There are 25 working days (5 weeks) of float available for design and specifications; 20 working days (4 weeks) of float available for researching alternative systems and for the procurement of equipment.

FIGURE 7-4 Engineering department responsibility for the Waste Heat Recovery Project.

```
PROJECT MANAGEMENT                        WASTE HEAT RECOVERY                              DETROIT, MICHIGAN
      REPORT TYPE :STANDARD LISTING                                  PRINTING SEQUENCE  :Earliest Activities First
                                                                    SELECTION CRITERIA : (FP)
      PLAN I.D.   :WHR      VERSION  5                               TIME NOW DATE       : 4/OCT/82
```

ACTIVITY DESCRIPTION	EARLIEST START	EARLIEST FINISH	LATEST START	LATEST FINISH	DURATION	FLOAT
4- 8 SELECT PHASE 2 PROJECT (FP)	15/NOV/82	26/NOV/82	3/JAN/83	14/JAN/83	10	35
8- 9 APPROVE PHASE 2 PROJECT (FP)	29/NOV/82	24/DEC/82	17/JAN/83	11/FEB/83	20	35
9- 10 PREPARE PHASE 2 PROJECT (FP)	27/DEC/82	4/MAR/83	14/FEB/83	22/APR/83	50	35

- Selection criteria (FP) represent the forward planning department's responsibility to install the waste heat recovery system and to develop the phase II plan.
- The forward planning department will concentrate on the installation of the system, which is the only critical item.
- The phase II planning efforts have 35 working days of float time; this allows the forward planning department adequate time to complete them while they are installing the waste heat recovery system.

FIGURE 7-5 Forward planning department responsibility for the Waste Heat Recovery Project.

```
PROJECT MANAGEMENT                              WASTE HEAT RECOVERY                          DETROIT, MICHIGAN
         REPORT TYPE :STANDARD LISTING                              PRINTING SEQUENCE :Earliest Activities First
                                                                   SELECTION CRITERIA :(IR)
         PLAN I.D.   :WHR      VERSION 5                            TIME NOW DATE     : 4/OCT/82
=================================================================================================================

         ACTIVITY DESCRIPTION              EARLIEST    EARLIEST    LATEST      LATEST      DURATION  FLOAT
                                           START       FINISH      START       FINISH
=================================================================================================================

      1-  4 DEVELOP ORGANIZATION (IR)       4/OCT/82   12/NOV/82    4/OCT/82   12/NOV/82     30       0 *
      4-  5 HIRE OPERATING PERSONNEL (IR)  15/NOV/82   10/DEC/82   15/NOV/82   10/DEC/82     20       0 *
      4-  6 SELECT OPERATING MANAGER (IR)  15/NOV/82   14/JAN/83   29/NOV/82   28/JAN/83     45      10
      5-  6 TRAIN OPERATING PERSONNEL (IR) 13/DEC/82   28/JAN/83   13/DEC/82   28/JAN/83     35       0 *
=================================================================================================================
```

- Selection criteria (IR) represent the industrial relations department's responsibility to develop organization and to select and train personnel.
- There are three critical work activities under their responsibility:
  - *Develop organization:* complete by 11/12/82
  - *Hire operating personnel:* complete by 12/10/82
  - *Train operating personnel:* complete by 1/28/83
- Although the industrial relations department has 10 working days (2 weeks) of float in which to select the operating manager, they will continue to schedule earliest start to allow for any possible delays that may occur.

FIGURE 7-6 Industrial relations responsibility for the Waste Heat Recovery Project.

Milestone Report

The computer-oriented milestone report (Figure 7-7) provides a condensed version or summary of the project status. It offers a number of features:

- The computer printout milestone listing provides a precise form for use in program monitoring.
- The computer program provides a milestone listing of activities, highlighting the items that must be expedited. (This is a good example of an exception report.)
- Additional milestones can be added during the course of the project as need arises.

Resource Reports

There are two major categories of resource reports available:

1. *Histogram* reports are drawn pictorially and show the demand for a specified resource. The histogram will show the resource demand based on the early start or late start schedule. The two options are shown separately.

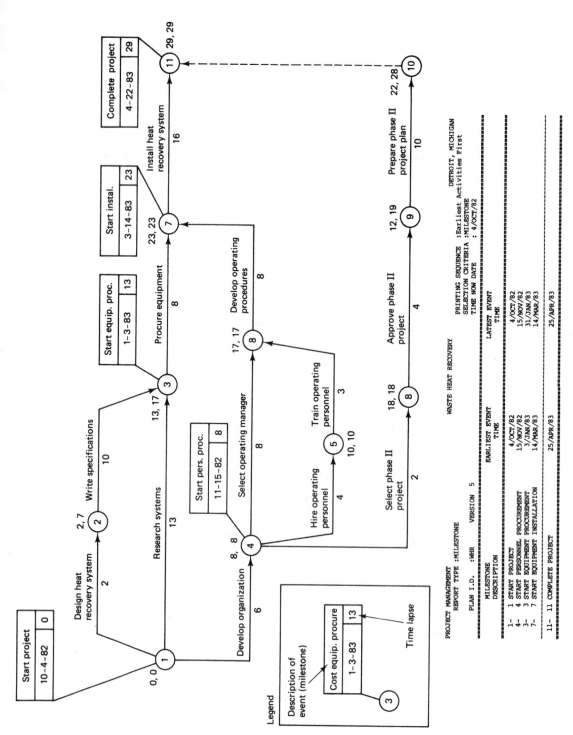

FIGURE 7-7 Planning diagram showing milestones and computer report showing milestone scheduled dates for the Waste Heat Recovery Project.

Histogram reports for the individual resources show the demand for a specified resource. Reports based on the early start schedule and the late start schedule are printed for planning purposes.

2. *Summary* reports give, for all resources (including cost), the level of demand according to a time scale. These reports can usually show detail on a daily basis, and average out the daily demand for each week. The level demand can be an early start schedule that sets all activities to start at their earliest possible start times and finish at their earliest possible finish times; or all activities start at their latest start times and finish at their latest finish times.

Comparing the *early start* and *late start* reports (which indicate the effect of float on resource demand) will help the planner view the degree of resource demand on the project (Figures 7-8 to 7-16).

EXERCISES

1. The planning diagram for relocating a manufacturing plant is shown below. Using a project management software package, produce a schedule report that provides the earliest and latest starts, earliest and latest finishes and the total float for the activities necessary to complete this project. The timing data for this project for input are as follows:

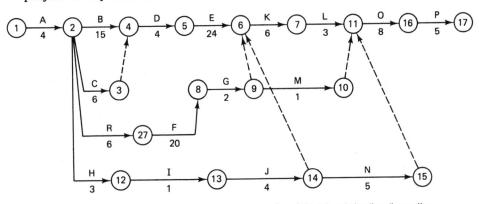

A	Prepare equipment layout	
B	Select architect/engineer; prepare construction, site drawings	
C	Prepare equipment installation drawings	
D	Select building construction; contractor and equipment installation cont.	
E	Construct bldg., install utilities	
F	Fabricate new equipment	
G	Deliver new equipment — 1 line	
H	Plan new plant startup	
I	Schedule existing line dismantling
J	Dismantle & move #1 line
K	Install #1 line
L	Startup #1 line
M	Deliver new equipment — #2 line
N	Dismantle & move #2 line
O	Install #2 line
P	Startup #2 line
R	Design new equipment

(Exercises continue on page 126)

```
PROJECT MANAGEMENT                              WASTE HEAT RECOVERY                          DETROIT, MICHIGAN
         REPORT TYPE :COMPLETE RESOURCES REPORT                          REPORT BASIS       :ACTIVITIES AT EARLY START
                    :AVERAGE DAILY DEMAND PER WEEK                       SELECTION CRITERIA :ALL
         PLAN I.D.  :WHR      VERSION  5                                 TIME NOW DATE      :4/OCT/82
=====================================================================================================================
    EN=ENGINEER                    SC=COST IN $(0)            TC=TENS OF DOLLARS          MT=MANAGEMENT TEAM
=====================================================================================================================

           ! EN ! SC ! TC ! MT !
---------------------------------------------------------------------------------------------------------------------
4/OCT/82   !  5! 118! 118!  4!
11/OCT/82  !  5! 118! 118!  4!
18/OCT/82  !  5! 133! 133!  4!
25/OCT/82  !  5! 133! 133!  4!
---------------------------------------------------------------------------------------------------------------------
1/NOV/82   !  5! 133! 133!  4!
8/NOV/82   !  5! 133! 133!  4!
15/NOV/82  !  5! 203! 203!  6!
22/NOV/82  !  5! 203! 203!  6!
---------------------------------------------------------------------------------------------------------------------
29/NOV/82  !  5! 193! 193!  7!
6/DEC/82   !  5! 193! 193!  7!
13/DEC/82  !  7! 233! 233!  9!
20/DEC/82  !  7! 233! 233!  9!
---------------------------------------------------------------------------------------------------------------------
27/DEC/82  !  3! 185! 185! 12!
3/JAN/83   !  6! 202! 202! 12!
10/JAN/83  !  6! 202! 202! 12!
17/JAN/83  !  6! 172! 172! 10!
---------------------------------------------------------------------------------------------------------------------
24/JAN/83  !  6! 172! 172! 10!
31/JAN/83  !  4! 302! 302!  8!
7/FEB/83   !  4! 302! 302!  8!
14/FEB/83  !   ! 282! 282!  8!
---------------------------------------------------------------------------------------------------------------------
21/FEB/83  !   ! 282! 282!  8!
28/FEB/83  !   ! 282! 282!  8!
7/MAR/83   !   ! 210! 210!  2!
14/MAR/83  !  2!  30!  30!   !
---------------------------------------------------------------------------------------------------------------------
21/MAR/83  !  2!  30!  30!   !
28/MAR/83  !  2!  30!  30!   !
4/APR/83   !  2!  30!  30!   !
11/APR/83  !  2!  30!  30!   !
---------------------------------------------------------------------------------------------------------------------
18/APR/83  !  2!  30!  30!   !
25/APR/83  !   !   !   !   !
=====================================================================================================================
```

- The resources report shows a summary of weekly average (based on requirements per day) of engineers and management team members when using the
  early start schedule.

- Engineer requirements range from two to seven over the life of the project,
  with no engineers required from the week of February 14 through the week of
  March 7, a period of 4 weeks.

- Management team requirements range from two to twelve from October 4 to
  March 7, and no management team members are required for the last 6 weeks
  of the project.

FIGURE 7-8 Engineers and management team requirements (early start schedule) for the
Waste Heat Recovery Project.

```
PROJECT MANAGEMENT                                    WASTE HEAT RECOVERY                          DETROIT, MICHIGAN
          REPORT TYPE :COMPLETE RESOURCES REPORT                       REPORT BASIS      :ACTIVITIES AT LATE START
                     :AVERAGE DAILY DEMAND PER WEEK                     SELECTION CRITERIA :ALL
          PLAN I.D.  :WHR        VERSION  5                             TIME NOW DATE     :4/OCT/82
==============================================================================================================================
    EN=ENGINEER                       $C=COST IN $(0)          TC=TENS OF DOLLARS          MT=MANAGEMENT TEAM
==============================================================================================================================

            ! EN ! $C  ! TC ! MT !

4/OCT/82    !    !  40!  40!  4!
11/OCT/82   !    !  40!  40!  4!
18/OCT/82   !    !  40!  40!  4!
25/OCT/82   !    !  40!  40!  4!
------------------------------------------------------------------------------------------------------------------------------
1/NOV/82    !  1!  43!  43!  4!
8/NOV/82    !  5! 118! 118!  4!
15/NOV/82   !  5! 118! 118!  2!
22/NOV/82   !  5! 133! 133!  2!
------------------------------------------------------------------------------------------------------------------------------
29/NOV/82   !  5! 163! 163!  4!
6/DEC/82    !  5! 163! 163!  4!
13/DEC/82   !  7! 203! 203!  6!
20/DEC/82   !  7! 203! 203!  6!
------------------------------------------------------------------------------------------------------------------------------
27/DEC/82   !  7! 203! 203!  6!
3/JAN/83    !  7! 243! 243!  8!
10/JAN/83   !  7! 243! 243!  8!
17/JAN/83   !  7! 233! 233!  9!
------------------------------------------------------------------------------------------------------------------------------
24/JAN/83   !  7! 233! 233!  9!
31/JAN/83   !  4! 260! 260!  5!
7/FEB/83    !  4! 260! 260!  5!
14/FEB/83   !  4! 302! 302!  8!
------------------------------------------------------------------------------------------------------------------------------
21/FEB/83   !  4! 302! 302!  8!
28/FEB/83   !  4! 302! 302!  8!
7/MAR/83    !  4! 302! 302!  8!
14/MAR/83   !  2! 102! 102!  6!
------------------------------------------------------------------------------------------------------------------------------
21/MAR/83   !  2! 102! 102!  6!
28/MAR/83   !  2! 102! 102!  6!
4/APR/83    !  2! 102! 102!  6!
11/APR/83   !  2! 102! 102!  6!
------------------------------------------------------------------------------------------------------------------------------
18/APR/83   !  2! 102! 102!  6!
25/APR/83   !    !    !    !   !
==============================================================================================================================
```

- The resources report shows a summary of weekly average (based on requirements per day) of engineers and management team members when using the late start schedule.
- Engineer requirements range from one to seven starting with the week of November 1. No engineers are needed for the first 4 weeks.
- Management team members range from two to nine over the life of the project.

FIGURE 7–9 Engineers and management team requirements (late start schedule) for the Waste Heat Recovery System.

```
PROJECT MANAGEMENT                              WASTE HEAT RECOVERY                              DETROIT, MICHIGAN
        REPORT TYPE :HISTOGRAM                                         REPORT BASIS      :ACTIVITIES AT EARLY START
                                                                       RESOURCE EXAMINED :ENGINEER
        PLAN I.D.   :WHR    VERSION  5                                 TIME NOW DATE     :4/OCT/82

71                                              **********
61                                              **********    *********************
51*********************************************************************    *********************
41*************************************************************************    ********************************
31*****************************************************************************************************************
21****************************************************************************************************************
11****************************************************************************************************************                ******
  ----------------------------------------------------------------------------------------------------------------------------
   ^      ^      ^      ^      ^      ^      ^      ^      ^      ^      ^      ^
   2  6  10  14  18  22  26  30  34  38  42  46  50  54  58  62  66  70  74  78  82  86  90  94  98 102 106 110 114 118
  4/OCT/82    20/OCT/82    5/NOV/82    23/NOV/82    9/DEC/82    27/DEC/82   12/JAN/83   28/JAN/83   15/FEB/83   3/MAR/83

PROJECT MANAGEMENT                              WASTE HEAT RECOVERY                              DETROIT, MICHIGAN
        REPORT TYPE :HISTOGRAM                                         REPORT BASIS      :ACTIVITIES AT EARLY START
        START DATE  :15/MAR/83                                         RESOURCE EXAMINED :ENGINEER
        PLAN I.D.   :WHR    VERSION  5                                 TIME NOW DATE     :4/OCT/82

71
61
51
41
31
21******************************
11******************************
  ----------------------------------------------------------------------------------------------------------------------------
   ^      ^      ^      ^      ^      ^      ^      ^      ^      ^      ^      ^
  118 122 126 130 134 138 142 146 150 154 158 162 166 170 174 178 182 186 190 194 198 202 206 210 214 218 222 226 230 234
  15/MAR/83   31/MAR/83   18/APR/83     ---         ---         ---         ---         ---         ---         ---
```

> - With the early start schedule, engineers are required from the week of October 4 to the week of April 18 (with the exception of the period from the week of February 14 to the week of March 7, when no engineers are required). There is a net total of 25 weeks when engineers are required in this schedule.
> - The number of engineers required ranges from a maximum of eight during the weeks of December 13 and 20 to a minimum of two during the weeks of March 14 to April 18. (*Note:* None are required during the period from the weeks of February 14 to March 7.)
> - There is a poor distribution of engineers required over the period October 4 to April 18.
> - With four engineers available, overtime will be needed from October 4 through the week of January 21.

FIGURE 7-10 Engineer utilization (early start schedule) for the Waste Heat Recovery Project.

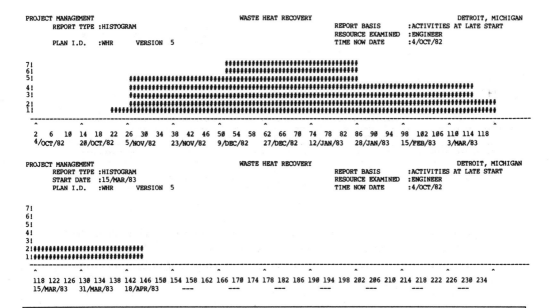

- With the late start schedule, engineers are required from the week of November 1 to the week of April 18, a period of 25 weeks.

- During the foregoing period the number of engineers required ranges from a maximum of eight during the weeks of December 13 to January 24 to a minimum of one during the week of November 1.

- There is a fair distribution of engineers required over the period November 1 to April 18.

- If four engineers are the maximum available daily, and if project completion during the week of April 18 needs to be maintained with the late start schedule, then overtime, added equipment, or expedited shipments are some items that need to be considered in 12 of the 29 weeks of this project.

FIGURE 7-11 Engineer utilization (late start schedule) for the Waste Heat Recovery Project.

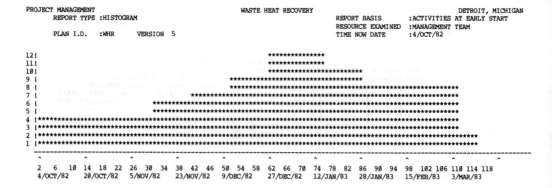

- With the early start schedule, management team members are required from the week of October 4 to the week of March 7, a total of 23 weeks.
- The number of management team members required ranges from a maximum of twelve during the weeks of December 27, January 3, and January 10, to a minimum of two during the week of March 7.
- There is a good distribution of management team members required during the weeks of October 4 to March 7.
- If six management team members are the maximum available, and if the project completion during the week of April 18 needs to be maintained with the early start schedule, then overtime, added equipment, or expedited shipments must be considered in 14 of the 29 weeks of this project.

FIGURE 7–12   Management team utilization (early start schedule) for the Waste Heat Recovery Project.

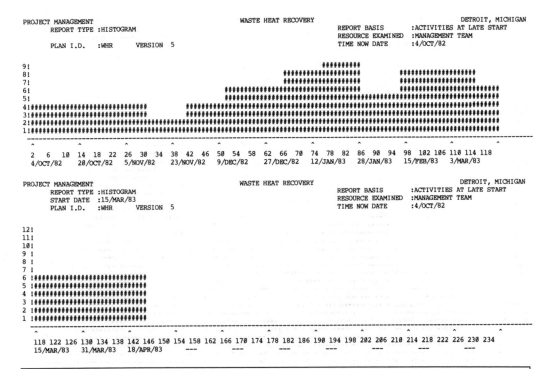

- With the late start schedule, management team members are required from the week of October 4 to the week of April 28, a total of 29 weeks.
- The number of management team members required ranges from a maximum of nine during the weeks of January 17 and 24 to a minimum of two during the weeks of November 15 and 22.
- There is a poor distribution of management team members required over the period October 4 to April 18.
- If six management team members are the maximum available, and if the project completion during the week of April 18 needs to be maintained with the late start schedule, then overtime, added equipment, or expedited shipments are some items that need to be considered in 8 of the 29 weeks of this project.

FIGURE 7-13   Management team utilization (late start schedule) for the Waste Heat Recovery Project.

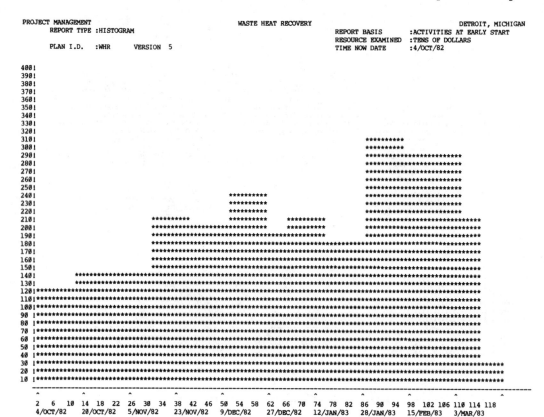

FIGURE 7-14 Daily cost histogram (early start schedule) for the Waste Heat Recovery Project (continued on next page).

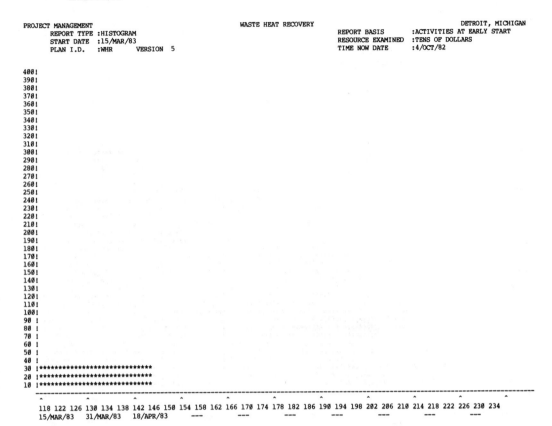

• The maximum daily rate is $3,100 for a 2-week period. The total cost is $31,000 for this peak period.

• The minimum daily rate is $300 for the final 7-week period. The total cost is $10,500 for this period.

• The total histogram area is $240,500.

FIGURE 7-14 (*Continued*)

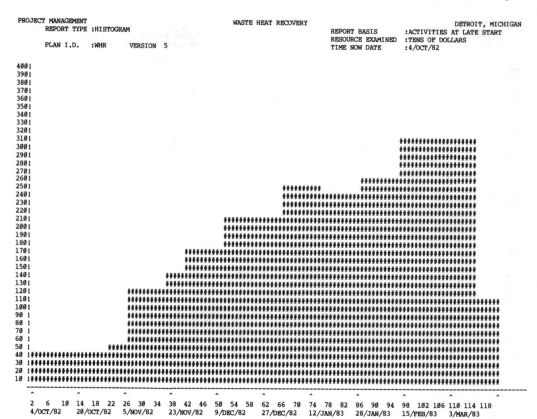

FIGURE 7–15 Daily cost histogram (late start schedule) for the Waste Heat Recovery Project (continued on next page).

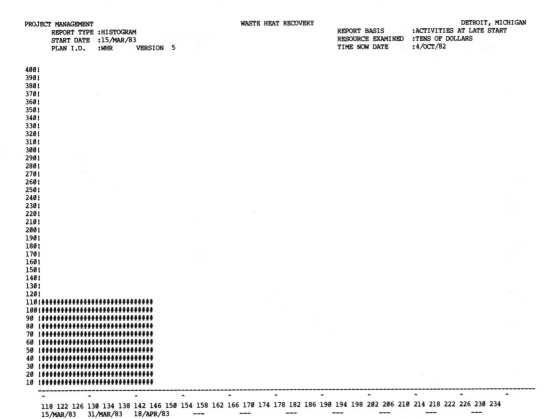

- The maximum daily rate is $3,100. For the 4-week peak period, the total cost is $62,000.
- There is a minimum daily rate of $400 for the first 4-week period. The total cost for this period is $8,000.
- The final 6-week period has a daily cost rate of $1,100. The total cost for this period is $33,000.
- The total cost histogram area is $240,500.

FIGURE 7–15 (*Continued*)

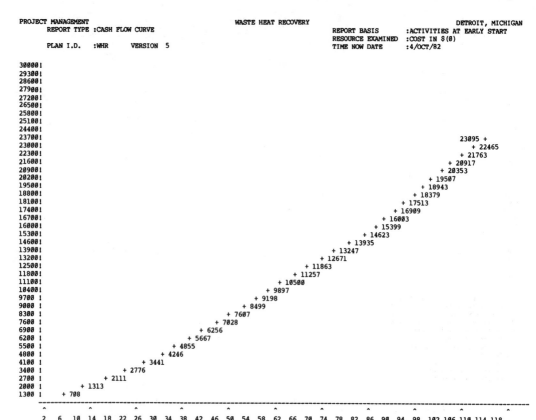

FIGURE 7–16 Accumulated costs (early start schedule) for the Waste Heat Recovery Project (continued on next page).

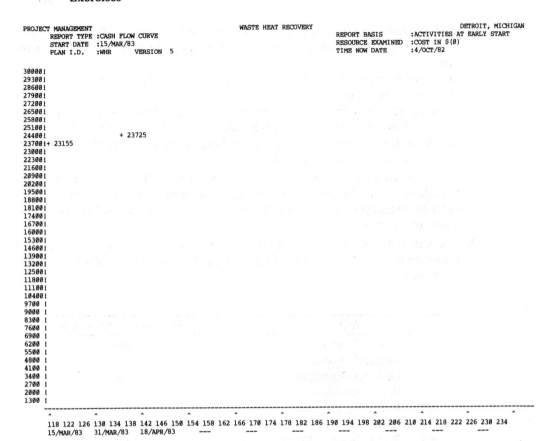

PROJECT MANAGEMENT   WASTE HEAT RECOVERY   DETROIT, MICHIGAN
        REPORT TYPE :CASH FLOW CURVE   REPORT BASIS   :ACTIVITIES AT EARLY START
        START DATE :15/MAR/83   RESOURCE EXAMINED   :COST IN $(0)
        PLAN I.D.   :WHR   VERSION 5   TIME NOW DATE   :4/OCT/82

```
30000!
29300!
28600!
27900!
27200!
26500!
25800!
25100!
24400!                        + 23725
23700!+ 23155
23000!
22300!
21600!
20900!
20200!
19500!
18800!
18100!
17400!
16700!
16000!
15300!
14600!
13900!
13200!
12500!
11800!
11100!
10400!
9700 !
9000 !
8300 !
7600 !
6900 !
6200 !
5500 !
4800 !
4100 !
3400 !
2700 !
2000 !
1300 !
     --------------------------------------------------------------------------------------------------------
     ^       ^       ^       ^       ^       ^       ^       ^       ^       ^       ^       ^       ^       ^
     118 122 126 130 134 138 142 146 150 154 158 162 166 170 174 178 182 186 190 194 198 202 206 210 214 218 222 226 230 234
     15/MAR/83   31/MAR/83   18/APR/83   ---       ---       ---       ---       ---       ---       ---
```

- The total project cost is $240,500. Rounding off causes a small discrepancy in the total cost curve, which is approximately 2%.

FIGURE 7-16 (*Continued*)

2. With the data provided in previous chapters for the Theater Planning Project, and using a project management software package, produce the following reports:

    (a) Schedule report (earliest and latest start, earliest and latest finish).

    (b) Project bar chart.

    (c) Resource distribution (or Histogram) for Stage Assistants and for Production Assistants for early start schedule; for the late start schedule.

    (d) What are the maximum number of Stage Assistants required; maximum number of Production Assistants?

3. The costs associated with the Theater Planning Project suggest that there are periods when the expenses are greater than the funds available. From the computer-generated cost data, determine the amount of funds required for every four weeks of the project.

4. The activities that make up the *Waste Heat Recovery Project* have been assigned responsibilities as follows: EG, Engineering; IR, Industrial Relations; and FP, Forward Planning.

i,j	Activity	Responsibility Code
1,2	Design Heat Recovery System	EG
1,3	Research Systems	EG
1,4	Develop Organization	IR
2,3	Write Specifications	EG
3,7	Procure Equipment	EG
4,5	Hire Operating Personnel	IR
4,8	Select Phase II Project	FP
5,6	Train Operating Personnel	IR
6,7	Develop Operating Procedures	IR
7,11	Install Heat Recovery System	EG
8,9	Approve Phase II Project	FP
9,10	Prepare Phase II Project Plan	FP

    (a) Prepare schedules for the total project, and each of the assigned responsibility sections (Engineering, Industrial Relations, Forward Planning)

    (b) Prepare a Milestone Report

    (c) Prepare a Management Report

Chapter 8

Southfork Building Project

Among the essential requirements for a construction project to succeed is a thorough plan. The plan should not only include a comprehensive "What work has to be done" exercise, the main objective, but also the interim objectives or milestones that must be met successfully to meet the specified date. In addition, meeting the cost budget is just as important. Time management and cost management are the very essence of project management in a construction project. To achieve success in these areas, a contractor must use project management disciplines in the planning phase.

In the first part of the chapter we use basic methods that a student of project management should go through in learning the essential elements. In the second part, the experienced contractor uses a computer to provide the necessary information to develop a plan and schedule, and then as an aid to implement the project—project control.

The size of the project permits the use of a microcomputer (personal computer). Available software packages are sufficient that the one selected can adequately fit the project needs. One essential requirement is that the timing and cost data input does not become a tough, tedious, and lengthy chore. After all, the contractor wants answers to the normal running of the project, and wants to run quickly through "what if" situations when certain changes to the project occur. And changes do occur.

BACKGROUND

The City of Southfork wants to construct a building addition to the Library Building at its Civic Center. The addition consists of a 10,000-square-foot structure with external and internal features similar to those of the main building. The construction drawings have been completed by S&E Associates, an architectural-engineering firm whose staff also administered solicitation of the bids for the construction of the addition. After review of the bids, the City of Southfork awarded the construction contract to Lawrence Construction Company, which submitted the lowest bid, $445,000. This bid provides for furnishing labor, equipment, and supervision. The City of Southfork will supply all the major building materials. (This is a somewhat unique arrangement for constructing a building, as normally the contractor provides everything. In this case, however, time was of the essence and the major building materials were procured as the building design was developing.) The terms of the contract provide for construction start by October 4, 1982. The project is to be completed by July 1, 1983, when the City of Southfork will begin occupancy.

PLANNING THE PROJECT

Under the terms of the contract, Lawrence Construction Company provided a detailed plan of action to satisfy the City of Southfork that the project completion would be met. They divided the project into three phases: planning, scheduling, and controlling.

The planning phase would follow these steps:

1. Establish objectives.
   a. The objectives would be derived from the requirements that motivated the project.
   b. Interim objectives or milestones that are significant in meeting the main objectives would also be established.
2. Develop a plan.
   a. All the jobs (or activities) that have to be done to complete the project would be listed.
   b. These jobs would be delineated by a specific procedure: After the jobs were decided upon, the relations between them are determined. This involves an analysis of each job.
3. Prepare the planning diagram.
   a. There are several basic tasks that must be performed before preparing the final planning diagram.
   b. These entail drawing preliminary subdiagrams and rough diagrams.

There are computer software programs that will draw the planning diagram after the data have been entered; however, none of them are as effective in portraying the plan as is a manual diagram to ensure a logical plan. Nevertheless, computer graphics used for diagramming the project is growing rapidly and eventually will have many advantages over manual drawing.

Establishing the Objectives

When setting the timing objectives, Lawrence Construction reviewed these with the designated subcontractors who are to be responsible, and emphasized that these milestones must be met. Assigning the objectives, milestones, and responsible subcontractors (Figure 8–1) constitutes the first steps taken in the planning process.

Identifying the Jobs Required

After establishing the objectives, the next step is to identify all the work items required to complete the project. Personnel who are to be actively engaged in this project, as well as those having specific responsibilities, will meet with the designated project manager and prepare a complete listing of the work items. The project manager, who represents Lawrence Construction, is well aware of the importance that *all* the jobs be accounted for and that they encompass all phases of the project.

A proper listing of *all* the work required is very important to the success of the planning phase. Omissions will cause inaccuracies in the scheduling phase and will probably result in failure to complete the project on time. Developing this portion is one of the most difficult, if not the most difficult, parts of the project management cycle.

Lawrence Construction personnel, with their subcontractors, completed the

ACTIVITY	DATE	RESPONSIBLE CONTRACTOR
Start project	October 4, 1982	
Complete excavation	October 25, 1982	Nardoni
Start concrete	December 20, 1982	Nardoni
Complete concrete	January 17, 1983	Nardoni
Complete steel erection	February 14, 1983	Kales
Complete roof deck	March 28, 1983	Kales
Complete masonry and woodwork	May 9, 1983	Nardoni
Obtain approval	July 1, 1983	Belvedere

FIGURE 8–1 Major objectives for the Southfork Building Project.

job description list for the major phases of the Southfork Building Project. The job description list is shown in Figure 8–2.

Group Jobs Into Major Sections of Work

As an expedient in establishing the relations between jobs, Lawrence Construction divided the project into groups of closely related functions. In the case of a construction project these groups usually identify the individual subcontractor's scope of work.

The major sections of work for the Southfork Building Project are shown in Figure 8–3.

Determining Relations between Activities; Drawing Subdiagrams

Establishing the relationships of the project activities generally involves a substantial amount of discussion among the responsible parties as to how the activities should be interrelated and then portrayed on the planning diagram. The benefit in doing this is the resulting agreement on the flow of work that should promote understanding of how various efforts and responsibilities tie together in the overall project.

As the responsible parties are working at determining the relations between the project jobs, Lawrence Construction personnel, acting as the project manager, prepare a number of subdiagrams of the major work sections. They have found from experience that combining the relationships of the project activities with the subdiagrams through a step-by-step procedure is useful in the formation of a complete planning diagram. Figure 8–4 shows the first and final steps of the subdiagramming efforts of Lawrence Construction.

Preparing the Planning Diagram

This is the final step in the planning process. When the subdiagram has finally been developed, it becomes the basis for completing the project plan by drawing the planning diagram. Drawing the diagram will be simplified if the subdiagram has been thoroughly prepared.

Lawrence Construction prepares the planning diagram using the arrow diagramming rules, which provide for a clear and concise diagram. Time schedulers, cost schedulers, and other resource analysts use this diagram, so it needs to be authentic. All responsible parties can now participate in the final review.

The procedure in drawing the planning diagram follows these steps:

1. Draw preliminary diagrams such as Figure 8–5a which permit making revisions expeditiously and sequentially until the final diagram takes shape.

2. Prepare a clear graphic portrayal as the final planning diagram (Figure 8–5b).

3. Check the final diagram for accuracy and effectiveness.

Activity	Description
1. Build floor forms	Construct and place foundation forms
2. Excavate	Survey site, clear site of brush and trees, grade and excavate for foundations
3. Prepare reinforcing steel	Sort out, clean rust from re-rod for foundations, walls
4. Build wall frames	Build wall frames before starting structural steel erection
5. Ship structural steel	Contract with steel supplier
6. Erect forms	Place forms in place after they are built
7. Install plumbing	Install underground plumbing before placement of concrete and continue with building plumbing requirements
8. Install floor electrical	Install floor conduit before placement of concrete and continue with building plumbing requirements
9. Place and tie reinforcing steel	Set and tie re-rod after forms are set and aligned
10. Place concrete	Place foundation and floor concrete at same time for a monolithic structure
11. Check forms	Check forms as concrete is being placed
12. Remove forms	Remove forms after concrete has reached required strength
13. Check floor	As concrete is placed, check floor before removing forms
14. Erect framework	Install concurrent with structural steel
15. Install wall electrical	Concurrent with framework erection, place wall conduit
16. Place masonry	Set masonry with framework and structural steel
17. Erect structural steel	After foundation is complete, begin erecting structural steel
18. Install roof and roofing	Install roofing after structural steel is complete
19. Complete woodwork	Finish carpentry completed before painting
20. Install ceiling electric	Start ceiling electric after wall electric is completed
21. Check walls	Make sure surface is clean as painting is started
22. Start painting	Begin painting after woodwork is completed
23. Install ceiling	Begin ceiling after ceiling electrical is completed
24. Clean site	Clean building interior and exterior
25. Finish painting	Finish painting and touch-up
26. Obtain final approval	All necessary inspections approved

FIGURE 8–2 Project work activities for the Southfork Building Project.

Major Work Sections

- Excavation, Concrete, Electrical
- Underground plumbing
- Reinforcing steel
- Floor, Walls, Painting
- Structural Steel and Roof
- Framework

Excavation, Concrete, Electrical (Nardoni)

- Excavate
- Install floor electrical (Lastar)
- Place concrete
- Remove forms
- Install ceiling electrical (Lastar)
- Install ceiling
- Clear site

Plumbing

- Install underground plumbing

Reinforcing Steel (Nardoni)

- Prepare reinforcing steel
- Place and tie reinforcing steel

Floor, Walls, Painting (Nardoni)

- Build floor forms
- Erect forms
- Check forms
- Check floor
- Place masonry
- Check walls
- Start painting
- Finish painting
- Obtain final approval

Structural Steel and Roof (Kales)

- Ship structural steel
- Erect structural steel
- Install roof deck and roofing

Framework (Belvedere)

- Build wall frames
- Erect framework
- Complete framework

FIGURE 8–3 Major work sections for the Southfork Building Project.

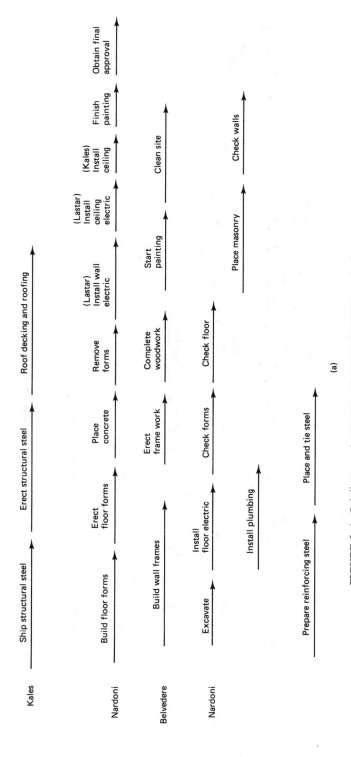

FIGURE 8–4 Subdiagrams for the Southfork Building Project: (a) first step; (b) final step (page 134).

133

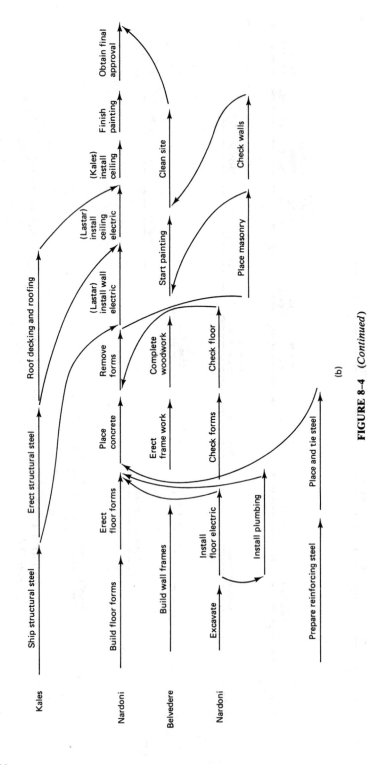

FIGURE 8-4 (*Continued*)

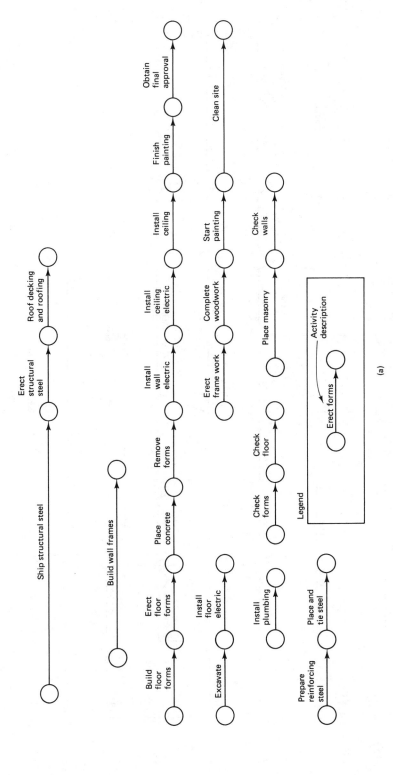

(a)

FIGURE 8-5 Planning diagrams for the Southfork Building Project: (a) first step; (b) final step (page 136).

135

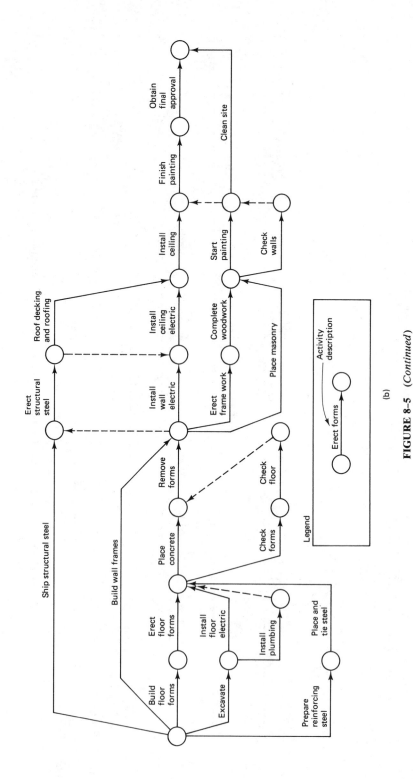

(b)

FIGURE 8-5 (*Continued*)

136

Lawrence Construction prepared several diagrams before completing the final planning diagram, and after reviews among their supervisory personnel and their subcontractors, submitted the building construction planning diagram to the City of Southfork.

It should be noted that for projects that may not be complex, fewer steps could be required in the preparation of the planning diagram. When there are several areas of responsibilities by different departments in the implementation of a project, using the step-by-step approach should be considered.

To summarize, the initial step in developing a project plan is to establish the objectives. The project plan is then developed by transforming the interconnecting activities of the project into a network diagram. The diagram is constructed in accordance with the stated rules so that the network will be accurate and allow for consistent interpretations.

The main advantage of developing a project plan by the arrow diagramming technique is that you must "think through" the project. Even though this approach is time consuming, it is extremely rewarding. After the city of Southfork approved the planning phase, Lawrence Construction began the scheduling phase.

SCHEDULING THE PROJECT

Despite many effective computer scheduling programs now available, scheduling by the manual method is used initially as a quick check on whether the project duration as defined by the objectives conforms with the planning diagram approved by the City of Southfork. Using the manual scheduling approach will also acquaint project planners with the analysis and logic used in scheduling projects by the planning network technique. And there may be times when availability of computer time may be limited or a relatively small project may make it not feasible to use a computer. Therefore, it is wise to become proficient in both methods of calculating schedules.

Following the pattern of many governmental agencies which require network planning diagrams and a detailed schedule compatible with the approved plan, the City of Southfork has asked for a detailed schedule. In this scheduling phase Lawrence Construction generally followed these steps:

1. After the sequence of jobs has been planned and laid out in a network diagram, this scheduling approach was followed:
   a. Estimate the *required time* to complete each job in the project.
   b. Calculate the schedule by computing the *available time* to complete each job.
   c. Identify the critical jobs by comparing the required time with the available time.
2. If the project duration that is calculated initially is not acceptable, make adjustments to the required time estimates and, if necessary, to the project plan so as to meet the timing objectives of the project.

3. Once the project duration is satisfied, establish a calendar schedule by preparing a bar chart that will portray the schedule effectively.

Preparing the Project Item Time Estimates

As time estimating is a very important part of the project scheduling phase, Lawrence Construction personnel considered all aspects necessary in getting time estimates for each job in the project. To arrive at acceptable estimates, there were many conferences with the subcontractors and others responsible for the work. A single time estimate that was finally decided upon was placed below each activity arrow of the approved planning diagram.

After confirming the adequacy of the time estimates, Lawrence Construction started the timing calculations. These timing calculations, which provide information necessary to schedule the Southfork Building Project, consist of determining the earliest start times, latest finish times, and the total float values of the project activities.

The manual method for calculating the earliest start times, latest finish times, and total floats was explained earlier. However, an explanation of each part will serve not only as a review, but will tend to maintain continuity in developing the calculations.

Timing Calculations: Earliest Start Time

The earliest start time at a node is the earliest time that any job can be started from that node. The beginning node of the project is assumed to start at time 0. For a given job, the earliest start time can be determined by adding the time estimate for the preceding job to the earliest start time for the preceding job.

Calculating the earliest start times follows these guidelines:

- The calculation of earliest start times begins with the first node at the beginning of the arrow diagram (time 0) and continues through each node to the end of the diagram.
- If only one arrow leads into a node, the earliest start time for jobs starting at the node is determined by adding the earliest start time for the preceding job to the time estimate for the preceding job.
- If more than one arrow leads into a node, the earliest start time calculation is made through each of the arrows. The highest value is the earliest start at that node.

Lawrence Construction used the following procedure and showed the estimates and the earliest start calculations for the Southfork Building Project on a network diagram (Figure 8–6).

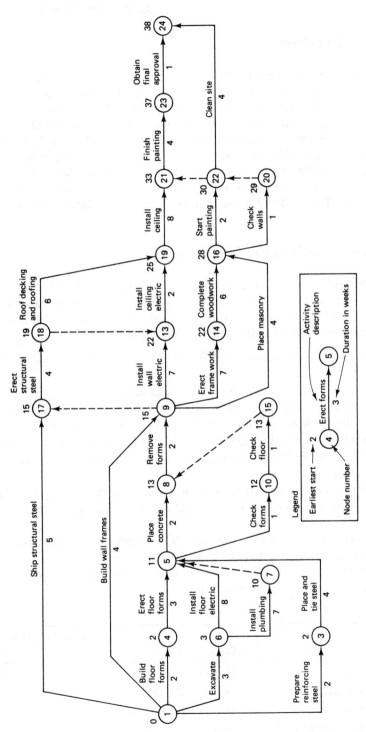

FIGURE 8-6 Network diagram: time estimates and earliest start times for the Southfork Building Project.

Project Duration

From the time estimates and the earliest start calculations, Lawrence Construction determined that the jobs on the longest path in this project, known as the *critical path,* totaled 38 weeks, which was the minimum project duration time for the plan that Lawrence Construction submitted and which was approved by the City of Southfork. Starting on October 4, 1982, a 38-week schedule would yield a June 27, 1983, completion, which satisfies the project objective of completing the project by July 1, 1983. If the objective were not met, the duration could be compressed by expediting some of the critical jobs of the project. Identifying the critical jobs will be possible after the latest finish time and total float values of the project jobs are calculated.

Timing Calculations: Latest Finish Times

The latest finish time is the latest time that an activity must be completed without lengthening the duration of the project. The latest finish time is required in identifying the activities on the critical path and in calculating float for jobs in the network. To determine the latest finish times, follow these guidelines:

- The project duration must first be determined by calculating the early start times.
- The calculation of latest finish times involves working from the end node back through each node to the first node in the project. The project duration is the latest finish time for the end node of the last job in the project.
- The latest finish time for an activity is determined by subtracting the time estimate of the succeeding activity from the latest finish time of this succeeding activity.
- If more than one arrow originates at a node, the calculation of latest finish time is made via each arrow and the *smallest* result is used.

Lawrence Construction followed this procedure and placed the latest finish time calculations on the network diagram (Figure 8–7).

At this stage the milestones that were established in the objectives can be checked against the calculated schedule:

| | | CALCULATED SCHEDULE | |
ACTIVITY	OBJECTIVE DATE	From time 0	Date
Start project	October 4, 1982	0	10/4/82
Complete excavation	October 25, 1982	3	10/25/82
Start concrete	December 20, 1982	11	12/20/82
Complete concrete	January 17, 1983	15	1/17/83

| | | CALCULATED SCHEDULE | |
		From time 0	Date
ACTIVITY	OBJECTIVE DATE	From time 0	Date
Complete steel erection	February 14, 1983	19	2/14/83
Complete roof deck	March 28, 1983	25	3/28/83
Complete masonry and woodwork	May 9, 1983	28	5/9/83
Obtain approval	July 1, 1983	38	6/27/83

A date calculator is used to convert the base weeks from time 0 (October 4, 1982) to calendar dates. Since the objective dates favorably match the calculated schedule dates, Lawrence Construction can proceed with completing the schedule, and particularly, with completing the float times of each item.

Timing Calculations: Total Float

With the earliest start and latest finish times completed for each activity of the project, Lawrence Construction personnel can now determine the float time available for each of the Southfork building project work items. Float figures make it possible to identify the project jobs that have optional starting and finishing dates. The total time for each job is the difference between the *time available* for performing a job and the *time required* for performing it.

A simple procedure is followed to arrive at these float values. For each activity, the time available is the latest finish time minus the earliest start time, and subtracting the activity duration from the time available will produce total float. Total float calculations for all the project activities are shown in Figure 8-8.

Tabulating the Schedule

The tabulated schedule (Figure 8-9) summarizes optional starting and finishing times and float values of the project items. To complete the optional times related to the float values and shown in the tabulated schedule, the latest start and the earliest finish times are needed. One method for calculating these optional times is through use of the following formulas:

$$\text{latest start} = \text{earliest start} + \text{total float}$$

$$\text{earliest start} = \text{latest finish} - \text{total float}$$

In the preparation of the tabulated schedule, one should include the timing values of the dummy activities in the initial tabulation. The intent is to check that the total planning diagram has been analyzed for the scheduling phase.

The final tabulation includes only the project items that contribute to the schedule. Although useful in this form, the schedule does have limitations. As tim-

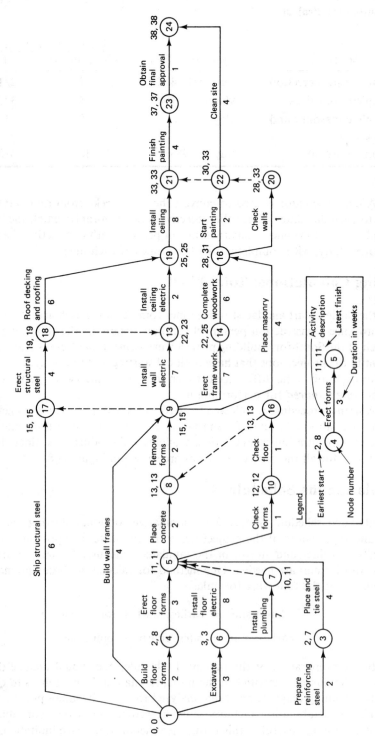

FIGURE 8-7 Time estimates, earliest start times, and latest finish times for the Southfork Building Project.

Job	Description	Latest Finish	−	Earliest Start	−	Duration	=	Total Float
1,9	Build wall frames	15		0		4		11
1,3	Prepare reinforcing steel	7		0		2		5
1,4	Build floor forms	8		0		2		6
1,6	Excavate	3		0		3		0*
1,17	Ship structural steel	15		0		5		10
3,5	Place and tie reinforcing steel	11		2		4		5
4,5	Erect floor forms	11		2		3		6
5,8	Place concrete	13		11		2		0*
5,10	Check forms	12		11		1		14
6,5	Install floor electrical	11		3		8		0*
6,7	Install plumbing	11		3		7		1
8,9	Remove forms	15		13		2		0*
9,13	Install wall electrical	23		15		7		1
10,15	Check floor	13		12		1		13
9,14	Erect wall framing	25		15		7		3
13,19	Install ceiling electrical	25		22		2		1
14,16	Complete woodwork	31		22		6		3
16,20	Check walls	33		28		1		4
9,16	Place masonry	31		15		4		12
17,18	Erect structural steel	19		15		4		0*
18,19	Install roof deck and roofing	25		19		6		0*
19,21	Install ceiling	33		25		8		0*
16,22	Start painting	33		28		2		3
21,23	Finish painting	37		33		4		0*
22,24	Clear site	38		30		4		4
23,24	Obtain final approval	38		37		1		0*
20,22	Dummy	33		29		0		4
7,5	Dummy	11		11		0		0*
22,21	Dummy	33		30		0		3
9,17	Dummy	15		15		0		0*
18,13	Dummy	23		19		0		4
15,8	Dummy	13		13		0		0*

*Critical path.

FIGURE 8-8 Computation of total float for the Southfork Building Project.

Job	Description	Duration (Weeks)	Earliest Start	Earliest Finish	Latest Start	Latest Finish	Float Total
1,9	Build wall frames	4	0	4	11	15	11
1,3	Prepare reinforcing steel	2	0	2	5	7	5
1,4	Build floor forms	2	0	2	6	8	6
1,6	Excavate	3	0	3	0	3	0
1,17	Ship structural steel	5	0	5	10	15	10
3,5	Place and tie reinforcing steel	4	2	6	7	11	5
4,5	Erect forms	3	2	5	8	11	6
6,5	Install floor electrical	8	3	11	3	11	0
6,7	Install plumbing	7	3	10	4	11	1
5,8	Place concrete	2	11	13	11	13	0
5,10	Check forms	1	11	12	11	12	0
8,9	Remove forms	2	13	15	13	15	0
10,15	Check floor	1	12	13	12	13	0
9,13	Install wall electrical	7	15	22	16	23	1
9,14	Erect framework	7	15	22	18	25	3
9,16	Place masonry	4	15	19	27	31	12
17,18	Erect structural steel	4	15	19	15	19	0
16,20	Check walls	1	28	29	32	33	4
14,16	Complete woodwork	6	22	28	25	31	3
13,19	Install ceiling electrical	2	22	24	23	25	1
18,19	Install roof deck and roofing	6	19	25	19	25	0
19,21	Install ceiling	8	25	33	25	33	0
16,22	Start painting	2	28	30	31	33	3
21,23	Finish painting	4	33	37	33	37	0
23,24	Obtain final approval	1	37	38	37	38	0
22,24	Clean site	4	30	34	34	38	4

FIGURE 8-9 Tabulated schedule for the Southfork Building Project.

ing usually relates to the calendar in developing the schedule, all the figures in the tabulated schedule need to be translated into calendar dates.

Preparing the Calendar Schedule

Lawrence Construction can now develop the schedule showing actual calendar dates (Figure 8–10) which will be used for not only future analysis but for developing bar chart schedules for use by the construction personnel in the field, ordering equipment, and monitoring the project. Its use will also become apparent in developing cost schedules and in the control of costs.

An expedient in translating tabulated schedule dates into calendar dates is the date calculator, one version of which is shown in Figure 8–11. Date calculators can be procured through bookstores or stationary stores. The arrow is set at the designated starting date, October 4 (time 0). Elapsed time in weekly units is read on the inner circle. For example, the *excavation* item that starts on October 4 has an estimated duration of 3 weeks and a finish date of October 25.

Lawrence Construction singled out those jobs showing no float and marked them with an asterisk. These jobs were then plotted on the network diagram shown in Figure 8–12 and represent the *critical path*.

Project items on the critical path are given special consideration by construction supervision. The sum of the project items on the critical path not only make up the longest path that represents the project duration, but the importance of each project item on the critical path is emphasized, as a timing change of any one of these items directly affects the project duration. The impact of float became apparent after Lawrence Construction completed the total tabulated schedule for the Southfork project. Once these timing values for the project item were checked, the calendar schedule was completed.

Preparing the Bar Chart Time Schedule

Although the network diagram could be used to graphically illustrate the schedule by applying the dates from the calendar schedule on the diagram, Lawrence Construction management is aware that field personnel are more comfortable when using a bar chart schedule. Furthermore, a network diagram has some limitations for scheduling jobs.

- At times the network can be difficult to interpret.
- A great deal of time is required to modify the diagram when there are changes to the schedule.

A bar chart recognizes these limitations when a graphic portrayal of the schedule is required. But it must be emphasized that the construction of a bar chart is dependent on the information derived from the network analysis developed previously. The bar chart has these advantages:

Job	Description	Time (Weeks)	Earliest Start	Earliest Finish	Latest Start	Latest Finish	Float Total
1,9	Build wall frames	4	10/4/82	11/1/82	12/20/82	1/17/83	11
1,3	Prepare reinforcing steel	2	10/4/82	10/18/82	11/8/82	11/22/82	5
1,4	Build floor forms	2	10/4/82	10/18/82	11/15/82	11/29/92	6
1,6	Excavate	3	10/4/82	10/25/82	10/4/82	10/25/82	0*
1,17	Ship structural steel	5	10/4/82	11/8/82	12/13/82	1/17/83	10
3,5	Place and tie reinforcing steel	4	10/18/82	11/15/82	11/22/82	12/20/82	5
4,5	Erect forms	3	10/18/82	11/8/82	11/29/82	12/20/82	6
6,5	Install floor electrical	8	10/25/82	12/20/82	10/25/82	12/20/82	0*
6,7	Install plumbing	7	10/25/82	12/13/82	11/1/82	12/20/82	1
6,8	Place concrete	2	12/20/82	1/3/82	12/20/82	1/3/82	0*
5,10	Check forms	1	12/20/82	12/27/82	3/28/83	4/4/83	14
8,9	Remove forms	2	1/3/83	1/17/83	1/3/83	1/17/83	0*
10,16	Check floor	1	1/3/83	1/10/83	4/4/83	4/11/83	13
9,13	Install wall electrical	7	1/17/83	3/7/83	1/24/83	3/14/83	1
9,14	Erect framework	7	1/17/83	3/7/83	2/7/83	3/28/83	3
15,16	Place masonry	4	1/17/83	2/14/83	4/11/83	5/9/83	12
17,18	Erect structural steel	4	1/17/83	2/14/83	1/17/83	2/14/83	0*
16,20	Check walls	1	4/18/83	4/25/83	5/16/83	6/23/83	4
14,16	Complete woodwork	6	3/7/83	4/18/83	3/28/83	5/9/83	3
13,19	Install ceiling electrical	2	3/7/83	3/21/83	3/14/83	3/28/83	4
18,19	Install roof deck and roofing	6	2/14/83	3/25/83	2/14/83	3/28/83	0*
19,21	Install ceiling	8	3/28/83	5/23/83	3/28/83	6/23/83	0*
16,22	Start painting	2	4/18/83	5/2/83	5/9/83	6/23/83	3
21,23	Finish painting	4	5/23/83	6/20/83	5/23/83	6/20/83	0*
23,24	Obtain final approval	1	6/20/83	6/27/83	6/20/83	6/27/83	0*
22,24	Clear site	4	5/2/83	5/30/83	5/30/83	6/27/83	4

FIGURE 8–10 Calendar schedule for the Southfork Building Project.

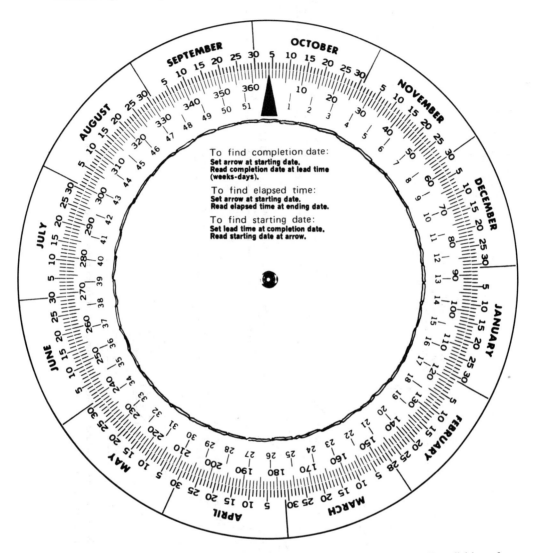

To find completion date:
Set arrow at starting date.
Read completion date at lead time (weeks-days).

To find elapsed time:
Set arrow at starting date.
Read elapsed time at ending date.

To find starting date:
Set lead time at completion date.
Read starting date at arrow.

FIGURE 8-11 Date calculator. (Designed and produced by PERRYGRAF, a division of Denney-Reyburn Co., Northridge, CA 91324.)

- The chart effectively displays the Southfork Building Project.
- Behind-schedule (and ahead-of-schedule) jobs can readily be depicted on the bar chart.
- Major milestones, including completion dates, can be noted specifically (several are shown in Figure 8–13).

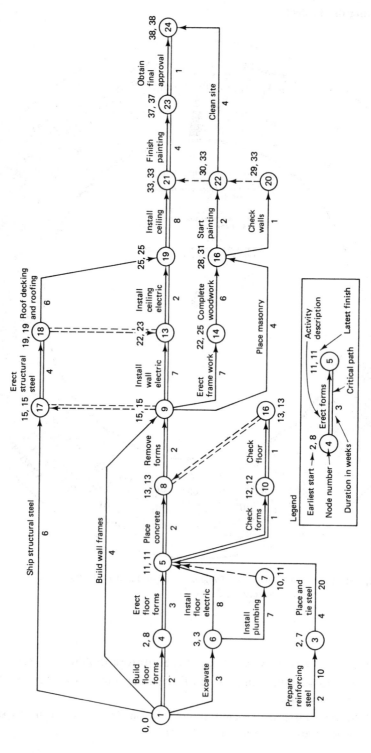

FIGURE 8-12 Time estimates, earliest start times, latest finish times, and critical path for the Southfork Building Project.

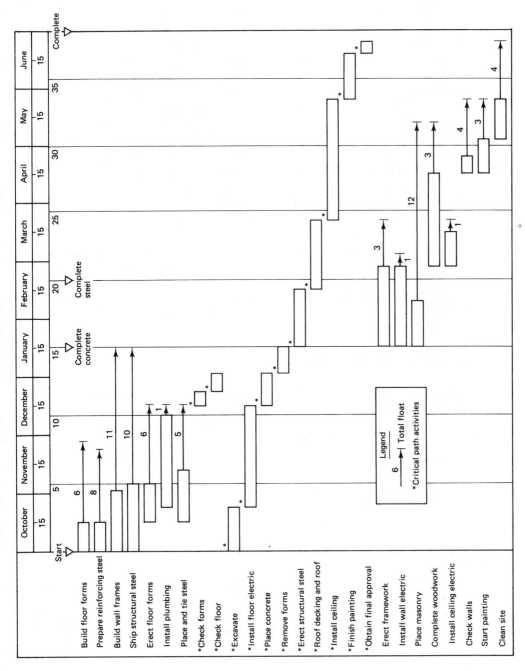

FIGURE 8-13 Bar chart time schedule for the Southfork Building Project.

Realizing the sensitivity of this project in that the planned project duration must be met, all of the jobs plotted on the bar chart reflect the earliest start schedule. The earliest start schedule bar chart, with appropriate float times, used by the Lawrence Construction as a "working" bar chart, is shown in Figure 8–13.

Lawrence Construction advises suppliers and subcontractors of delivery dates, starting dates, and completion dates reflecting the earliest start schedule. The earliest start schedule allows for Lawrence Construction to maintain complete control of the float times of the project activities. When equipment is projected not to be received on the planned schedule date, or a subcontract cannot start on the predetermined starting date, Lawrence Construction will know how much time can be tolerated before these deviations will affect the planned completion date of the project.

An expedient used by Lawrence Construction that is shown in Figure 8–13 is the placement of the float times for each project item shown by an arrow with the float value above it. Critical items have an asterisk (*) placed adjacent to them. This type of bar chart is for use by the owner or general contractor. A bar chart without the designated float times is distributed to the supplier or subcontractor. Suppliers and subcontractors who have access to their respective float times for the project items for which they are responsible will have a tendency to use the latest start or latest finish times that could absorb all or most of the float too early in the project. To maintain timing discipline for this project, Lawrence Construction requires that all the suppliers and subcontractors use the early start schedule as a basis for their work schedule.

Benefits of Timing Calculations

Summarizing this scheduling approach, Lawrence Construction lists the principal benefits that are derived from the technique as follows:

- Establishes a supportable project duration for the plan.
- Identifies the critical activities that make up the longest path (or critical path) through the project.
- Identifies the jobs where there is scheduling flexibility without changing the project duration.

MONITORING THE PROJECT SCHEDULE

Under the terms of the construction contract, the City of Southfork requires Lawrence Construction to submit status reports every 5 weeks on the progress of the building project. Whether or not this contract provision existed, Lawrence Construction management would still have set up some project control disciplines, as monitoring the progress of each project item is an essential phase of project management.

Lawrence Construction prepares two types of status reports: the progress schedule, which monitors the progress of earliest start times for use by their personnel, suppliers, and subcontractors, and the summary schedule of latest start times, which is prepared for the City of Southfork.

Preparing the Progress Schedule

The progress report used by Lawrence Construction personnel is predicated on the early start–early finish philosophy. This principle is used to install the discipline for completing the job on time. In this manner, during project implementation, there is a built-in allowance for reasonable delays on those jobs that have float values, and they will not contribute to any lengthening of the project duration. However, any delays on critical jobs have a direct effect on the project duration. To illustrate, Lawrence Construction's review of the work activities at the end of *week 20* indicated the following status:

Activity	Weeks Behind
Install wall electrical	2
Erect framework	3
Install roof deck and roofing	1
Place masonry	5

All other work activities are progressing as planned. This review is shown on the bar chart time schedule by filling in the bars in accordance with the status of the work activities. The completed progress schedule is shown in Figure 8-14.

Lawrence Construction uses the progress schedule to assess the timing status by reviewing how those specific jobs that are behind schedule actually affect the project completion date. A simple tabulation provides the answers.

	Weeks Behind	Weeks Float	Effect on Project Duration
Install wall electrical	2	13	11 weeks float remaining
Erect framework and woodwork	3	3	0 weeks float remaining
Install roof deck and roofing	1	0	Can extend project 1 week
Place masonry	5	12	7 weeks float remaining

Progress report date

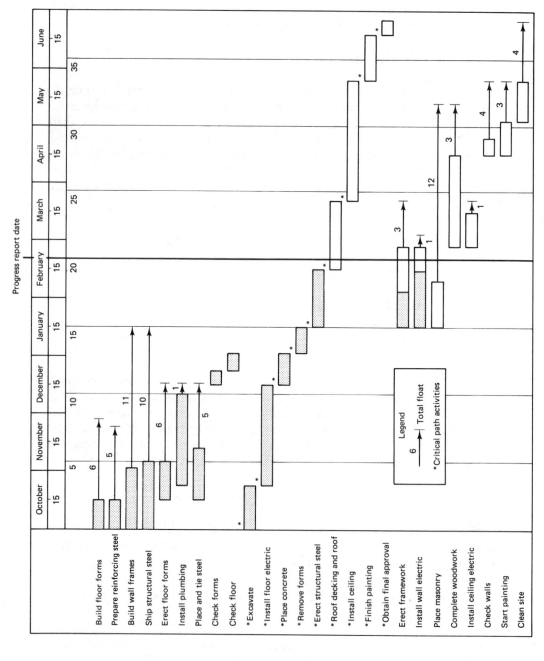

FIGURE 8-14 Progress schedule for the Southfork Building Project (end of week 20, February 21, 1983).

152

The next step in the analysis is to determine the reasons for the delays that have caused the project to fall behind schedule. The findings are tabulated below.

ACTIVITY	REASONS FOR DELAY
Install wall electrical	Did not start as scheduled
Erect framework and woodwork	Layout changes slowed work
Install roof deck and roofing	Layout changes slowed work
Place masonry	Layout changes slowed work

From the timing status and the reasons for the delays, Lawrence Construction recognized that although the electrical and framing jobs need some attention to be expedited, the main concern is the roof deck and roofing. So the action taken was the following:

- Subcontractor for framework is submitting proposal for overtime charges that would restore its work to original schedule.
- Electrical subcontractor not required to consider overtime, as their present 2-week delay will not affect the project duration in view of the 11-week float time remaining after consideration of the 2-week delay.
- Roof deck and roofing subcontractor requested to submit overtime schedule to recover 1-week delay.

Lawrence Construction has other options that they are considering concurrently. These options, which may be recommended for future action in order to restore the original plan, are the following:

- Negotiate with electrical subcontractor on overtime costs, as they have to assume some liability since they did not start as scheduled. This approach may recover at least 1 week.
- Review masonry subcontractor's proposal to recover 2 weeks of the 3-week delay.
- Investigate future critical work activities with the purpose of reducing 1 week from the schedule so that the project duration will remain as planned.

Although it appears that Lawrence Construction is "on top" of the problems, they recognize that at least 18 weeks of this project remains, and that other "crises" will probably occur. This situation, which is typical of many, makes project control a very important part of project management.

Preparing the Summary Schedule

The basic difference between the summary schedule and the progress schedule is that the summary schedule uses the latest start–latest finish philosophy and is used by Lawrence Construction to show progress to the owner, whereas the progress schedule is used by Lawrence Construction and its subcontractors for day-to-day operations, and employs the early start–early finish philosophy.

In either case, Lawrence Construction management uses the status report to evaluate and then submit corrective action for any potential delays. This is an application of the management-by-exception technique. Exception reporting is an important aspect of status reporting. Status reporting raises these important points:

- Which jobs, specifically, are behind schedule? How much will this extend the project completion date if not corrected?
- What are the reasons for the delays that have caused the project to fall behind schedule?
- What steps have been or are being taken to restore the situation, and what results have been obtained or are expected?
- What are the recommendations for further action that will restore the correct situation?

The summary schedule approach by which Lawrence Construction project personnel communicate project status to all levels of their management and to the City of Southfork is essentially a project status report. This status report will generally contain the following documents: (1) cover letter, (2) executive highlights, and (3) summary progress schedule (bar chart).

Cover Letter. The cover letter shown in Figure 8–15 is an overview of the status of the project to date. Lawrence Construction will use this letter to summarize the progress, provide anticipated completion dates of major events, and make brief statements concerning the status of critical items and potential solutions to problems.

Executive Highlights. The executive highlights section employed by Lawrence Construction emphasizes the status of the important aspects of the project in the form of a bullet (•) listing (Figure 8–16). Each bullet point consists of a brief sentence or a maximum of two sentences. For a relatively small project, or if the progress status report is to be brief, the highlights can be included with the cover letter.

Summary Progress Schedule (Bar Chart). The summary schedule depicting progress in a summary form allows the City of Southfork the opportunity to review the overall project on one sheet. The countless delays associated with the day-to-day activities are summarized, and the management-by-exception technique of drawing attention to the most critical items is applied. Lawrence Construction prepares the summary bar chart to accomplish the following:

March 1, 1983

TO: City of Southfork

SUBJECT: February, 1983 Status Report
                    Southfork Building Project

The Southfork building project at this time is projected to be delayed 1 week from the planned June 27 to the present projected July 3 date. The 1-week delay is due primarily to the roof deck and roofing work, which was late in starting because of changes that had been approved in the building layout design.

Negotiations are under way with the subcontractors of the roof deck and roofing subcontractors as well as the framework and woodwork contractor on extra overtime costs in an effort to expedite their work so that contract schedules can be maintained.

The attached program executive highlights and summary progress schedule will provide you with additional details.

Please advise if you wish further information.

Lawrence Construction

FIGURE 8-15   Cover letter for Southfork Building Project.

- Portray graphically any projected extensions beyond the planned completion date.
- Show the actual progress status to the original plan.
- Show the status of major milestones.

After a review of the work activities at the end of week 20, Lawrence Construction graphically portrayed the status on a summary bar chart (Figure 8-17).

By using the latest start–latest finish approach (which utilizes the float values of the project activities), Lawrence Construction management and the City of Southfork officials are subject to only the major problems. Those project items in the critical path that are "in trouble" and those project items whose float times have been used up represent the problems that make up most of the attention.

Lawrence Construction management realizes the importance of communication—of keeping the City of Southfork and their own personnel informed of the performance of the Southfork Building Project. The expedients that they employ to assist them in appraising project performance and objectively evaluating the problem areas have been shown in part in this section.

Use of the computer for monitoring the project and preparing updates has proved to be invaluable. The role of the computer is explained in a later section.

- Concrete work completed on schedule; forms have been removed, and the minor patchwork is done.
- Electrical work continues to "drift." Although there is yet no critical situation, because of the remaining float time, there have been several meetings conducted with the electrical subcontractor to find solutions to problems creating delays.
- Masonry work behind the early start schedule by 3 weeks, but adequate float time for this activity keeps project items on time.
- Framework construction has been delayed because of changes in the design of the partitions. Investigating additional cost impact of overtime authorization to reduce construction time.
- Roof deck and roofing projected to be delayed 1 week; to be completed first week in April. Subcontractor asked to submit overtime costs to recover this 1-week delay.
- Timing of ceiling and painting work activities being investigated for possible "compression" to help in bringing project back on schedule.
- Significant milestones that need to be met to keep project on schedule:
  - Complete electrical   3/28
  - Complete roof deck and roofing   3/28 (4/4 present projection)
  - Complete framework and woodwork   5/9
  - Complete masonry   5/9

FIGURE 8-16 Executive highlights of progress of the Southfork Building Project.

Reporting Status Using Milestones

The milestone approach is an excellent "tool" for reporting project status in a summary form to higher management, as it summarizes the status of the major events. They are selected events that are of a major importance toward achieving objectives. They are key events usually showing the completion date of a major phase of the project, the delivery date of a major equipment item, or the date of a key management decision to make the project maintain a successful completion sequence. These events may or may not be on the critical path.

Milestones are noted on a network diagram and represent the key starting and/or completion dates of major events. A display of this kind can be helpful in summarizing a planning diagram. See Figure 8-18 for an example on the use of milestones for the Southfork Building Project. Milestones can be identified on the planning diagram by a rectangular block showing description and dates.

Using the milestone approach for monitoring and controlling project timing becomes quite effective with the use of computer software. Most project manage-

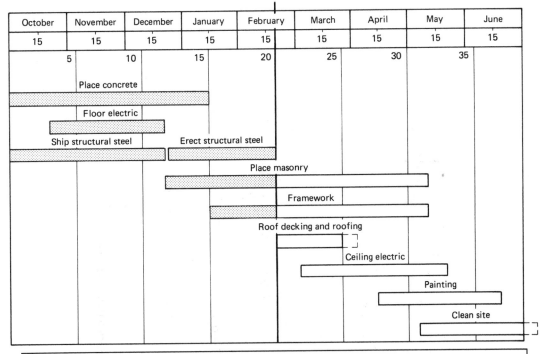

Progress to Date

- Concrete completed on schedule.
- Plumbing and floor electrical completed on schedule.
- Structural completed on schedule.
- Masonry on schedule; however, drifting needs to be checked. Overtime may have to be considered.
- Framework and woodwork on schedule; however, drifting has placed this work on the critical path. Further drifting will cause project delay, and overtime may have to be considered.
- Roof deck and roofing have been delayed 1 week and may cause a 1-week delay from the present project completion date unless there is a correction, such as overtime.
- Remainder of project items appear to be on schedule.

Milestone Report

ACTIVITY	PLANNED	PROJECTED
Complete electrical	3/28	3/28
Complete roof deck and roofing	3/28	4/5
Complete framework and woodwork	5/9	5/9
Complete masonry	5/9	5/9
Complete project	6/29	7/4

FIGURE 8-17 Summary progress schedule for the Southfork Building Project (end of week 20, February 21, 1983).

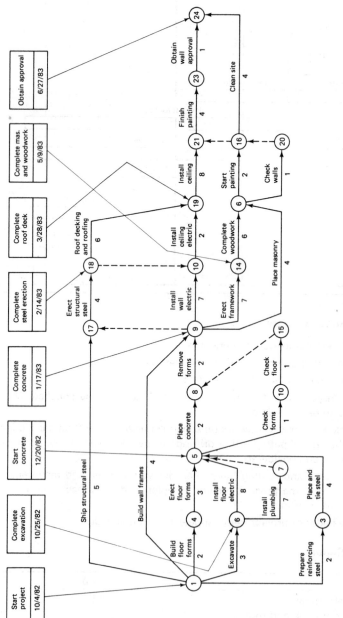

FIGURE 8–18 Milestones for the Southfork Building Project.

ment packages have the milestone status feature. We cover the computer-oriented milestone status report in the section "Using the Computer for Planning and Scheduling" (along with several other project control features, one of which is the "management review" bar chart that is developed from the MR activities shown on Figure 8–29).

CONTROLLING PROJECT COSTS

Lawrence Construction knows that to stay in business, they must operate at a profit. Knowledge of the status of their costs is important. The financial integrity of their organization is dependent on controlling the funds allocated for this project.

After the costs for each project activity have been established, Lawrence Construction is interested in knowing how these costs are distributed over the project. Knowing the cost distribution, such as monthly or quarterly costs, allows Lawrence Construction to plan their cash flow over the length of the project. Lawrence Construction can also use cost distribution as a basis to measure cost performance during the course of the project.

Lawrence Construction starts the procedure for controlling costs the moment the timing schedule is formulated. The costs associated with each project activity are placed on a bar chart time schedule such as that shown on Figure 8–19.

Controlling costs follows a specific procedure. This procedure uses the base document: the bar chart time schedule with the project costs added to the chart and placed with their respective activities. From this reference chart Lawrence Construction produces the various cost schedules needed for effective cost scheduling, including method for payment of work completed. Controlling Southfork Building Project costs starts here as well.

The reference chart showing the float times will allow for making adjustments, with little difficulty, in the cost schedule if there are timing changes. This is especially helpful during the planning phase, when costs for specific periods may need adjustment but with attention to project timing.

Setting up the cost schedule requires the unit cost of each activity. For the Southfork project the unit cost is expressed in dollars per week. Another term for expressing the unit cost is the cost slope. The cost slope tabulation is shown in Figure 8–20.

The cost slope calculation essentially reduces the calculations eventually needed for the tabulated cost schedule. Instructions for the cost slope calculations format are as follows:

- *Activity* is the description of the project activity.
- *Cost* is the total cost in dollars of performing the project activity.
- *Duration* is the total duration time of the project activity. For this project the time is weeks. The *cost slope* is the *cost* divided by the *duration* and is expressed in dollars per week.

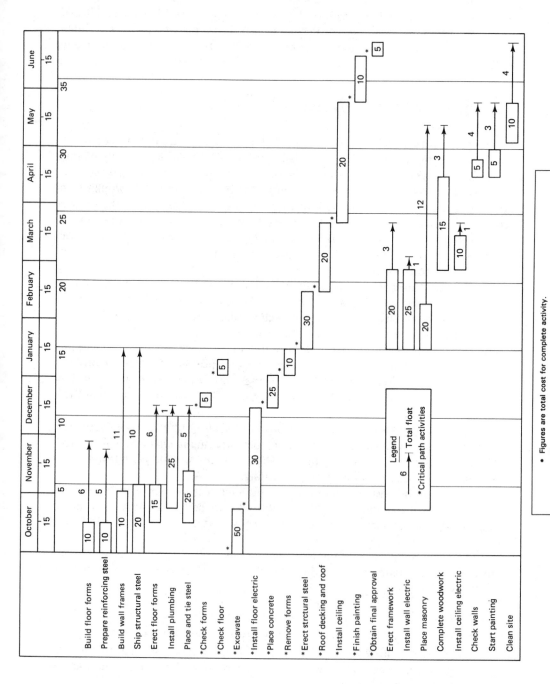

FIGURE 8-19 Bar chart cost schedule for the Southfork Building Project.

ACTIVITY	COST (DOLLARS)	DURATION (WEEKS)	COST SLOPE (DOLLARS/WEEK)
Build wall frames	$ 10,000	4	$ 2,500
Prepare reinforcing steel	10,000	2	5,000
Build floor forms	10,000	2	5,000
Excavate	50,000	3	16,667
Ship structural steel	20,000	5	4,000
Place and tie reinforcing steel	25,000	4	6,250
Erect forms	15,000	3	5,000
Install floor electrical	30,000	8	3,750
Install plumbing	25,000	7	3,571
Place concrete	25,000	2	12,500
Check forms	5,000	1	5,000
Remove forms	10,000	2	5,000
Check floor	5,000	1	5,000
Install wall electrical	25,000	7	3,571
Erect framework	20,000	7	2,857
Place masonry	20,000	4	5,000
Erect structural steel	40,000	4	10,000
Check walls	5,000	1	5,000
Complete woodwork	15,000	6	2,500
Install ceiling electrical	10,000	2	5,000
Install roof deck and roofing	20,000	6	3,333
Install ceiling	20,000	8	2,500
Start painting	5,000	2	2,500
Finish painting	10,000	4	2,500
Obtain final approval	5,000	1	5,000
Clear site	10,000	4	2,500
	$445,000		

FIGURE 8-20   Calculating the cost slope for the Southfork Building Project.

While monthly cost schedules are most common, for this project, Lawrence Construction prepares this particular cost schedule on a 5-week basis. Both the bar chart cost schedule and the cost slope tabulation are used to develop the tabulated cost schedule shown in Figure 8–21. The explanation of the cost schedule calculations shown in the figure are as follows:

- *Activity* is the description of the project activity.
- *Activity time* is the period of time that is desired to determine the costs (or expenditures). If project costs appear critical, as little as 2-week periods

Activity	Activity Time (Weeks)	Cost Slope (Dollars/Week)	Expenditures (Dollars)
Excavate	3	$16,667	$ 50,000
Install floor electrical	2	3,750	7,500
Install plumbing	2	3,571	7,142
Build wall frames	4	2,500	10,000
Prepare reinforcing steel	2	5,000	10,000
Place and tie reinforcing steel	3	6,250	18,750
Build floor forms	2	5,000	10,000
Erect forms	3	5,000	15,000
Ship structural steel	5	4,000	20,000
Total 0–5 (10/4–11/5)			$148,392
Install floor electrical	5	3,750	18,750
Install plumbing	5	3,571	17,855
Place and tie reinforcing steel	1	6,250	6,250
Total 6–10 (11/5–12/10)			$ 42,855
Install floor electrical	1	3,750	3,750
Place concrete	2	12,500	25,000
Remove forms	2	5,000	10,000
Check forms	1	5,000	5,000
Check floor	1	5,000	5,000
Total 11–15 (12/10–1/14)			$ 48,750
Install wall electrical	5	3,571	17,855
Erect framework	5	2,857	14,285
Place masonry	4	5,000	20,000
Erect structural steel	4	10,000	40,000
Install roof deck and roofing	1	3,333	3,333
Total 16–20 (1/14–2/18)			$ 95,473
Install wall	2	3,571	7,142
Complete woodwork	3	2,500	7,500
Install ceiling electrical	2	5,000	10,000
Erect framework	2	2,857	5,714
Check walls	1	5,000	5,000
Install roof deck and roofing	5	3,333	16,665
Total 21–25 (2/18–3/25)			$ 52,021
Check walls	1	5,000	5,000
Complete woodwork	3	2,500	7,500
Start painting	2	2,500	5,000
Install ceiling	5	2,500	12,500
Total 26–30 (3/25–4/29)			$ 30,000
Install ceiling	3	2,500	7,500
Finish painting	1	2,500	2,500
Clean site	3	2,500	7,500
Total 31–35 (4/29–6/3)			$ 17,500
Finish painting	2	2,500	5,000
Obtain final approval	1	5,000	5,000
Total 36–38 (6/3–6/27)			$ 10,000
Total project costs			$444,991
		(rounded)	($445,000)

FIGURE 8-21   Calculating the cost schedule for the Southfork Building Project.

may be required; for the Southfork job, a 5-week period is used. In any event, the time period remains constant for the total project duration.

- *Cost slope* was developed previously.
- *Expenditures* is the result of multiplying the *activity time* column by the *cost slope* column. The expenditures within each time period are then totaled.

The total cost of this project will equal the sum of the total time period expenditures. The expenditures developed from this cost schedule format will serve as the basis for cost control when comparing actual project expenditures during a given period to arrive at the variance. This procedure is explained in a later section.

Preparing the Cost Distribution Graph

As an expedient for effective review of the cost schedule, Lawrence Construction prepares the cost distribution graph shown in Figure 8–22, which is a graphic portrayal of the total project costs broken down into costs for each period.

After a review of the cost distribution graph, Lawrence Construction is concerned about the outlay of $148,000 the first 5 weeks of the project. This amounts to one-third of the total project cost of $445,000. The fourth 5-week period also has a high outlay, almost 20% of the total cost. If these large expenditures cause

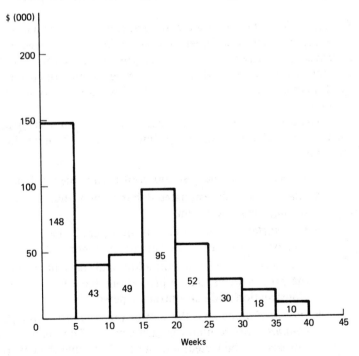

FIGURE 8-22 Cost distribution graph for the Southfork Building Project.

potential cash flow problems, Lawrence Construction would evaluate the possibility of adjusting the earliest start dates of those project jobs that have float availability. As this cost distribution graph is based on the earliest start schedule, consideration may be given to using the latest start schedule of several selected project items as the implementation schedule if the cost expenditures from the latest start schedule show a cash flow more conducive to the financial strategy of the Southfork project.

- *Build wall frames.* Total cost of $10,000 and 11-week float can be scheduled to start in the second 5-week period.

- *Prepare reinforcing steel* and *place and tie reinforcing steel.* Can be scheduled in second 5-week period, which shifts $28,750 from first 5-week period (these items have 11 weeks of float).

- *Ship structural steel.* Can be scheduled to start in second 5-week period if supplier agrees to delaying shipment. This can shift $20,000 without affecting schedule, as this item has a 10-week float.

This same approach can be used for the fourth 5-week period, where it may be necessary to reduce costs by about $20,000. *Erect frame work* and *Install wall electrical* are the float items that can be investigated.

Preparing the Indicated Cost Outcome Report

Lawrence Construction uses a cost control device, known as the indicated cost outcome report, that is designed to ensure that project spending is contained within approved (authorized) amounts. The report is used to review and evaluate the spending status of projects, to determine if project commitments are in line with authorized amounts, and to determine if (and when) additional authorizations may be required.

The cost outcome format indicated is simple to develop and is a valuable tool for Lawrence Construction management. The major items in its development are the following:

- *Project item* is the description of each project job activity.

- *Authorized* is the estimated dollar amount that has been approved for completing the project item.

- *Committed to date* for each project item is the amount that has been spent and/or ordered as of the date of the report.

- *Future commitments* are the additional costs that will be needed to complete the project items. These projections have to be determined by Lawrence Construction and subcontractor personnel.

- *Indicated outcome* is the sum of the *committed to date* column and *future commitments* column for each activity. This figure is compared to the authorized (or budgeted) amount to determine the cost performance of each item. All of the indicated outcomes of the activities are added algebraically, and this total is compared with the total budgeted cost.

- *Variance* is the difference between *authorized* column and *indicated outcome* column.
- *Percent of variance* is the result of dividing the difference between *authorized* column amount and *indicated outcome* column by the *authorized* column amount. (Multiply by 100 to arrive at percent amounts.)

The indicated cost outcome exercise is done every 5 weeks for the Southfork project. Figure 8–23 shows the indicated cost outcome report of February 21 (week 20).

The seven items noted below contribute to $25,000 of the $32,000 overrun. It will be the task of Lawrence Construction to determine the absolute need for these items to be overrun. And they have an additional responsibility of reviewing all other project items remaining to be done to determine whether there can be any "thrifting," that is, reduce some features or introduce some efficiencies.

With 18 weeks of this project remaining, it is quite evident that Lawrence Construction will need to be very cost-control conscious to maintain an efficient project. The important tool to be used in reporting cost performance will be the indicated cost outcome report. In view of the critical cost situation, Lawrence Construction may decide to prepare this report every 2 weeks instead of the present every 5 weeks.

In week 20 this project shows an overrun of 7.2%. There is an indicated cost of $467,000, the amount that is expected to be spent to complete the project. This is $32,000 over the authorized amount of $445,000.

As Lawrence Construction views this additional cost, or overrun, as a serious concern, they need to evaluate the project items that have the greatest overruns and determine if their projected costs can be reduced enough to bring the total project costs back into line. The project items that will be evaluated are the following:

ACTIVITY	AUTHORIZED AMOUNT	INDICATED OUTCOME
Install wall electrical	$ 25,000	$ 28,000
Erect structural steel	40,000	45,000
Complete woodwork	15,000	20,000
Install ceiling electrical	10,000	12,000
Install ceiling	20,000	22,000
Finish painting	10,000	14,000
Clean site	10,000	14,000
	$130,000	$155,000

Reporting date: Week 20   Start date: Week 0   Completion date: Week 38

Project Item	Authorized (Budgeted)	Committed to Date	Future Commitments	Indicated Outcome	Variance (Over) or Under	Percent (Over) or Under
Build wall frames	$ 10	$ 10	$–	$ 10	$–	$–
Prepare reinforcing steel	10	10	–	10	–	–
Build floor forms	10	10	–	10	–	–
Excavate	50	45	–	45	5	11.1
Ship structural steel	20	30	–	30	(10)	(50)
Place and tie reinforcing steel	25	30	–	30	(5)	(20)
Erect forms	15	15	–	15	–	–
Install floor electrical	30	30	–	30	–	–
Install plumbing	25	25	–	25	–	–
Place concrete	25	20	–	20	(5)	(20)
Check forms	5	5	–	5	–	–
Remove forms	10	10	–	10	–	–
Check floor	5	5	–	5	–	–
Install wall electrical	25	24	4	28	(3)	(12)
Erect framework	20	12	6	18	2	10
Place masonry	20	14	3	17	3	15
Erect structural steel	40	45	–	45	(5)	(12.5)
Check walls	5	–	5	–	–	–
Complete woodwork	15	18	2	20	(5)	(33.3)
Install ceiling electrical	10	10	2	12	(2)	(20)
Install roof deck and roofing	20	12	6	18	(2)	(10)
Install ceiling	20	1	21	22	(2)	(10)
Start painting	5	1	4	5	–	–
Finish painting	10	–	14	14	(4)	(40)
Obtain final approval	5	–	4	4	1	20
Clear site	10	–	14	14	(4)	(40)
	$445	$382	$85	$467	$32	(7.2)

Note: Costs in thousands of dollars.

FIGURE 8–23   Indicated cost outcome as of February 21, 1983 (week 20) for the Southfork Building Project.

PLANNING FOR LABOR AND PERSONNEL

Lawrence Construction recognizes the need for planning and scheduling personnel and labor resources similar to the approach used in planning and scheduling costs. Although there are many similarities, there are several other aspects that are unique to the labor and personnel that will be used on the Southfork project. This project requires, for the most part, carpenters and ironworkers. Because of requirements of other projects, Lawrence Construction will make available a maximum of six carpenters and four ironworkers.

In the labor and personnel planning phase, Lawrence Construction has established two major objectives:

1. Maintain the project schedule with the personnel available.
2. Maintain a uniform level of personnel throughout the length of the project.

A good plan produces effective leveling, which will reduce peaks and valleys in demands, minimize crew sizes, and avoid, or at least minimize, idle time or downtime. For a successful project, managers of an organization such as Lawrence Construction know that they need to achieve these goals. They recognize that there are advantages for an organization to strive to balance the overall requirements over reasonable periods of time. A business or industrial firm should be hiring an employee to work the life of the project, making workers feel that once hired, there is reasonable assurance of consistent employment. A firm's efficiency is reduced through layoffs and rehires. Meeting peak demands can provide problems that can possibly be avoided with effective leveling procedures.

All sorts of intuitive methods for leveling (or normalizing) labor for project purposes have been tried, usually with only partial success. Satisfactory results are obtained more often when intuitive methods are supported by a disciplined approach. The first step in allocating personnel is to determine the requirements when using the early start schedule. If the leveling is not satisfactory, the late start schedule is considered. If neither of these schedules provides an adequate level, schedules are adjusted using the float values. The leveling procedure follows these steps:

1. The first adjustments are made with the noncritical jobs, that is, those with the most float time.
2. Adjustment is made with the jobs almost on the critical list.
3. If leveling is not achieved, then adjusting the highest-priority jobs, those on the critical path, may be necessary to satisfy the leveling process. In most cases, adjusting jobs on the critical path involves lengthening the duration of the project.

The resource leveling program is a valuable tool for the project planner, and when used together with cost and timing factors, Lawrence Construction expects to arrive at the desirable project plan.

Lawrence Construction starts the personnel and labor plan by showing the requirements on the network diagram in Figure 8–24a and on the bar chart time schedule that shows the earliest start schedule, which is shown on Figure 8–24b. Using this bar chart made it fairly simple for Lawrence Construction to total the weekly carpenter and ironworker daily requirements. Figure 8–25 is a tabulation of these requirements if the project is to be scheduled using the earliest start schedule. By graphing the labor requirements, Lawrence Construction could readily observe the "peaks and valleys" and the time periods when requirements exceeded availability.

After an analysis of the earliest start time schedule charts and tabulations, Lawrence Construction concludes that the earliest start schedule was not personnel/labor efficient:

- *Poor continuity.* There were no ironworkers required from week 7 to week 15 and from week 32 to week 37, yet immediately preceding and succeeding these periods, two to four ironworkers are required.
- *Not a normal level work force.* The number of required carpenters ranges from a high of thirteen to a low of two in the first half of the project (19 weeks). The second half ranges from eight to one. During the periods that ironworkers are required, the maximum required is six; the minimum is two.
- *Exceeds number of carpenters and ironworkers available.* Six carpenters are available, whereas the schedule requires more than six carpenters for 6 of the 38 weeks. The number of ironworkers required (four) is exceeded during 5 weeks.

To correct this situation suggests an excessive amount of overtime costs, which the project budget may not be able to afford. Before calculating the added costs associated with this schedule, Lawrence Construction took the necessary steps to review the latest start schedule, which adjusts the earliest start schedule by changing all the noncritical jobs to their latest starts.

Lawrence Construction followed the same steps used in the earliest start schedule to develop the data needed to analyze the labor and personnel allocation in the event the latest start schedule is used. The following charts and tabulations were prepared:

- Bar chart time schedule showing the latest start times of all work items, including the skilled labor required for each work item, of the Southfork project (Figure 8–26)
- Weekly tabulation of skilled labor requirements, when using the latest start schedule, for the Southfork project (Figure 8–27)
- Graphic load charts of the skilled labor requirements, when using the latest start schedule, for the Southfork project (Figure 8–28)

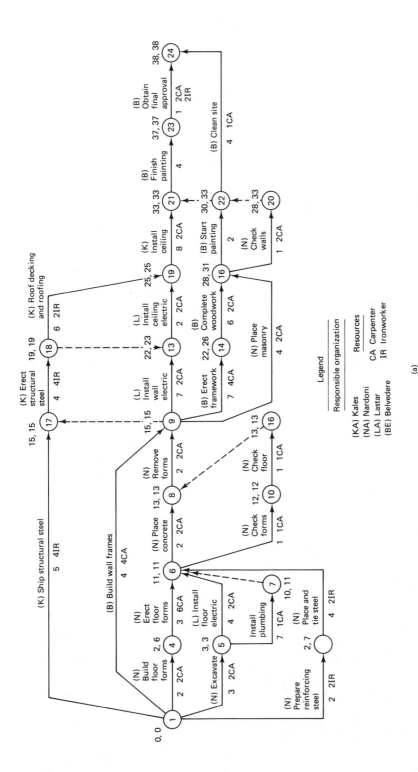

FIGURE 8-24 Labor allocation for the Southfork Building Project: (a) network diagram showing the initial labor allocation; (b) bar chart time schedule (earliest start time).

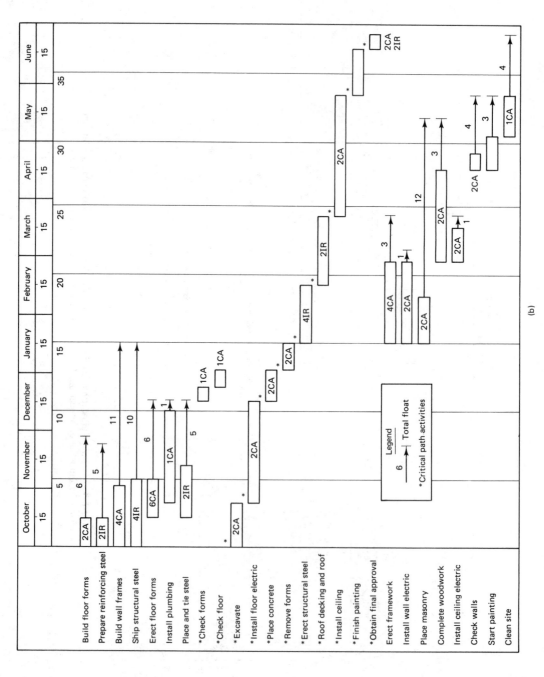

FIGURE 8-24 (*Continued*)

(b)

170

							Week											
	1-2	3	4	5	6	7-10	11	12-13	14-15	16-18	19	20-24	25	26-31	32-33	34-37	38
Carpenter (CA)	8	12	13	9	3	3	2	3	2	4	8	6	4	4	2	1	2
Ironworker (IR)	6	6	6	6	2	0	0	0	0	4	4	4	2	2	0	0	2

FIGURE 8-25 Tabulation of carpenters and ironworkers' requirements (earliest start schedule) for the Southfork Building Project.

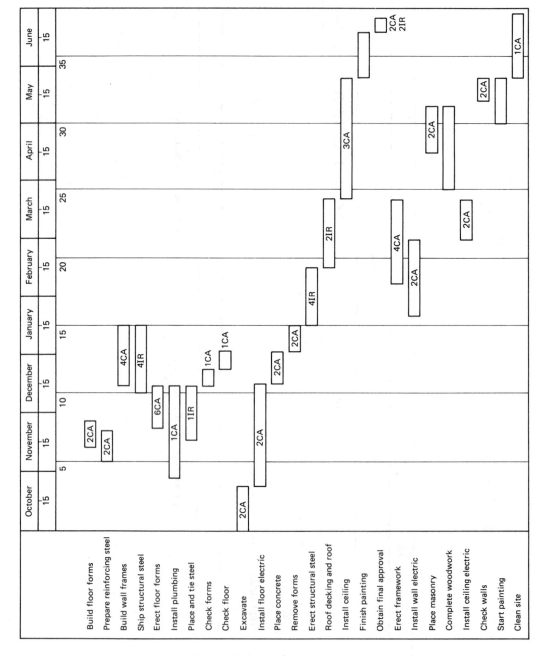

FIGURE 8-26 Labor leveling: bar chart time schedule (latest start time) for the Southfork Building Project.

	Week																	
	1–4	5	6	7–8	9–10	11	12–13	14–15	16	17–18	19	20–25	26–27	28–31	32–33	34	35–37	38
Carpenter (CA)	2	3	5	9	9	7	6	—	2	6	6	4	6	2	—	—	1	3
Ironworker (IR)	—	—	2	2	2	6	4	4	2	4	4	2	—	—	—	—	—	2

FIGURE 8-27 Tabulation of weekly labor requirements (latest start dates) for the Southfork Building Project.

173

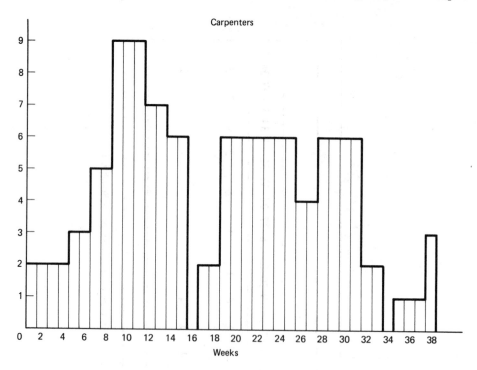

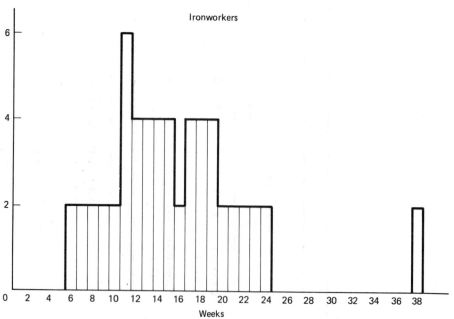

FIGURE 8-28 Graphic load charts of labor allocation (latest start time) for the Southfork Building Project.

An analysis of the charts and tabulations showing the labor allocations based on latest start times did not give Lawrence Construction any better solution than the earliest start times. Although this schedule is more efficient than the early start schedule, it cannot be considered a good schedule.

- *Not a normal level work force.* Requirements for carpenters range from nine to one. There are two separate weeks where no carpenters are required. When they are required, ironworkers range from six to two.
- *Exceeds number of skilled tradesmen that are available.* There are five weeks in this schedule when more than six carpenters are required. There is one week when more than four ironworkers are required.

To make up for the excessive requirements, less overtime is needed for this schedule than for the earliest start schedule, and Lawrence Construction may decide to use this schedule. The main drawback is that there would be no allowance for any drift in the project schedule. All project items are now on the critical path.

Further leveling efforts can be done but become time consuming and tedious without the aid of a computer software package specifically designed for resource leveling. Lawrence Construction will delay making a decision on how the personnel and labor concerns will affect the planning and scheduling of the Southfork project until after an analysis has been completed using the computer software packages that are available.

USING THE COMPUTER
FOR PLANNING AND SCHEDULING

During the planning and scheduling of the Southfork project, Lawrence Construction acquired a computer software package that they used for the planning, scheduling, and monitoring of the timing, costs, and personnel/labor requirements of this project. To phase in the computer system for use on a permanent basis, Lawrence Construction wanted to compare its merits with those of the manual methods that were being used for the Southfork project.

There are several ways that computer systems accept input data to be read into the computer. For example, if Lawrence Construction had a remote terminal available in their field office, they might make use of an *interactive* input as well as a reporting system that should simplify inserting the input data and facilitate examination of the output results by having the central office generate the reporting requirements.

Field personnel of Lawrence Construction use a personal computer to schedule and control several aspects of the Southfork project. The software packages available for personal computers have improved appreciably during recent years and now contain most of the software used previously with mainframe computer systems.

There are many benefits to use of the personal computer for schedule calculations rather than time-consuming manual methods. Bar charts can be generated and changes made in a fraction of the time. "What if" situations can be analyzed without disturbing the base schedule. The ability to compare personnel required with available skilled personnel becomes a valuable asset with the use of the personal computer.

The software package used is typical of the many packages that are now available. Software suppliers are constantly upgrading and improving their products. Lawrence Construction chose this package primarily because of its compatibility with the arrow diagramming technique used by Lawrence Construction in planning the project. The software package used by Lawrence Construction can accept input either for the method used in arrow diagramming or in a precedence charting network. Since Lawrence Construction has used the arrow diagramming (or i,j) method in the past, they will continue this approach.

Using the Computer Printout Reports

For the Southfork Building Project, Lawrence Construction selected essentially the same reports to be generated from the computer calculations that were developed from manual calculations. However, computer-generated reports will provide more information, which can be used to better analyze the plan and schedule of the project, and to analyze the skilled trades requirement.

The reports produced for Lawrence Construction, accompanied with an analysis, are shown as follows:

- A tabulated schedule for each project item shows the earliest and latest start dates, earliest and latest finish dates, duration, and float times.
- A bar chart schedule graphically portrays the information shown in the tabulated schedule. Both the tabulated and bar chart schedules become planning and scheduling tools for Lawrence Construction.
- A milestone report and a management review bar chart summarizes the plan and schedule. These are for reporting status to management and to review the overall program from a management-by-exception approach to detect the critical items.
- Tabulated and bar chart schedules that the subcontractors will receive will show just the project items for which they are responsible. Lawrence Construction will design these schedules so that the subcontractors will need to comply with the early start schedule.
- Cost histograms and cash flow curves allow Lawrence Construction to plan and analyze against the availability of funds allotted for this project.
- Lawrence Construction and the subcontractors will use resource histograms and summary resource reports to compare the required number of critical skilled tradesmen with the number initially made available for this project. Where the computer reports show that more labor time is required than is

available, Lawrence Construction and the subcontractors will need to decide on the best course of action: revise plan, extend schedule, authorize overtime, or make additional personnel available during these periods.

The individual reports shown in Figures 8-29 to 8-35 are structured to allow the contractor and subcontractors to review the timing, cost, and resource schedules based on the plan developed. There are commentaries included with each report that simulate the thought process leading to decision making, where required.

```
BUILDING CONSTRUCTION PROJECT                SOUTHFORK LIBRARY ADDITION
     REPORT TYPE :MILESTONE                               PRINTING SEQUENCE  :Earliest Activities First
                                                          SELECTION CRITERIA :MILESTONE
     PLAN I.D.  :SOLA    VERSION  14                       TIME NOW DATE     : 4/OCT/82
====================================================================================================
       MILESTONE                       EARLIEST EVENT              LATEST EVENT
       DESCRIPTION                          TIME                       TIME
====================================================================================================
    1-   1 START PROJECT                  4/OCT/82                   4/OCT/82
    5-   5 START CONCRETE                20/DEC/82                  20/DEC/82
    8-   8 COMPLETE EXCAVATION            3/JAN/83                   3/JAN/83
    9-   9 COMPLETE CONCRETE             17/JAN/83                  17/JAN/83

   18-  18 COMPLETE STEEL ERECTION       14/FEB/83                  14/FEB/83
   19-  19 COMPLETE ROOF DECK            28/MAR/83                  28/MAR/83
   16-  16 COMPLETE MASONRY & WOODWORK   18/APR/83                   9/MAY/83
   24-  24 OBTAIN FINAL APPROVAL         27/JUN/83                  27/JUN/83
----------------------------------------------------------------------------------------------------

====================================================================================================
```

(a)

```
BUILDING CONSTRUCTION PROJECT                SOUTHFORK LIBRARY ADDITION
     REPORT TYPE :COMPRESSED PERIOD BARCHART               PRINTING SEQUENCE  :Earliest Activities First
                                                          SELECTION CRITERIA ::MR
     PLAN I.D.  :SOLA    VERSION  14                        TIME NOW DATE     : 4/OCT/82
========================================1982=================1983===================================
  PERIOD COMMENCING DATE        14    11    16    13    17    17    14    12    16    I
  MONTH                       IOCT  INOV  IDEC  IJAN  IFEB  IMAR  IAPR  IMAY  IJUN    I
  PERIOD COMMENCING TIME UNIT   12   122   147   167   192  1112  1132  1152  1177    I
====================================================================================================
  1-  25 COMPLETE CONCRETE :MR      ICCCCCC ICCCCCCCCC ICCCCCCC ICCCC    I      I     I     I     I
 17-  19 COMPLETE S.S.& ROOF DECK :MR   I      I      I      I    CCCCC ICCCCCC ICCCCCC I   I     I
  9-  26 COMPLETE MAS/WDWK :MR      I      I      I      I   =====I=====I=====I====...I..   I     I
 19-  24 COMP BLDG :MR             I      I      I      I      I     I    CC ICCCCCCC ICCCCCCCC ICCCCCCCI>
----------------------------------------------------------------------------------------------------

====================================================================================================
Barchart Key:-   CCC :Critical Activities   === :Non Critical Activities   NNN :Activity with neg float   ... :Float
```

(b)

- Of the nine major events (or milestones) in the Southfork project, seven represent critical dates that need to be met for the project to stay on schedule.
- The other two milestones have optional start and/or finish dates:
  - *Excavation* can *start* as late as November 15, 1982, although the planned start date is October 4, 1982.
  - *Masonry* and *woodwork* can be completed any time between April 15 and May 6, 1983, without affecting the project completion date.

FIGURE 8-29 (a) Milestone report and (b) management review bar chart for the Southfork Building Project.

```
BUILDING CONSTRUCTION PROJECT              SOUTHFORK LIBRARY ADDITION
     REPORT TYPE :STANDARD LISTING
                                                        PRINTING SEQUENCE  :Earliest Activities First
                                                        SELECTION CRITERIA :ALL
     PLAN I.D.   :SOLA     VERSION  14                   TIME NOW DATE      : 4/OCT/82
```

ACTIVITY DESCRIPTION	EARLIEST START	EARLIEST FINISH	LATEST START	LATEST FINISH	DURATION	FLOAT
1- 6 EXCAVATE :NA	4/OCT/82	22/OCT/82	4/OCT/82	22/OCT/82	15	0 *
1- 25 COMPLETE CONCRETE :MR	4/OCT/82	14/JAN/83	4/OCT/82	14/JAN/83	75	0 *
1- 3 PREPARE REINFORCING STEEL :NA	4/OCT/82	15/OCT/82	8/NOV/82	19/NOV/82	10	25
1- 4 BUILD FLOOR FORMS :NA	4/OCT/82	15/OCT/82	15/NOV/82	26/NOV/82	10	30
1- 17 SHIP STRUCTUAL STEEL :KA	4/OCT/82	5/NOV/82	13/DEC/82	14/JAN/83	25	50
1- 9 BUILD WALL FRAMES :BE	4/OCT/82	29/OCT/82	20/DEC/82	14/JAN/83	20	55
3- 5 PLACE AND TIE REINFORCING STEEL :NA	18/OCT/82	12/NOV/82	22/NOV/82	17/DEC/82	20	25
4- 5 ERECT FLOOR FORMS :NA	18/OCT/82	5/NOV/82	29/NOV/82	17/DEC/82	15	30
6- 5 INSTALL FLOOR ELECTRICAL :LA	25/OCT/82	17/DEC/82	25/OCT/82	17/DEC/82	40	0 *
6- 7 INSTALL PLUMBING	25/OCT/82	10/DEC/82	1/NOV/82	17/DEC/82	35	5
5- 10 CHECK FORMS :NA	20/DEC/82	24/DEC/82	20/DEC/82	24/DEC/82	5	0 *
5- 8 PLACE CONCRETE :NA	20/DEC/82	31/DEC/82	20/DEC/82	31/DEC/82	10	0 *
10- 15 CHECK FLOORS :NA	27/DEC/82	31/DEC/82	27/DEC/82	31/DEC/82	5	0 *
8- 9 REMOVE FORMS :NA	3/JAN/83	14/JAN/83	3/JAN/83	14/JAN/83	10	0 *
17- 19 COMPLETE S.S.& ROOF DECK :MR	17/JAN/83	25/MAR/83	17/JAN/83	25/MAR/83	50	0 *
17- 18 ELECT STRUCTURAL STEEL :KA	17/JAN/83	11/FEB/83	17/JAN/83	11/FEB/83	20	0 *
9- 13 INSTALL WALL ELECTRICAL :LA	17/JAN/83	4/MAR/83	24/JAN/83	11/MAR/83	35	5
9- 14 ERECT WALL FRAMING :BE	17/JAN/83	4/MAR/83	7/FEB/83	25/MAR/83	35	15
9- 26 COMPLETE MAS/WDWK :MR	17/JAN/83	15/APR/83	7/FEB/83	6/MAY/83	65	15
9- 16 PLACE MASONRY :NA	17/JAN/83	11/FEB/83	11/APR/83	6/MAY/83	20	60
18- 19 INSTALL ROOF DECK & ROOFING :KA	14/FEB/83	25/MAR/83	14/FEB/83	25/MAR/83	30	0 *
13- 19 INSTALL CEILING ELECTRICAL :LA	7/MAR/83	18/MAR/83	14/MAR/83	25/MAR/83	10	5
14- 16 COMPLETE WOODWORK :BE	7/MAR/83	15/APR/83	28/MAR/83	6/MAY/83	30	15
19- 24 COMP BLDG :MR	28/MAR/83	24/JUN/83	28/MAR/83	24/JUN/83	65	0 *
19- 21 INSTALL CEILING :KA	28/MAR/83	20/MAY/83	28/MAR/83	20/MAY/83	40	0 *
16- 22 START PAINTING :BE	18/APR/83	29/APR/83	9/MAY/83	20/MAY/83	10	15
16- 20 CHECK WALLS :NA	18/APR/83	22/APR/83	16/MAY/83	20/MAY/83	5	20
22- 24 CLEAN SITE :BE	2/MAY/83	27/MAY/83	30/MAY/83	24/JUN/83	20	20
21- 23 FINISH PAINTING :BE	23/MAY/83	17/JUN/83	23/MAY/83	17/JUN/83	20	0 *
23- 24 OBTAIN FINAL APPROVAL :BE	20/JUN/83	24/JUN/83	20/JUN/83	24/JUN/83	5	0 *

FIGURE 8-30 Standard listing report (early start schedule) for the Southfork Building Project (continued on next page).

A milestone report and a management review bar chart (Figure 8-29) that summarize the plan and schedule are used for reporting status to management and to review the overall program from a management-by-exception approach, to detect the critical items of the project. Updating the project work activities will cause the milestone report to be adjusted automatically if there are timing changes to those activities that affect these milestones.

The reports shown in Figures 8-36 to 8-39 are generated from a project management software package to analyze the critical resources, carpenter and ironworker skilled tradesmen, comparing availability with requirements. Lawrence Construction prepares this report as a service for the subcontractors to use as a planning tool. As the graphic plan of action is a superior planning tool, so are the graphic histograms generated by the computer a superior resource allocation tool. These histograms are an improvement over the manually prepared load charts (or histograms) shown previously.

There is a scheduling similarity between the manually prepared and computer-generated histograms. At this time the computer software package provides require-

- The Southfork project is planned to start on October 4, 1982.
- Based on a 5-day work week and the earliest start schedule, there are five activities that will start October 4:
  - *Excavate.*
  - *Prepare reinforcing steel.*
  - *Build floor forms.*
  - *Ship structural steel.*
  - *Build wall frames.*

  Critical activities, designated 0* in the *float* column, must start and finish on the designated dates in order for the project to be completed on June 24, 1983.

ACTIVITY	START	FINISH
Excavate	4/Oct/82	22 Oct/82
Install floor electric	25/Oct/82	17/Dec/82
Place concrete	20/Dec/82	31/Dec/82
Remove forms	3/Jan/83	14/Jan/83
Erect structural steel	17/Jan/83	11/Feb/83
Roof decking and roofing	14/Feb/83	25/Mar/83
Install ceiling	28/Mar/83	20/May/83
Finish painting	23/May/83	17/Jan/83
Obtain final approval	20/Jun/83	24/Jun/83

- Based on the earliest start schedule, this project is to be completed on June 24, 1983, when the activity *obtain final approval* is completed.

FIGURE 8-30   (*Continued*)

ments based only on the early start schedule and, if required, the late start schedule. (Improvements are now being implemented to produce leveling features that allow float times of selected project activities. This feature is incorporated in several software packages for personal computers, and many others are in the process of installing this feature to remain competitive.)

As Lawrence Construction and their subcontractors are concerned over the availability of carpenters (six made available for this project) and ironworkers (four made available), they have gone through an exercise on both early and late start schedules to determine the best schedule—one that has the fewest "peaks and valleys" and where the available and required skilled trades are about the same throughout the project.

Lawrence Construction's analysis of the early start schedule reveals a poor

```
BUILDING CONSTRUCTION PROJECT                SOUTHFORK LIBRARY ADDITION
    REPORT TYPE :COMPRESSED PERIOD BARCHART                                    PRINTING SEQUENCE  :Earliest Activities First
                                                                              SELECTION CRITERIA :ALL
    PLAN I.D.   :SOLA      VERSION  14                                        TIME NOW DATE       : 4/OCT/82
================================================1982================1983=============================================
    PERIOD COMMENCING DATE            14     11      16      13      17      17      14      12      16      1
    MONTH                             !OCT   !NOV    !DEC    !JAN    !FEB    !MAR    !APR    !MAY    !JUN    !
    PERIOD COMMENCING TIME UNIT       !2     !22     !47     !67     !92     !112    !132    !152    !177    !
    -------------------------------------------------------------------------------------------------------------
    1-  6 EXCAVATE :NA                !CCCCC !       !       !       !       !       !       !       !       !
    1- 25 COMPLETE CONCRETE :MR       !CCCCCC!CCCCCCCCC!CCCCCCC!CCCC !       !       !       !       !       !
    1-  3 PREPARE REINFORCING STEEL :NA  !===..!.......!       !       !       !       !       !       !       !
    1-  4 BUILD FLOOR FORMS :NA       !===..!.......! !       !       !       !       !       !       !       !

    1- 17 SHIP STRUCTUAL STEEL :KA    !=====!===.....!......!....!  !       !       !       !       !       !
    1-  9 BUILD WALL FRAMES :BE       !=====!=........!......!....!  !       !       !       !       !       !
    3-  5 PLACE AND TIE REINFORCING STEE !  ===!====.....!....!   !       !       !       !       !       !
    4-  5 ERECT FLOOR FORMS :NA       !   ===!====.....!....!   !       !       !       !       !       !

    6-  5 INSTALL FLOOR ELECTRICAL :LA  !   C!CCCCCCCCC!CCCC !       !       !       !       !       !       !
    6-  7 INSTALL PLUMBING            !   =!========!==.. !       !       !       !       !       !       !
    5- 10 CHECK FORMS :NA             !       !       ! CC ! !       !       !       !       !       !
    5-  8 PLACE CONCRETE :NA          !       !       ! CCC!C !       !       !       !       !       !

    10- 15 CHECK FLOORS :NA           !       !       ! C!C   !       !       !       !       !       !
    8-  9 REMOVE  FORMS :NA           !       !       ! !CCCC !       !       !       !       !       !
    17- 19 COMPLETE S.S.& ROOF DECK :MR !     !       !   !  CCCCC!CCCCCCC!CCCCCC !       !       !       !
    17- 18 ELECT STRUCTURAL STEEL :KA !       !       !   !  CCCCC!CC !       !       !       !       !

    9- 13 INSTALL WALL ELECTRICAL :LA !       !       !       !   ====!=!=====!=.....!   !       !       !
    9- 14 ERECT WALL FRAMING :BE      !       !       !       !   ====!=!=====!=..... !       !       !
    9- 26 COMPLETE MAS/WDWK :MR       !       !       !       !   ====!=!=====!=======!====...!..   !       !
    9- 16 PLACE MASONRY :NA           !       !       !       !   ====!==...!......!......!..   !       !

    18- 19 INSTALL ROOF DECK & ROOFING :K !   !       !       !   ! CCCCC!CCCCCC !       !       !       !
    13- 19 INSTALL CEILING ELECTRICAL :LA !   !       !       !   !=====..! !       !       !       !
    14- 16 COMPLETE WOODWORK :BE      !       !       !       !   !=======!====..!..   !       !       !
    19- 24 COMP BLDG :MR              !       !       !       !       !  CC!CCCCCCCC!CCCCCCCCC!CCCCCC!>

    19- 21 INSTALL CEILING :KA        !       !       !       !       !   !  CC!CCCCCCCC!CCCCC   !       !
    16- 22 START PAINTING :BE         !       !       !       !       !   !  CC!CCCCCCCC!CCCCC   !       !
    16- 20 CHECK WALLS :NA            !       !       !       !       !       !  ===!.....   !       !
    22- 24 CLEAN SITE :BE             !       !       !       !       !       !  ===.!..     !       !
                                      !       !       !       !       !       !     !======.!......!>

    21- 23 FINISH PAINTING :BE        !       !       !       !       !       !       !       ! CCC!CCCC  !
    23- 24 OBTAIN FINAL APPROVAL :BE  !       !       !       !       !       !       !       !    ! CCC!>
================================================================================================================
Barchart Key:-  CCC :Critical Activities   === :Non Critical Activities   NNN :Activity with neg float   ... :Float
```

- The bar chart shows graphically the information on the standard listing (or tabulated schedule).

- The legend at the bottom of the chart identifies critical and noncritical activities and activities by negative float (behind schedule activities).

- This project is scheduled to start on October 4, 1982 (the second working day of the month) and to complete on June 24, 1983 (the 191st working day of the project).

FIGURE 8-31 Bar chart (early start schedule) for the Southfork Building Project.

```
BUILDING CONSTRUCTION PROJECT                        SOUTHFORK LIBRARY ADDITION
    REPORT TYPE :STANDARD LISTING                             PRINTING SEQUENCE  :Earliest Activities First
                                                              SELECTION CRITERIA :BE
    PLAN I.D.   :SOLA      VERSION 14                         TIME NOW DATE      : 4/OCT/82
=================================================================================================================
    ACTIVITY DESCRIPTION                  EARLIEST     EARLIEST     LATEST      LATEST      DURATION  FLOAT
                                          START        FINISH       START       FINISH
=================================================================================================================
    1-  9 BUILD WALL FRAMES :BE           4/OCT/82     29/OCT/82    20/DEC/82   14/JAN/83      20       55
    9- 14 ERECT WALL FRAMING :BE          17/JAN/83    4/MAR/83     7/FEB/83    25/MAR/83      35       15
   14- 16 COMPLETE WOODWORK :BE           7/MAR/83     15/APR/83    28/MAR/83   6/MAY/83       30       15
   16- 22 START PAINTING :BE              18/APR/83    29/APR/83    9/MAY/83    20/MAY/83      10       15
   -------------------------------------------------------------------------------------------------------------
   22- 24 CLEAN SITE :BE                  2/MAY/83     27/MAY/83    30/MAY/83   24/JUN/83      20       20
   21- 23 FINISH PAINTING :BE             23/MAY/83    17/JUN/83    23/MAY/83   17/JUN/83      20       0 *
   23- 24 OBTAIN FINAL APPROVAL :BE       20/JUN/83    24/JUN/83    20/JUN/83   24/JUN/83       5       0 *
=================================================================================================================


BUILDING CONSTRUCTION PROJECT                        SOUTHFORK LIBRARY ADDITION
    REPORT TYPE :COMPRESSED PERIOD BARCHART                   PRINTING SEQUENCE  :Earliest Activities First
                                                              SELECTION CRITERIA ::BE
    PLAN I.D.   :SOLA      VERSION 14                         TIME NOW DATE      : 4/OCT/82
===========================================1982=================1983=============================================
    PERIOD COMMENCING DATE        !4       !1       !6       !3       !7       !7       !4       !2       !6     !
    MONTH                         !OCT     !NOV     !DEC     !JAN     !FEB     !MAR     !APR     !MAY     !JUN    !
    PERIOD COMMENCING TIME UNIT   !2       !22      !47      !67      !92      !112     !132     !152     !177    !
=================================================================================================================
    1-  9 BUILD WALL FRAMES :BE   !=====!=........!......!.....  !         !         !         !         !       !
    9- 14 ERECT WALL FRAMING :BE  !        !        !        !  =====!=====!=!.....  !         !        !       !
   14- 16 COMPLETE WOODWORK :BE   !        !        !        !       !=======!=...!..  !        !        !       !
   16- 22 START PAINTING :BE      !        !        !        !       !         !       ! ====!.....  !        !   !
   -------------------------------------------------------------------------------------------------------------
   22- 24 CLEAN SITE :BE          !        !        !        !       !         !       !       !=====.!......!>   !
   21- 23 FINISH PAINTING :BE     !        !        !        !       !         !       !       !  CCC!CCCC   !    !
   23- 24 OBTAIN FINAL APPROVAL :BE !      !        !        !       !         !       !       !        !  CCC!>  !
=================================================================================================================
Barchart Key:-  CCC :Critical Activities   === :Non Critical Activities   NNN :Activity with neg float   ... :Float
```

- BE is the abbreviation code for Belvedere Construction, the subcontractor responsible for the finish carpentry and painting for this project.
- Lawrence Construction has also made Belvedere Construction responsible for handling all the work necessary to obtain final approval.
- Lawrence Construction has informed Belvedere Construction of the critical activities for which they are responsible. The timing is critical, and their earliest finish dates must be met.
- The completion dates of the critical activities are
  - *Painting* (second phase)   6/17/83
  - *Final approval* (project completion)   6/24/83
- Belvedere Construction is responsible for five noncritical activities, and although there is float time available for these project items, they will still be required to comply with the early start–early finish schedule.
- Lawrence Construction will require all subcontractors to comply with the early start–early finish schedule. This procedure permits timing flexibility for any schedule problems that may occur during the course of the project.

FIGURE 8-32 Belvedere Construction responsibility for the Southfork Building Project.

```
BUILDING CONSTRUCTION PROJECT              SOUTHFORK LIBRARY ADDITION
    REPORT TYPE :STANDARD LISTING                                    PRINTING SEQUENCE  :Earliest Activities First
                                                                     SELECTION CRITERIA :KA
    PLAN I.D.   :SOLA     VERSION  14                                TIME NOW DATE        : 4/OCT/82
==================================================================================================================
       ACTIVITY DESCRIPTION                 EARLIEST    EARLIEST     LATEST      LATEST      DURATION  FLOAT
                                            START       FINISH       START       FINISH
==================================================================================================================
   1-  17 SHIP STRUCTURAL STEEL :KA          4/OCT/82    5/NOV/82    13/DEC/82   14/JAN/83     25        50
  17-  18 ELECT STRUCTURAL STEEL :KA        17/JAN/83   11/FEB/83    17/JAN/83   11/FEB/83     20         0 *
  18-  19 INSTALL ROOF DECK & ROOFING :KA   14/FEB/83   25/MAR/83    14/FEB/83   25/MAR/83     30         0 *
  19-  21 INSTALL CEILING :KA               28/MAR/83   20/MAY/83    28/MAR/83   20/MAY/83     40         0 *
------------------------------------------------------------------------------------------------------------------
==================================================================================================================
```

```
BUILDING CONSTRUCTION PROJECT              SOUTHFORK LIBRARY ADDITION
    REPORT TYPE :COMPRESSED PERIOD BARCHART                          PRINTING SEQUENCE  :Earliest Activities First
                                                                     SELECTION CRITERIA ::KA
    PLAN I.D.   :SOLA     VERSION  14                                TIME NOW DATE        : 4/OCT/82
===============================1982========================1983====================================================
  PERIOD COMMENCING DATE        14     11     16     13     17     17     14     12     16     !
  MONTH                        !OCT   !NOV   !DEC   !JAN   !FEB   !MAR   !APR   !MAY   !JUN    !
  PERIOD COMMENCING TIME UNIT   !2     !22    !47    !67    !92   !112   !132   !152   !177    !
==================================================================================================================
   1-  17 SHIP STRUCTURAL STEEL :KA    !======!===....!.......!....   !      !      !      !      !      !
  17-  18 ELECT STRUCTURAL STEEL :KA   !      !      !      !      !CCCCC!CC    !      !      !      !
  18-  19 INSTALL ROOF DECK & ROOFING :K !    !      !      !      !     !CCCCC!CCCCCC !     !      !
  19-  21 INSTALL CEILING :KA          !      !      !      !      !      !     !CC!CCCCCCC!CCCCC  !      !
------------------------------------------------------------------------------------------------------------------
==================================================================================================================
Barchart Key:-  CCC :Critical Activities   === :Non Critical Activities   NNN :Activity with neg float   ... :Float
```

- KA is the abbreviation code for Kales Construction, the subcontractor for the structural steel, roof, and ceiling work.
- All the project items that Kales Construction is responsible for are critical, with the exception of *ship structural steel,* which has 10 weeks of float time.
- So that the structural steel does not stay out in the weather for 10 weeks, the amount of float time, Kales may elect to ship a week or two prior to *steel erection.*
- This decision may depend on the steel fabricator. In this case Kales Construction is also the fabricator, so they have total control of the shipment and can dictate shipment date.
- This might be a tougher decision to make where the steel supplier does not have a good record for timely deliveries.
- Kales' roof decking and roofing suppliers must have their materials on the job site by 3/28/83 so that the project can stay on schedule.
- Roof decking and roofing suppliers should furnish a milestone schedule that can be checked for periodic delivery status.

FIGURE 8-33 Kales Construction responsibility for the Southfork Building Project.

```
BUILDING CONSTRUCTION PROJECT                   SOUTHFORK LIBRARY ADDITION
     REPORT TYPE :STANDARD LISTING                                   PRINTING SEQUENCE  :Earliest Activities First
                                                                    SELECTION CRITERIA ::LA
     PLAN I.D.   :SOLA      VERSION  14                             TIME NOW DATE      : 4/OCT/82
================================================================================================================
     ACTIVITY DESCRIPTION                    EARLIEST      EARLIEST      LATEST        LATEST      DURATION  FLOAT
                                             START         FINISH        START         FINISH
================================================================================================================
  6-   5 INSTALL FLOOR ELECTRICAL :LA        25/OCT/82     17/DEC/82     25/OCT/82     17/DEC/82      40       0 *
  9-  13 INSTALL WALL ELECTRICAL :LA         17/JAN/83     4/MAR/83      24/JAN/83     11/MAR/83      35       5
 13-  19 INSTALL CEILING ELECTRICAL :LA      7/MAR/83      18/MAR/83     14/MAR/83     25/MAR/83      10       5
================================================================================================================
BUILDING CONSTRUCTION PROJECT                   SOUTHFORK LIBRARY ADDITION
     REPORT TYPE :COMPRESSED PERIOD BARCHART                         PRINTING SEQUENCE  :Earliest Activities First
                                                                    SELECTION CRITERIA ::LA
     PLAN I.D.   :SOLA      VERSION  14                             TIME NOW DATE      : 4/OCT/82
======================================1982====================1983==============================================
     PERIOD COMMENCING DATE          14     11      16     13      17     17      14     12      16   I
     MONTH                           1OCT   1NOV    1DEC   1JAN    1FEB   1MAR    1APR   1MAY    1JUN I
     PERIOD COMMENCING TIME UNIT     12     122     147    167     192    1112    1132   1152    1177 I
================================================================================================================
  6-   5 INSTALL FLOOR ELECTRICAL :LA    I   C1CCCCCCCCC1CCCC   I      I       I      I       I      I       I
  9-  13 INSTALL WALL ELECTRICAL :LA     I       I       I      I   =====I=====I=..   I       I      I       I
 13-  19 INSTALL CEILING ELECTRICAL :LA I       I       I      I      I   I====..  I      I       I      I
================================================================================================================
Barchart Key:-  CCC :Critical Activities   === :Non Critical Activities   NNN :Activity with neg float  ... :Float
```

- LA is the abbreviation for Lastar Electric, the electrical subcontractor for the Southfork project.
- Lastar Electric will comply with the same earliest start–earliest finish schedule as Belvedere Construction and the other subcontractors.
- Although *install floor electric* is the critical item, the other two project items that Lastar Electric is responsible for have only 5 days of float time; therefore, Lastar Electric should consider these to be just as critical.
- Since the project work items of Lastar Electric are not continuous, Lawrence Construction must coordinate and make all affected subcontractors aware of the lengthy "gaps" of Lastar Electrics work.
- There is 1-month interruption between completion of electrical installation and start of *wall electrical* installation.
- When all electrical installation is completed on Friday, March 4, 1983, Lastar's electrical installation crew can come right back on the job on Monday, March 7, 1983, to start the *ceiling electrical* work.
- (Having a "sort" schedule showing the individual schedules of each subcontractor offers the opportunity to identify specific scheduling concerns, such as those noted above.)

FIGURE 8-34 Lastar Electric work schedule report.

BUILDING CONSTRUCTION PROJECT   SOUTHFORK LIBRARY ADDITION
    REPORT TYPE :STANDARD LISTING
                                                                        PRINTING SEQUENCE :Earliest Activities First
                                                                        SELECTION CRITERIA ::NA
    PLAN I.D.   :SOLA   VERSION 14   TIME NOW DATE   : 4/OCT/82

ACTIVITY DESCRIPTION	EARLIEST START	EARLIEST FINISH	LATEST START	LATEST FINISH	DURATION	FLOAT
1- 6 EXCAVATE :NA	4/OCT/82	22/OCT/82	4/OCT/82	22/OCT/82	15	0 *
1- 3 PREPARE REINFORCING STEEL :NA	4/OCT/82	15/OCT/82	8/NOV/82	19/NOV/82	10	25
1- 4 BUILD FLOOR FORMS :NA	4/OCT/82	15/OCT/82	15/NOV/82	26/NOV/82	10	30
3- 5 PLACE AND TIE REINFORCING STEEL :NA	18/OCT/82	12/NOV/82	22/NOV/82	17/DEC/82	20	25
4- 5 ERECT FLOOR FORMS :NA	18/OCT/82	5/NOV/82	29/NOV/82	17/DEC/82	15	30
5- 10 CHECK FORMS :NA	20/DEC/82	24/DEC/82	20/DEC/82	24/DEC/82	5	0 *
5- 8 PLACE CONCRETE :NA	20/DEC/82	31/DEC/82	20/DEC/82	31/DEC/82	10	0 *
10- 15 CHECK FLOORS :NA	27/DEC/82	31/DEC/82	27/DEC/82	31/DEC/82	5	0 *
8- 9 REMOVE FORMS :NA	3/JAN/83	14/JAN/83	3/JAN/83	14/JAN/83	10	0 *
9- 16 PLACE MASONRY :NA	17/JAN/83	11/FEB/83	11/APR/83	6/MAY/83	20	60
16- 20 CHECK WALLS :NA	18/APR/83	22/APR/83	16/MAY/83	20/MAY/83	5	20

BUILDING CONSTRUCTION PROJECT   SOUTHFORK LIBRARY ADDITION
    REPORT TYPE :COMPRESSED PERIOD BARCHART
                                                                        PRINTING SEQUENCE :Earliest Activities First
                                                                        SELECTION CRITERIA ::NA
    PLAN I.D.   :SOLA   VERSION 14   TIME NOW DATE   : 4/OCT/82

```
============================1982============================1983================================
PERIOD COMMENCING DATE     !4    !1    !6    !3    !7   !7   !4   !2   !6   !
MONTH                      !OCT  !NOV  !DEC  !JAN  !FEB !MAR !APR !MAY !JUN  !
PERIOD COMMENCING TIME UNIT !2   !22   !47   !67   !92  !112 !132 !152 !177  !
================================================================================================
1-  6 EXCAVATE :NA                  !CCCCC !     !     !     !    !    !    !    !    !
1-  3 PREPARE REINFORCING STEEL :NA !====..!.....!     !     !    !    !    !    !    !
1-  4 BUILD FLOOR FORMS :NA         !====..!.......!   !     !    !    !    !    !    !
3-  5 PLACE AND TIE REINFORCING STEE !   ==!====.....!....!   !    !    !    !    !    !
------------------------------------------------------------------------------------------------
4-  5 ERECT FLOOR FORMS :NA         !     ==!===....!.....!   !    !    !    !    !    !
5- 10 CHECK FORMS :NA               !      !     !  CC !     !    !    !    !    !    !
5-  8 PLACE CONCRETE :NA            !      !     !  CCC!C    !    !    !    !    !    !
10- 15 CHECK FLOORS :NA             !      !     !  C!C     !    !    !    !    !    !
------------------------------------------------------------------------------------------------
8-  9 REMOVE FORMS :NA              !      !     !     !CCCC !    !    !    !    !    !
9- 16 PLACE MASONRY :NA             !      !     !     !  =====!==....!.......!.......!..!   !
16- 20 CHECK WALLS :NA              !      !     !     !     !    !    !  ===.!.....!   !
================================================================================================
```

Barchart Key:- CCC :Critical Activities === :Non Critical Activities   NNN :Activity with neg float   ... :Float

FIGURE 8-35 Nardoni Construction responsibility for the Southfork Building Project (continued on next page).

distribution of carpenters, and the number of carpenters required far exceeds the number that are available in an exceptional number of weeks. Lawrence Construction will next review the computer-generated late start schedule shown in Figure 8-37.

Lawrence Construction can summarize the histograms that show the distribution of carpenters and ironworkers with another report available with the software package. This is a complete resources report and can be generated for both the early start and the late start schedule. These summaries allow Lawrence Construction to complete their planning analysis of the critical skilled trades, carpenters and ironworkers.

Concerns such as personnel required compared with personnel available, extent of time when no personnel are required, and extent of time of the maximum requirements are seen on these complete resources reports. All the resources are summarized on the complete resources report. Skilled labor summaries are shown in Figure 8-40 for the early start schedule and Figure 8-41 for the late start schedule.

- The abbreviation code NA represents Nardoni Construction, the major subcontractor, responsible for the excavating, concrete, and masonry work.
- Lawrence Construction has also contracted with Nardoni to handle the *interior framing* and *underground plumbing* work.
- With the early start schedule, Nardoni has five critical items with no float and two with 1 week float that can be considered critical as well. This represents 50% of their total work activity.

ACTIVITY	REQUIRED COMPLETION
No float	
Excavate	10/22/82
Check forms	12/24/82
Place concrete	12/31/82
Check floor	12/31/82
Remove forms	1/14/83
1-week float: *Install plumbing*	12/10/82

- Nardoni will need to comply with the early starts of the remaining 50% of the project items that are now considered as noncritical. In coordinating all of the Southfork project items, Lawrence Construction will inform Nardoni if there can be any float allowed on these items, that is, if they can start later (within the late start date) or can take longer to complete the work (within the late finish date).

FIGURE 8-35   (*Continued*)

As shown in the complete resources report and the histograms, the late start schedule provides a better labor distribution as well as better control of the maximum requirements. By using bar charts and histograms, Lawrence Construction may be able to do some further limited schedule adjustment which may reduce maximum requirements and normalize requirements.

When Lawrence Construction finally complete the carpenter and ironworker utilization review, they prepare the comparison chart shown in Figure 8-42 to determine the best schedule if labor requirements become the major issue.

The skilled trades requirements analysis shown in Figure 8-42 is reviewed, and the analysis shows that the late start schedule provides the least overtime costs—105 overtime hours less than the overtime needed with the early start schedule—and there are also fewer peaks and valleys with this schedule. Lawrence Construction needs to decide whether the reduced overtime costs of the late start schedule are

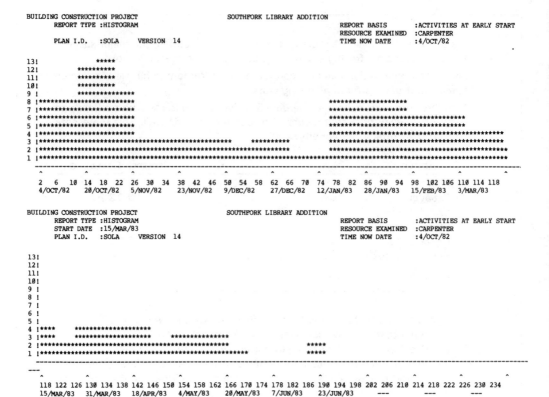

```
BUILDING CONSTRUCTION PROJECT                    SOUTHFORK LIBRARY ADDITION
     REPORT TYPE :HISTOGRAM                                                      REPORT BASIS      :ACTIVITIES AT EARLY START
                                                                                RESOURCE EXAMINED :CARPENTER
     PLAN I.D.   :SOLA      VERSION  14                                          TIME NOW DATE     :4/OCT/82
```

- The number of carpenters ranges from thirteen during the week of October 25 to a minimum of one during the week of May 2 (excluding weeks when none are required.)

- The heaviest load is during the first 5 weeks of the project, when 250 carpenter weeks are required; 150 carpenter weeks are available. (There is another 4-week period, January 17 to February 7, when personnel required exceeds personnel available.)

- One possible solution is overtime for the six available carpenters in the first 5 weeks. Six 12-hour days would handle the work load.

- This schedule shows 30% of the work load to be performed in the first 5 weeks of the project. There is a total of 825 carpenter days during the length of this project.

- There are "peaks and valleys" throughout the project—a poor distribution.

FIGURE 8–36 Carpenter utilization (early start schedule) for the Southfork Building Project.

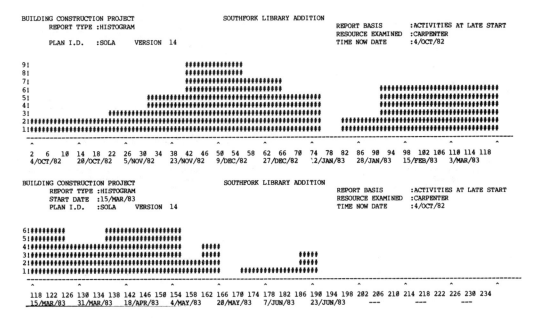

- With the late start schedule, carpenters are required from the week of October 4, 1982, to the week of June 20, 1983, with the exception of the weeks of January 17 and May 23, 1983, when no carpenters are required. There is a net total of 37 weeks when no carpenters are required.
- The number of carpenters required daily ranges from nine during the weeks of November 29 to December 13 to one during the weeks of May 30 to June 13 (excluding weeks when no carpenters are required).
- There are 4 weeks when the number of carpenters available (six) exceeds the number required. By working 15 hours of overtime per week, each available carpenter can make up the additional work load during these weeks.

FIGURE 8–37 Carpenter utilization (late start schedule) for the Southfork Building Project.

```
BUILDING CONSTRUCTION PROJECT            SOUTHFORK LIBRARY ADDITION
      REPORT TYPE :HISTOGRAM                                      REPORT BASIS       :ACTIVITIES AT EARLY START
                                                                 RESOURCE EXAMINED  :IRONWORKER
      PLAN I.D.   :SOLA    VERSION  14                           TIME NOW DATE      :4/OCT/82

6I**************************
5I**************************
4I**************************
3I**************************
2I****************************       **************************************************
1I****************************       **************************************************
   --------------------------------------------------------------------------------------------
   ^    ^    ^    ^    ^    ^    ^    ^    ^    ^    ^    ^    ^    ^    ^    ^    ^    ^    ^   ^
   2    6   10   14   18   22   26   30   34   38   42   46  50   54   58   62  66  70  74  78  82   86  90  94  98  102 106 110 114 118
   4/OCT/82     20/OCT/82     5/NOV/82    23/NOV/82    9/DEC/82    27/DEC/82   12/JAN/83    28/JAN/83   15/FEB/83   3/MAR/83


BUILDING CONSTRUCTION PROJECT            SOUTHFORK LIBRARY ADDITION
      REPORT TYPE :HISTOGRAM                                      REPORT BASIS       :ACTIVITIES AT EARLY START
      START DATE  :15/MAR/83                                      RESOURCE EXAMINED  :IRONWORKER
      PLAN I.D.   :SOLA    VERSION  14                           TIME NOW DATE      :4/OCT/82

6I
5I
4I
3I
2I*********                          *****
1I*********                          *****
   --------------------------------------------------------------------------------------------
   ^    ^    ^    ^    ^    ^    ^    ^    ^    ^    ^    ^    ^    ^    ^    ^    ^    ^    ^   ^
  118  122  126  130  134  138  142  146  150  154  158  162  166 170 174 178 182 186 190 194 198 202 206 210 214 218 222 226 230 234
  15/MAR/83    31/MAR/83     18/APR/83    4/MAY/83     20/MAY/83    7/JUN/83    23/JUN/83       ---         ---         ---
```

- With the early start schedule, ironworkers are needed 16 of the 38 working weeks. No ironworkers are used from November 12, 1982, to January 17, 1983. If the early start schedule is used, the ironworkers would be available for other projects during these periods.

- When ironworkers are needed, requirements range from a maximum of six to a minimum of two. There are 25 working days (5 weeks) when more than four ironworkers, the number available for this project, are required.

- There is a fair distribution of ironworkers during the times when they are required.

FIGURE 8-38 Ironworker utilization (early start schedule) for the Southfork Building Project.

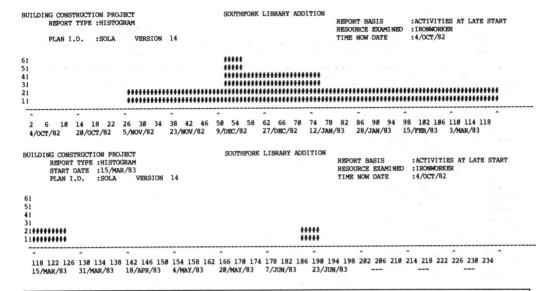

- Ironworkers are needed during 21 of the 38 working weeks. The four iron-workers are available 17 working weeks for other projects. Six ironworkers are needed for 1 week, four are needed for 8 weeks, and the remainder of the time, two ironworkers are needed.
- This is a good distribution, slightly better than the distribution generated from the early start schedule.
- There appears to be little problem in meeting this schedule, as far as available ironworkers are concerned. For the one week (week of December 13) when overtime is required, each of the four ironworkers would work 10 hours of overtime.

FIGURE 8-39 Ironworker utilization (late start schedule) for the Southfork Building Project.

BUILDING CONSTRUCTION PROJECT   SOUTHFORK LIBRARY ADDITION
    REPORT TYPE :COMPLETE RESOURCES REPORT   REPORT BASIS   :ACTIVITIES AT EARLY START
               :AVERAGE DAILY DEMAND PER WEEK   SELECTION CRITERIA :ALL
    PLAN I.D. :SOLA   VERSION 16   TIME NOW DATE   :4/OCT/82

CA=CARPENTER $D=CASH FLOW IN HUNDREDS   DP=DAILY COST IN HUNDREDS   IR=IRONWORKER

	CA	$D	DP	IR
4/OCT/82	8	66.33	66.33	6
11/OCT/82	8	66.33	66.33	6
18/OCT/82	12	68.83	68.83	6
25/OCT/82	13	50.14	50.14	6
1/NOV/82	9	45.14	45.14	6
8/NOV/82	3	27.14	27.14	2
15/NOV/82	3	14.64	14.64	
22/NOV/82	3	14.64	14.64	
29/NOV/82	3	14.64	14.64	
6/DEC/82	3	14.64	14.64	
13/DEC/82	2	7.50	7.50	
20/DEC/82	3	35.00	35.00	
27/DEC/82	3	35.00	35.00	
3/JAN/83	1	10.00	10.00	
10/JAN/83	1	10.00	10.00	
17/JAN/83	8	42.85	42.85	2
24/JAN/83	8	42.85	42.85	2
31/JAN/83	8	42.85	42.85	2
7/FEB/83	8	42.85	42.85	2
14/FEB/83	6	19.52	19.52	2
21/FEB/83	6	19.52	19.52	2
28/FEB/83	6	19.52	19.52	2
7/MAR/83	4	21.67	21.67	2
14/MAR/83	4	21.67	21.67	2
21/MAR/83	2	11.67	11.67	2
28/MAR/83	4	10.00	10.00	
4/APR/83	4	10.00	10.00	
11/APR/83	4	10.00	10.00	
18/APR/83	4	20.00	20.00	
25/APR/83	2	10.00	10.00	
2/MAY/83	3	10.00	10.00	
9/MAY/83	3	10.00	10.00	
16/MAY/83	3	10.00	10.00	
23/MAY/83	1	10.00	10.00	
30/MAY/83		5.00	5.00	
6/JUN/83		5.00	5.00	
13/JUN/83		5.00	5.00	
20/JUN/83	2	10.00	10.00	2

FIGURE 8–40 Weekly average of carpenters' and ironworkers' requirements using the early start schedule.

BUILDING CONSTRUCTION PROJECT   SOUTHFORK LIBRARY ADDITION
     REPORT TYPE :COMPLETE RESOURCES REPORT   REPORT BASIS   :ACTIVITIES AT LATE START
                 :AVERAGE DAILY DEMAND PER WEEK   SELECTION CRITERIA :ALL
       PLAN I.D.   :SOLA   VERSION 16   TIME NOW DATE   :4/OCT/82

CA=CARPENTER $D=CASH FLOW IN HUNDREDS   DP=DAILY COST IN HUNDREDS   IR=IRONWORKER

	CA	$D	DP	IR
4/OCT/82	2	33.33	33.33	
11/OCT/82	2	33.33	33.33	
18/OCT/82	2	33.33	33.33	
25/OCT/82	2	7.50	7.50	
1/NOV/82	3	14.64	14.64	
8/NOV/82	3	24.64	24.64	2
15/NOV/82	5	34.64	34.64	2
22/NOV/82	5	37.14	37.14	2
29/NOV/82	9	37.14	37.14	2
6/DEC/82	9	37.14	37.14	2
13/DEC/82	9	45.14	45.14	6
20/DEC/82	7	48.00	48.00	4
27/DEC/82	7	48.00	48.00	4
3/JAN/83	5	23.00	23.00	4
10/JAN/83	5	23.00	23.00	4
17/JAN/83		20.00	20.00	2
24/JAN/83	2	27.14	27.14	2
31/JAN/83	2	27.14	27.14	2
7/FEB/83	6	32.85	32.85	2
14/FEB/83	6	19.52	19.52	2
21/FEB/83	6	19.52	19.52	2
28/FEB/83	6	19.52	19.52	2
7/MAR/83	6	19.52	19.52	2
14/MAR/83	6	22.38	22.38	2
21/MAR/83	6	22.38	22.38	2
28/MAR/83	4	10.00	10.00	
4/APR/83	4	10.00	10.00	
11/APR/83	6	20.00	20.00	
18/APR/83	6	20.00	20.00	
25/APR/83	6	20.00	20.00	
2/MAY/83	6	20.00	20.00	
9/MAY/83	2	10.00	10.00	
16/MAY/83	4	20.00	20.00	
23/MAY/83		5.00	5.00	
30/MAY/83	1	10.00	10.00	
6/JUN/83	1	10.00	10.00	
13/JUN/83	1	10.00	10.00	
20/JUN/83	3	15.00	15.00	2

FIGURE 8–41 Weekly average of carpenters' and ironworkers' requirements using the late start schedule.

SKILLED PERSONNEL (AVAILABLE)	NET WEEKS REQUIRED	PERSONNEL DISTRIBUTION	RANGE* [ ]		OVERTIME REQUIREMENTS (WEEKS)
			MAX	MIN	
Carpenters (6)					
Early start	35	Poor	13	1	5
Late start	27	Fair	9	1	5
Ironworkers (4)					
Early start	17	Fair	6	2	5
Late start	17	Good	6	2	1

*Not including weeks when no skilled personnel are required.

FIGURE 8–42 Personnel requirements comparison of early start and late start for the Southfork Building Project.

better than the risk of a delayed project. A late start schedule means that all project activities are on the critical path—all are critical activities. Delayed starts and late schedule deliveries can result in late project completion. Projections of daily and cumulative cost such as those shown in Figures 8–43 to 8–46 are a critical part of the resource analysis.

When Lawrence Construction compared the 105 overtime hours, about 2% of the total carpenter and ironworker hours, that are required when using the early start schedule, they decided that this is a reasonable price to pay to reduce the risk of a project delay when using the late start schedule. They and the subcontractors need to assess the peaks and valleys further so that there will be more continuous employment, either by checking further on the possibility of using the available personnel on project activities to reduce durations, or by placing them on another project until they are needed on this project. The decision is to go with the early start schedule. The risk of delay, thereby possibly causing ill feelings with the City of Southfork, was the overriding factor.

EXERCISES

1. The present construction plan allows for completion of the project on May 20, 1983. The owner, the City of Southfork, has asked the contractor, Lawrence Construction Company, to reduce the completion time by 3 weeks (May 2) without any additional costs, such as overtime or additional equipment. What changes in the plan could possibly be made to comply with the request by the

(Exercises continue on p. 197)

```
BUILDING CONSTRUCTION PROJECT              SOUTHFORK LIBRARY ADDITION
       REPORT TYPE :HISTOGRAM                                          REPORT BASIS      :ACTIVITIES AT EARLY START
                                                                      RESOURCE EXAMINED :DAILY COST IN HUNDREDS
       PLAN I.D.  :SOLA     VERSION 16                                TIME NOW DATE     :4/OCT/82

70!          *****
68!***************
66!***************
64!***************
62!***************
60!***************
58!***************
56!***************
54!***************
52!********************
50!********************
48!*********************
46!**************************
44!**************************                          *********************
42!**************************                          *********************
40!**************************                          *********************
38!**************************                          **********************
36!**************************          **********      **********************
34!**************************          **********      **********************
32!**************************          **********      **********************
30!**************************          **********      **********************
28!********************************    **********      **********************
26!********************************    **********      **********************
24!********************************    **********      **********************
22!********************************    **********      *********************            **********
20!********************************    **********      ****************************************
18!********************************    **********      ****************************************
16!**********************************************      **********************************************
14!**********************************************      **********************************************
12!**********************************************      *************************************************
10!********************************************************************************************************
8 !********************************************************************************************************
6 !********************************************************************************************************
4 !********************************************************************************************************
2 !********************************************************************************************************
  ----------------------------------------------------------------------------------------------------------
   ^     ^     ^      ^      ^       ^       ^       ^       ^      ^        ^       ^      ^
   2   6  10  14 18  22  26 30  34  38 42  46  50 54  58  62 66  70  74  78  82  86  90  94  98  102 106 110 114 118
   4/OCT/82    20/OCT/82    5/NOV/82    23/NOV/82   9/DEC/82   27/DEC/82   12/JAN/83   28/JAN/83   15/FEB/83   3/MAR/83


BUILDING CONSTRUCTION PROJECT              SOUTHFORK LIBRARY ADDITION
       REPORT TYPE :HISTOGRAM                                          REPORT BASIS      :ACTIVITIES AT EARLY START
       START DATE  :15/MAR/83                                         RESOURCE EXAMINED :DAILY COST IN HUNDREDS
       PLAN I.D.  :SOLA     VERSION 16                                TIME NOW DATE     :4/OCT/82

70!
68!
66!
64!
62!
60!
58!
56!
54!
52!
50!
48!
46!
44!
42!
40!
38!
36!
34!
32!
30!
28!
26!
24!
22!****
20!****            *****
18!****            *****
16!****            *****
14!****            *****
12!********        *****
10!*********************************************************      *****
8 !*********************************************************      *****
6 !**************************************************************
4 !**************************************************************
2 !**************************************************************
  ----------------------------------------------------------------------------------------------------------
   ^       ^        ^        ^        ^        ^        ^        ^        ^        ^        ^
   118 122 126 130 134 138 142 146 150 154 158 162 166 170 174 178 182 186 190 194 198 202 206 210 214 218 222 226 230 234
   15/MAR/83   31/MAR/83   18/APR/83   4/MAY/83   20/MAY/83   7/JUN/83   23/JUN/83      ---         ---         ---
```

FIGURE 8-43 Daily cost of project (in hundreds of dollars) using the early start schedule.

BUILDING CONSTRUCTION PROJECT
    REPORT TYPE :HISTOGRAM

      PLAN I.D.   :SOLA   VERSION 16

SOUTHFORK LIBRARY ADDITION

REPORT BASIS   :ACTIVITIES AT LATE START
RESOURCE EXAMINED :DAILY COST IN HUNDREDS
TIME NOW DATE   :4/OCT/82

```
70!
68!
66!
64!
62!
60!
58!
56!
54!
52!
50!
48!                                   ##########
46!                               ##################
44!                               ##################
42!                               ##################
40!                               ##################
38!                       ##############################
36!                       ##############################
34!################       ##############################              #####
32!################       ##############################              #####
30!################       ##############################              #####
28!################       ##############################         ##############
26!################   ##################################         ##############
24!################   ######################################     ##############
22!################   ######################################     ##############              ######
20!################   ##########################################################              ######
18!################   ##############################################################################
16!           ######################################################################################
14!################################################################################################
12!################################################################################################
10!################################################################################################
 8 !################################################################################################
 6 !################################################################################################
 4 !################################################################################################
 2 !################################################################################################
   ----------------------------------------------------------------------------------------------
     ^       ^       ^       ^       ^       ^       ^       ^       ^       ^       ^
     2   6  10  14  18  22  26  30  34  38  42  46  50  54  58  62  66  70  74  78  82  86  90  94  98  102 106 110 114 118
     4/OCT/82    20/OCT/82   5/NOV/82    23/NOV/82   9/DEC/82    27/DEC/82   12/JAN/83   28/JAN/83   15/FEB/83   3/MAR/83
```

BUILDING CONSTRUCTION PROJECT
    REPORT TYPE :HISTOGRAM
    START DATE :15/MAR/83
    PLAN I.D.   :SOLA   VERSION 16

SOUTHFORK LIBRARY ADDITION

REPORT BASIS   :ACTIVITIES AT LATE START
RESOURCE EXAMINED :DAILY COST IN HUNDREDS
TIME NOW DATE   :4/OCT/82

```
70!
68!
66!
64!
62!
60!
58!
56!
54!
52!
50!
48!
46!
44!
42!
40!
38!
36!
34!
32!
30!
28!
26!
24!#########
22!#########
20!#########          ####################    #####
18!#########          ####################    #####
16!#########          ####################    #####                      #####
14!#########          ####################    #####                      #####
12!#########          ####################    #####                      #####
10!################################################################################
 8 !##########################################################################
 6 !##########################################################################
 4 !##########################################################################
 2 !##########################################################################
   ----------------------------------------------------------------------------------------------
     ^       ^       ^       ^       ^       ^       ^       ^       ^       ^       ^
     118 122 126 130 134 138 142 146 150 154 158 162 166 170 174 178 182 186 190 194 198 202 206 210 214 218 222 226 230 234
     15/MAR/83   31/MAR/83   18/APR/83   4/MAY/83    20/MAY/83   7/JUN/83    23/JUN/83   ---         ---         ---
```

FIGURE 8-44 Daily cost of project (in hundreds of dollars) using the late start schedule.

194

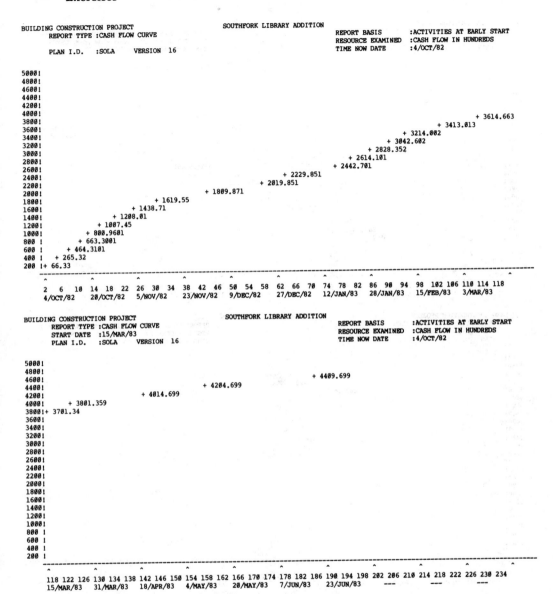

FIGURE 8–45 Accumulative cost of project (in hundreds of dollars) using the early start schedule.

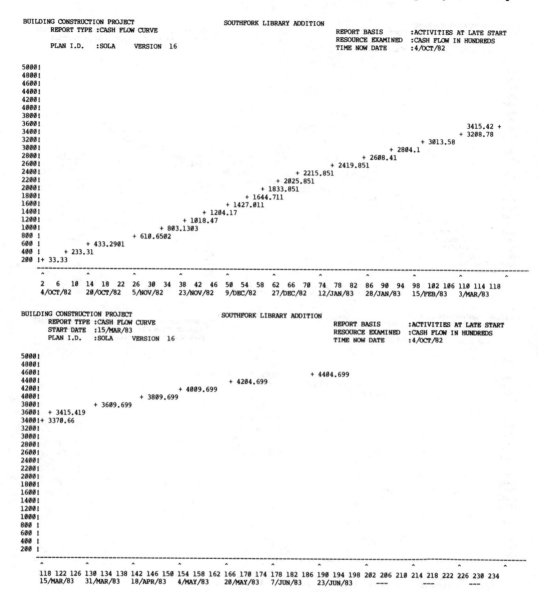

BUILDING CONSTRUCTION PROJECT
        REPORT TYPE :CASH FLOW CURVE   SOUTHFORK LIBRARY ADDITION
                                                                        REPORT BASIS   :ACTIVITIES AT LATE START
                                                                        RESOURCE EXAMINED   :CASH FLOW IN HUNDREDS
        PLAN I.D.   :SOLA   VERSION 16   TIME NOW DATE   :4/OCT/82

BUILDING CONSTRUCTION PROJECT
        REPORT TYPE :CASH FLOW CURVE   SOUTHFORK LIBRARY ADDITION
        START DATE :15/MAR/83   REPORT BASIS   :ACTIVITIES AT LATE START
        PLAN I.D.   :SOLA   VERSION 16   RESOURCE EXAMINED   :CASH FLOW IN HUNDREDS
                                                                        TIME NOW DATE   :4/OCT/82

FIGURE 8-46 Accumulative cost of project (in hundreds of dollars) using the late start schedule.

City of Southfork? (Check what project items can be separated into phases such that subsequent items can be done concurrently, particularly in the interior of the constructed building.)

2. The project completion date developed from the original plan and schedule is May 20, 1983. The owner desired occupancy 3 weeks (May 2) prior to May 20. Assume no change in the project plan.
   (a) What project items should be considered for possible reduction in duration times?
   (b) Explain why those project items that were chosen were the most appropriate to use.
   Hint: Select those items that are started early in the project.

3. From the calendar schedule (prepared from the tabulated schedule), complete a milestone report.

Event Description	Earliest Event Time	Latest Event Time

4. Assume that the City of Southfork delayed awarding the contract to Lawrence Construction until February 2, 1987. Prior to the award, Southfork Construction requested from Lawrence Construction revised timing and costs. Lawrence Construction, in turn, notified the subcontractors of the new contract. In light of the above, prepare the following materials.
   (a) A milestone report showing the key events and corresponding timing, including the project start and project completion dates.
   (b) A computer-generated schedule showing earliest start and finish dates, latest start and finish dates, and float for each work activity.
   (c) Computer-generated detail bar chart schedules for (1) the total project and (2) each subcontractor.
   (d) From the information above, prepare a letter to the City of Southfork outlining the timing schedule using the start date of February 2, 1987. Include in this letter the key event dates that Lawrence Construction expects to meet and the subcontractors who will be used on this project. Total costs for this project should also be shown (since 5 years has elapsed, there needs to be an escalation factor—about an overall 8% per year increase may be a reasonable assumption).

5. A 5-year delay creates a cost penalty—prices have escalated. Using an 8% per year increase, prepare a new cost schedule using the computer-generated cost histogram and cash flow report.

6. From the report, develop a monthly cash disbursement schedule.

Chapter 9

Installing an Energy Management System

Project management techniques, normally applied to achieve more productive project implementation, are also used to great advantage in other applications. One case is that of preparing a plan and schedule for a feasibility study as an expedient for project approval. The study follows the same procedure as that used in completing the plan and follows these general steps:

1. Prepare an initial plan of action.
2. Conduct an audit.
3. Gather fact-finding data for the present system.
4. Design an improved system.
5. Compare features, including costs of the improved system with the present system and alternative systems.
6. Structure a feasibility report.
7. Obtain management approval.

These steps can become milestones by designating their start and/or completion dates. In preparation for this program, a comprehensive background report was generated so that the reader could fully appreciate the underlying reasons for installing an energy management system.

BACKGROUND

MAS Products is an international manufacturer of a component part for the automotive industry. Its major facility is located in the south-central part of the United

States. Built 20 years ago, this plant has expanded several times. It is now a complex of office areas and manufacturing facilities, employing 2500 people, occupying 2 million square feet of covered floor area, and situated on a 200-acre plot of land.

Figure 9-1 shows the facility as it is presently situated. The main building houses the manufacturing operations, office space, and maintenance and storage areas. There is a separate powerhouse building for the compressors, steam boilers, and primary electrical substation. Another building houses the millwater supply pumps and controls for the water clarification system.

Production at the MAS Products facility has been decreasing gradually in the past 5 years due to loss of sales, and its management is reviewing means to reduce operating costs in order to maintain profits. As production is energy intensive at MAS Products, energy costs making up 20% of total costs, a review of energy costs revealed a disturbing trend over the past 5 years. A graphic distribution of this trend of unit energy costs and performance is shown in Figure 9-2.

What was more disturbing was the graphic illustration in Figure 9-3 which compared the energy performance of MAS Products with the average energy performance of the industry group of which MAS Products is a part. This comparison is very important, as it provides a yardstick of the total efficiency among the competition. In this case MAS Products needs considerable improvement to meet the com-

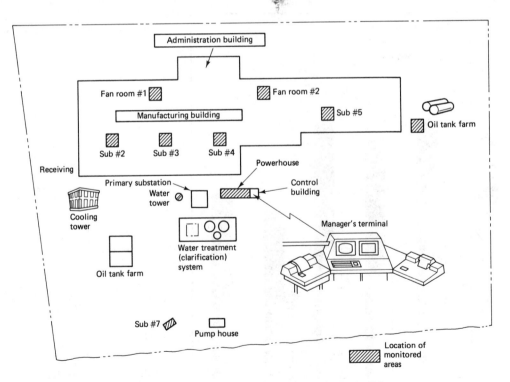

FIGURE 9-1 Plan of MAS manufacturing facilities.

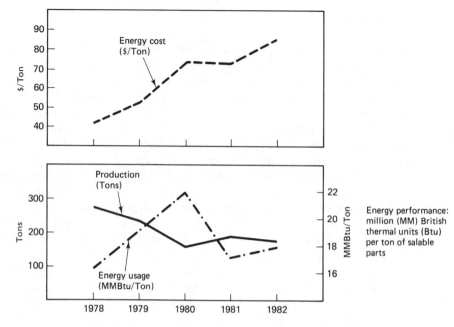

FIGURE 9–2 Yearly energy efficiency trend at MAS Products.

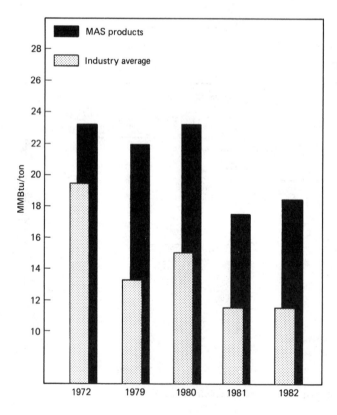

FIGURE 9–3 Energy performance MAS Products versus industry.

petitors' performance. Whereas the industry as a group is performing favorably, a 42% improvement over 5 years, MAS Products is experiencing only a 22% improvement for the same period.

This energy measurement began as a result of a report prepared by the General Accounting Office, stressing the need for federal action to promote energy conservation and more efficient energy consumption. The GAO report points out that conservation programs in national energy planning have been drastically underemphasized. Highlighted was the industrial sector, which consumes 40% of all U.S. energy, and is the largest sector for potential energy savings given effective conservation programs.

The GAO report called for stronger systems used in setting voluntary targets, and setting more challenging efficiency goals. It also recommended better systems to monitor industrial conservation efforts through establishing milestones and a plan to monitor and evaluate continuously each portion of the energy conservation program's contribution to meeting its goals. Specifically, GAO made these recommendations:

1. Establish an energy conservation goal for each industry.
2. Develop an adequate measure of the progress of each industry in achieving established goals.
3. Establish specific milestones to assess each industry's progress toward the goals.
4. Develop standby programs to implement if milestones are not being met.

The industrial sector, which includes private and governmental activities consuming energy in manufacturing, mining, construction, and agriculture, is the largest energy-consuming sector. The federal government has developed two major programs to encourage industry to conserve energy voluntarily. These programs are (1) an industrial energy conservation program, directed to all industrial companies, and (2) an energy-efficiency-improvement targeted program, directed at the 10 most energy-consumptive industries.

The voluntary industrial energy conservation program was initiated to persuade industries, through their trade associations, to adopt energy management programs and report achievements to the federal government. As a result of the program, at least 40 industry trade associations through industrial representatives have reported energy-efficiency data to the federal government.

Under this program the Department of Energy (DOE) was to establish voluntary energy efficiency improvement targets for each of the 10 most energy-consumptive industries. The targets were to be established at the level which represents the maximum feasible improvement over the base year which each industry could achieve in the next 8 years.

Companies that used at least 1 trillion Btu of energy a year and were among the 50 largest energy consumers in each industry were required to report annually to the federal government on the progress being made to improve their energy efficiency. This reporting could be done directly to DOE or through industry trade associations or industrial representatives.

Final industrial energy-efficiency targets for each of the 10 industries were established. The industries, ranked in order of energy consumption, and the final targets are shown below.

INDUSTRY	PERCENT IMPROVEMENT
Chemicals and allied products	14
Primary metal industries	9
Petroleum and coal products	12
Stone, clay, and glass products	16
Paper and allied products	20
Food and kindred products	12
Fabricated metal products	24
Transportation equipment	16
Machinery, except electrical	15
Textile mill products	22

MAS Products requested from DOE an analysis of their industry group's energy conservation activity in the past year. DOE submitted a detail accounting of improvement areas. These are noted as follows:

- *Operational changes.* These involve housekeeping and "belt-tightening" measures: reduced lighting, equipment tune-ups, repair of steam and air leaks, and other measures requiring little or no cost. The amount of energy saved from these operational changes may be difficult to calculate because either (1) energy consumption data collected are not in sufficient detail or form to make such an assessment, or (2) the data are considered proprietary.

- *Capital investments.* There has been considerable activity by the industry group in installing energy conservation facilities, such as waste heat recovery, cogeneration, energy management systems, and more efficient industrial processes and operational changes.

- *Waste heat recovery systems.* This generally involves capturing heat from manufacturing processes and recirculating it for some other use. A popular application is capturing the heat that would normally escape from very high temperature furnaces and kilns into the atmosphere. The heat that is recovered can be converted into steam for plant heating and/or producing hot water for process and/or domestic use; or it can be transferred via ducting to heat other plant areas. In this industry group about 20% of its annual energy requirement entails installing proper heat recovery equipment.

- *Cogeneration.* This is a process by which (1) waste heat generated in making electricity is recycled and used in an industrial application, (2) waste from an industrial or fuel combustion process is recycled to generate electricity, or (3) a cheaper fuel is used to generate steam for use in generating electricity, and using the spent steam for heating. Some examples of cogeneration facilities are (1) a utility company which sells its waste heat from power generation for industrial, commercial, or space-heating purposes, and (2) an industry that uses the waste heat of its industrial processes to generate electricity on-site for its own consumption or for sale to a utility company.

There is a decided attractiveness to the energy-saving benefits from cogeneration, but company decisions to realize these savings have been precluded by barriers of a technical, financial, institutional/regulatory, or attitudinal nature.

- *Energy management systems* are becoming more popular as the reliability of the equipment improves and as electrical price rates continue to escalate. The underlying principle is to control electrical usage by setting a limit on the demand. With good automatic control of the energy management system, noncritical equipment can be shut down temporarily in steps, to avoid high electrical readings.
- *Industrial process changes* offer significant potential for reducing energy consumption in the industrial sector. In many cases, introducing an industrial process change is a long-term effort, interrelated with a number of factors: for example, technological, financial, and marketing constraints, such as capital costs to replace major equipment or change facilities; future availability of suitable fuels; research and development time required to commercialize processes; environmental constraints; and return on investment.

From the results of DOE's reports, MAS Products managers were concerned over their energy performance in the last 5 years. While production personnel had made some improvements in labor and overhead through facility with robots, automated equipment, and many sophisticated controls to bring MAS Products back to a competitive position, energy proved to be a problem, as energy "cannot be seen" and very little attention was given to the operation of the major utilities.

The results of energy conservation measures being monitored by the Department of Energy will be given due consideration by MAS Industries. The next step is to adopt an organizational structure that will direct an energy conservation program of operational changes, investments, and industrial process changes. An immediate move by management is to authorize the organization of an energy conservation committee. The main objective of the energy conservation committee will be to develop and implement a program for the planning and control of energy usage and the conservation of energy. The committee is also dedicated to stimulating, encouraging, and motivating plant personnel to save energy. This is done through publicity, periodic talks with department heads, energy information presented to all managers through scheduled "energy awareness" meetings, and through informal discussions. Other specific measures are:

- Reducing energy waste in existing operations.
- Implementing a preventive maintenance program directed toward effecting corrective action as rapidly as possible so that utilities are not wasted because of lack of maintenance. Scheduled inspections to detect, tag, and correct leaks on an ongoing basis are essential to maintaining a successful energy conservation program. Systems to be inspected are steam, compressed air, water supply, and fuels.
- Maintaining a "watch" that MAS Products is receiving from utilities the best possible rates for natural gas, electricity, and potable water.
- Increasing awareness on the part of all personnel of the importance of energy conservation.

Having the people in the plant participate in the energy programs is considered to be very important. The various ways to communicate under consideration by the committee are as follows:

- *Distribute an in-house publication.* This would be a separate publication, published monthly, featuring significant energy accomplishments over the past month. It would include productivity news and cost-savings achievements, including information on energy savings installations.
- *Employ "spot" energy promotions.* These serve as an expedient to keep the people in the plant aware of the benefits of energy savings and to be cooperative in obtaining the maximum benefits.
    Consider energy slogans to be posted on bulletin boards. The source of these slogans can be contests conducted in the plant.
    Place on the bulletin board letters from the plant manager that have energy conservation themes.
- Show films and tapes provided by government or private sources.
- Solicit energy conservation suggestions. Provide cash awards for acceptable suggestions. The energy conservation committee will announce that top priority will be given to suggestions submitted by persons in the plant. Such incentives as a credit-card calculator will be given for turning in any reasonable suggestion. Place energy conservation suggestion forms in suggestion displays at various locations.

A good example of complementing the existing employee suggestion award program is shown in Figure 9–4.

MAKE ENERGY SUGGESTIONS PAY

Starting immediately, a drive will be conducted to solicit energy conservation suggestions.

Not only will your suggestions be given top priority by the energy conservation commission, and cash adjustments promptly awarded, but during this drive, each person will receive a credit-card calculator, just for turning in a reasonable suggestion!

All you have to do is fill out an energy conservation suggestion form, located in the suggestion displays, and turn it in to the Personnel Office. You will then receive your free pocket calculator. The only stipulations are that the suggestion must be written on an official energy conservation suggestion form and be a realistic effort at saving energy, and that there be no duplication of ideas. Only one calculator will be awarded per employee.

These calculators would also make an excellent gift for someone. If your suggestion is accepted and deemed appropriate for utilization and a cash award, you make possible presenting yourself with some gifts!

FIGURE 9-4   Special energy conservation award notice.

Energy Conservation Committee Members

The original committee was made up mostly of plant management, as there was direction and visibility from top corporate levels. The designated committee had four principal members:

- Plant manager, chairman
- Assistant plant manager
- Plant engineering manager
- Plant energy coordinator, secretary

At the "kickoff" meeting, the committee met to act on the following:

- Scope and goals of the program
- How the committee will function
- Who will be serving on the committee
- Responsibilities of the committee
- Training requirements

The advantage of this managerial type of committee was to gain a sense of credibility for its purpose, but it did lag in achieving results. It did not concentrate on the locations where energy is actually used.

A more meaningful group is a working committee made up of people from various functions. This committee will have more of an impact in furthering accomplishments. People in the plant who will participate represent such functions as engineering, plant utility services, and maintenance and production departments. From six to twelve persons make up an effective working committee, with both skilled tradespersons and first-level supervisors represented.

Committee meetings will be held at least once per month, and more often as energy conservation programs are initiated. Important assignments initiate action on the part of committee members. A full-time energy coordinator is appointed to guide this committee. This person prepares the agenda, defines problems, assigns work among the members, and maintains the records. The energy coordinator, who may also be known as the energy committee secretary, assumes these responsibilities:

- Establish committee meeting schedule and agenda.
- Prepare committee meeting minutes and report on the status of the plant energy management program.
- Report to the committee the status of plant energy conservation projects— energy and dollars savings achieved, capital costs, and so on.
- Serve as the contact with plant management.

The meeting minutes are published for distribution among committee members and management, and are placed on bulletin boards at various plant locations. The energy coordinator will also place "Newsflash" energy highlights on the bulletin boards to call attention to important energy actions.

The energy coordinator becomes the key figure in energy conservation activities. Included among his or her duties are:

- *Identify and prioritize potential energy conservation opportunities.* There are two major energy conservation classifications: operation and maintenance improvements, and capital improvements. Among the operational and maintenance improvements the energy coordinator needs to outline are effective housekeeping and preventive maintenance procedures, and development of shutdown procedures. The first step in recommending capital improvements for energy conservation opportunities is to make an analysis of the individual plant processes and their associated energy systems.
- *Implement the identified energy conservation actions.* The energy coordinator will prepare the plan of action for the operations and maintenance supervision to implement. To get funds approved for capital projects, the coordinator needs to prepare feasibility studies, which includes investigating, evaluating, and recommending. Once funds have been approved, the coordinator must act as project engineer to supervise implementation. (The major energy conservation project illustrated in this book, the energy management system, elaborates on these duties of a project engineer that are required to complete this project successfully.)

- *Maintain energy operating records and energy costs.* The energy coordinator collects energy supply and consumption data. Keeping utility rates and recording energy performance costs to note trends are important to the overall energy programs. From the historical records, the coordinator prepares supply and cost forecasts using governmental and corporate information on supply and cost projections. Publishing energy conservation reports on a periodic basis allows those participating in implementing these programs to learn how they are performing.
- *Prepare specifications and review designs of capital projects.* When there are building expansions, or machinery and equipment installations, the energy coordinator becomes actively involved to see that efficient utilization of energy is incorporated. He or she prepares design guidelines that can quantify the energy impact of new facilities.

The coordinator will review and analyze proposals for new energy-related facilities so that the most cost-effective and energy efficient will be implemented:

- *Implement a continuing program of energy ideas and plans.* Enlist the support and participation of the people working in the plant through the use of communicative methods: news flashes, special suggestion programs, bulletin board notices, and so on.
- *Evaluate and monitor the energy management program.* The coordinator will evaluate the energy conservation goals and consider modifications and refinements. He or she will periodically report the energy savings, offering comments on the status of the program and proposing recommendations designed to keep the program on target. Evaluating the energy management program includes reviewing energy demands in terms of supplies, and analyzing rate schedules. The coordinator will develop a forecasting procedure that will reflect the anticipated utility rates and their effect on the future operating costs.
- *Serve as managing secretary for the energy management committee.*

MAS realizes that an energy committee with a full-time energy coordinator is essential. One underlying reason is that energy rates are high. State regulatory commissions maintain controls that distort the rate structure. Natural gas is deregulated and rates have been reduced dramatically. Yet electric rates, which are regulated, are skyrocketing. The cost of energy has been the fastest-growing item in the operating cost budget. MAS is dedicated to reducing these costs.

Energy Management System

The energy coordinator has recommended to the energy conservation committee that the most effective energy conservation facility for this operation is the installation of an energy management sytem. The energy coordinator defines an energy management system (EMS) as the process through which energy consumption is intelligently managed by either manual, semiautomatic, or automatic modes of operation situated either on a local control or in a central control location. These systems can be as simple as the manual operation of turning off individual equipment, when not needed, or as complex as the computerized control systems installed in relatively large industrial plants and office buildings.

A manual system continues to be the most popular method for data gathering and control; however, manual operation of many units is not easily accomplished, as the equipment may not be readily available or accessible. For example, heating and ventilating units mounted on the underside of roofs are difficult to control. Yet the manual method of operation can be used and can be cost-effective with the enforcement of adequate procedures and if the equipment is located in close proximity to other operations.

A step up from manual operation is the semiautomatic system. This operation uses remote-control equipment and a master control panel with audible alarms and/ or visible indication of equipment operation. Usually, these systems require a crew of plant services operators on a full-time basis to maintain and handle the equipment controls.

The automatic, computer-controlled system is generally considered currently as an energy management system (EMS). An EMS consists of a computerized control console from which a wiring loop extends throughout the facility to interface with energy-consuming equipment to be monitored and controlled. This type of automatic system is currently being utilized at many varied operational areas, with substantial energy cost reductions.

There are other computerized systems that can be installed either concurrently or subsequently which will realize additional facility cost savings. Such systems include:

- Closed-circuit TV monitoring of production and service equipment
- Monitoring process equipment by the use of sensors
- Quality reporting
- Production control (including warehousing)

An EMS is most effective for programming controls of production and plant services equipment which can then be turned off and on automatically to coordinate with off-shifts that are not operating, shift changes, periodic shutdowns, lunch hours, and so on.

The computerized EMS needs to be handled with care. Computer control will be only as good as the personnel responsible for its operation. Inexperience in the use of EMS is shown in this scenario: EMS was programmed for *eight-hour* shifts based on scheduled production, and the system functioned with regularity and accuracy. At a subsequent time, sales increased and it was decided to run production for 10 hours. Employees were informed, maintenance schedules adjusted, and other details were handled—all except the computer. As a result, at the end of eight hours and one minute, lights went off, ventilating fans ceased to operate, and entire systems were scheduled off. In this particular incident, quick-thinking operating personnel switched to the manual mode of operation (which was provided in the system) and rescheduled lighting, heating, ventilating, and the necessary production functions for a 10-hour shift.

An energy management system can also monitor all the key elements of dust collection operations. Various points, such as dampers, are monitored to assure that the dust collection systems are operating satisfactorily and air quality is maintained.

A complete management system essentially encompasses the total energy operation at the MAS facility. Every energy system—electrical, natural gas, compressed air, water supply, steam, lighting, heating, ventilating, and air conditioning—will need to be investigated for adaptation to the energy management systems.

DEVELOPING A PLAN OF ACTION

As this type of program follows the same arrangement as a typical project, the initial step is to develop a plan of action. MAS will eventually need to select a task force for implementing the energy management system, and at this time one person is selected to start the program. This person may be a staff member or the appointed project manager, who will prepare the overall plan and develop a plan of action. The plan of action as shown on the network plan (Figure 9–5) consists of the following major activities: (1) *set objectives,* (2) *select a task force,* (3) *draft a general plan of action,* and (4) *prepare a network plan.*

Setting Objectives

Setting the objectives on what is expected to be accomplished needs as much thought and effort as any other part of the project. This is more than a general statement such as "complete an energy management system." Objectives need to be clearly stated, especially in the case of an energy management system, where the basic objectives in the feasibility report will express the savings and benefits to be realized with the new system. These savings and benefits may include reduced costs, better production and process control, improved quality, increased productivity, and a more efficient and effective operation.

If there are savings, they need to be identified at the outset, since they will be instrumental in selling the program. The preliminary savings exercise will help to rule out any alternatives that may not have an acceptable rate of return. While the savings objectives are needed primarily to sell the project, the main thrusts are setting time and cost objectives. Timing objectives need to be established before costs or any other resource.

From the preliminary savings exercise, the overall project costs can be determined and these are also listed in the objectives as the budgeted amount that needs

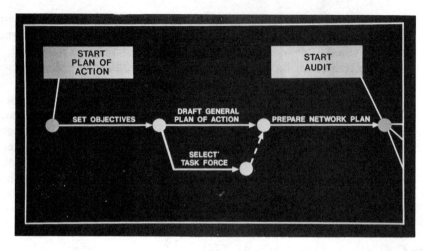

(a)

PROJECT MANAGEMENT   ENERGY MANAGEMENT SYSTEM   SOUTHEAST UNITED STATES
     REPORT TYPE :STANDARD LISTING   PRINTING SEQUENCE   :Earliest Activities First
                                                    SELECTION CRITERIA ::PA
     PLAN I.D.   :IEMS   VERSION   24   TIME NOW DATE   :12/MAR/84

ACTIVITY DESCRIPTION	EARLIEST START	EARLIEST FINISH	LATEST START	LATEST FINISH	DURATION	FLOAT
:PA SET OBJECTIVES	12/MAR/84	16/MAR/84	12/MAR/84	16/MAR/84	5	0 *
:PA SELECT TASK FORCE	19/MAR/84	23/MAR/84	19/MAR/84	23/MAR/84	5	0 *
:PA DRAFT GENERAL PLAN OF ACTION	19/MAR/84	23/MAR/84	19/MAR/84	23/MAR/84	5	0 *
:PA PREPARE NETWORK PLAN	26/MAR/84	13/APR/84	26/MAR/84	13/APR/84	15	0 *

(b)

PROJECT MANAGEMENT   ENERGY MANAGEMENT SYSTEM   SOUTHEAST UNITED STATES
     REPORT TYPE :COMPRESSED PERIOD BARCHART   PRINTING SEQUENCE   :Earliest Activities First
                                                SELECTION CRITERIA ::PA
     PLAN I.D.   :IEMS   VERSION   24   TIME NOW DATE   :12/MAR/84

```
========================================1984=========================1985==================================
PERIOD COMMENCING DATE     11212  17   14  12   16  13   11   15  13   17   14  14  11   16  13  11   15   1
MONTH                      1MAR   1MAY 1JUN1JUL 1AUG1SEP 1OCT 1NOV1DEC 1JAN 1FEB1MAR1APR 1MAY1JUN1JUL 1AUG  1
PERIOD COMMENCING TIME UNIT 18 123  148  168 188  11131133 1153 11781198 1223 12431263128 3 130813281348 1373 1
============================================================================================================
:PA SET OBJECTIVES          1C 1    1    1    1    1    1    1    1    1    1    1    1    1    1    1    1    1
:PA SELECT   TASK FORCE     1CC1    1    1    1    1    1    1    1    1    1    1    1    1    1    1    1    1
:PA DRAFT GENERAL PLAN OF ACTION 1CC1  1    1    1    1    1    1    1    1    1    1    1    1    1    1    1  1
:PA PREPARE NETWORK PLAN    1 C 1CCC 1   1    1    1    1    1    1    1    1    1    1    1    1    1    1    1
============================================================================================================
```

Barchart Key:-   CCC :Critical Activities   ══ :Non Critical Activities   NNN :Activity with neg float   ... :Float

(c)

FIGURE 9-5   Plan of action phase: (a) planning diagram; (b) computer-generated schedule; (c) bar chart.

to be contained. The cost items may have to be modified once the feasibility study has been completed, but in any event, they are an essential part of the objectives.

Selecting a Task Force

When major timing events (also known as milestones) are established, there are parties assigned who will be responsible for these milestones with their respective specific dates to be met. Members of the task force will be assigned to the project activities, and through this exercise the task force organization can be developed.

A very important part of the plan of action is to determine the responsible parties for the work that is to be completed. It is most desirable to have the task force made up of members who eventually will be responsible for various areas of the operation of the new facility. This task force type of an organization is popular for installing important facilities.

Another likely task force organization for a relatively smaller facility can be made up of persons of various skills and disciplines. In the case of the project for an energy management system, the head of the project will determine who will be required to assist in implementing the project. The first choice will be engineers—mechanical and electrical—because of the technical emphasis of this project. For overall project control and for the construction work, the task force leader will choose as a project engineer one who has overall project administration experience and a construction engineering background. The project engineer will have the responsibility for maintaining communication among the task force and implementing project control.

Drafting a General Plan of Action

The task force representatives developed the initial milestones shown in Figure 9-6. It is important, while developing the milestones, to maintain communication with the management organization, the energy conservation committee, and key operating personnel who will be using the energy management system.

After the task force leader starts selecting task force members and begins drafting a general plan of action, the next step is to prepare a network plan that will graphically portray the plan of action. (Although important, costs for the project will be deferred until the initial task force selection and plan of action is completed.)

A good deal of the work analysis has been completed prior to starting the network plan. Drawing the graphical plan that portrays the work analysis can be done with conventional drafting methods. There is one major benefit about this part of the work effort—you have to *think through* the project.

It is essential to prepare a graphic plan of action. It will help you achieve successful completion of the project. It is of equal importance to document this plan of action concurrent with preparing a graphic portrayal of the network plan. Going through such an exercise creates a "thorough" thought process ("thinking

```
PROJECT MANAGEMENT                           ENERGY MANAGEMENT SYSTEM                          SOUTHEAST UNITED STATES
      REPORT TYPE :MILESTONE                                        PRINTING SEQUENCE  :Earliest Activities First
                                                                    SELECTION CRITERIA :MILESTONE
      PLAN I.D.   :IEMS    VERSION  26                              TIME NOW DATE      :12/MAR/84
================================================================================================================
         MILESTONE                      EARLIEST EVENT            LATEST EVENT
         DESCRIPTION                         TIME                     TIME
================================================================================================================
PROJECT START                             12/MAR/84                 12/MAR/84
START AUDIT                                16/APR/84                 16/APR/84
START FEASBILITY REPORT                    28/MAY/84                 28/MAY/84
COMPLETE FEASIBILITY REPORT                16/JUL/84                 16/JUL/84
----------------------------------------------------------------------------------------------------------------
PROJECT APPROVAL                           20/AUG/84                 20/AUG/84
START EQUIPMENT DESIGN                      10/SEP/84                 10/SEP/84
START SITE DESIGN & CONSTRUCTION            8/OCT/84                  8/OCT/84
START EQUIPMENT DESIGN & INSTALLATION       8/OCT/84                  7/JAN/85
----------------------------------------------------------------------------------------------------------------
SYSTEM COMPLETE START TRYOUT               20/MAY/85                 20/MAY/85
SYSTEM OPERATIONAL                         12/AUG/85                 12/AUG/85
================================================================================================================
```

FIGURE 9-6 Computerized milestone report for the Energy Management System.

through" the project), and also a reference tool is now available for the continuous project planning and replanning that a dynamic project requires.

Preparing a Network Plan

A graphic plan of action offers operations personnel a chance to review the program and provide suggestions for improvements *before* operations start. Once the task force leader drafts a general plan of action and the task force is approved, they begin the network plan. This plan will be used to plan and schedule the energy management system. The general plan was established when the task force leader prepared the objectives and milestones. His or her detailed milestones act as a guide to establish the major sections of the project: The task force now develops the activities associated with each major section:

1. Prepare plan of action.
   - Set objectives.
   - Draft general plan of action.
   - Select task force.
   - Prepare network plan.
2. Conduct energy audit of operating systems.
   - Investigate present systems:
     a. Heating and ventilation
     b. Air conditioning
     c. Lighting
     d. Electrical
     e. Water supply
     f. Steam supply
     g. Compressed air
   - Lay out improvements/costs of improvements:
     a. Heating and ventilation

    b. Air conditioning

    c. Lighting

    d. Electrical

    e. Water supply

    f. Steam supply

    g. Compressed air

- Collect present energy rates.
- Project future energy rate trends.
- Investigate present utility metering.
- Lay out metering system improvements.
- Determine costs for improved metering systems.

3. Prepare feasibility report.
   - Compare improved with present system.
   - Examine alternative systems.
   - Structure feasibility report.
     - **a.** Review economics feasibility.
     - **b.** Review engineering feasibility.
     - **c.** Review operating feasibility.
   - Prepare project appropriation request.

4. Obtain management approvals.
   - Prepare project appropriation request.
   - Submit project for approval.

5. Plan and schedule implementation.
   - Notify task force.
   - Plan and schedule implementation.

6. Procure, install, and try out equipment.
   - Prepare equipment designs and specifications.
   - Prepare equipment schedules.
   - Solicit and review supplier proposals.
   - Fabricate, deliver, and assemble equipment.
   - Prepare equipment installation designs and specifications.
   - Solicit and review installation contractors' bids.
   - Install equipment.
   - Try out equipment.

7. Design and construct site.
   - Prepare site designs and specifications.
   - Solicit and review contractors' bids.
   - Construct site: phase I.
   - Construct site: phase II.

8. Try out and launch energy management system.
   - Assign and train operating personnel.
   - Complete installation of system.
   - Try out system.

- Launch system.
- Phase out existing systems.

The task force realizes that it is not practical to include every conceivable activity in the network plan. The major activities were accounted for and any more activities to be added will be the result of further detail as the project progresses. The activities that have been listed are for use by management in directing the project.

The next step is to prepare the network plan that shows the interrelationships of all the activities listed. The network plan will also show the major events or milestones that will be useful when monitoring the project. Shown in Figure 9–7 is the completed network plan, including the milestones. This plan will provide the guidelines for the project leader and the task force to schedule the project and to direct its implementation.

Once the network plan is completed, individual members of the task force were assigned to the project activities. The task force leader, who had selected the members of the task force based on their skills, now assigned each of them to a specific work activity. They will be responsible to ensure successful completion of their activity.

From the network plan each task force member is able to identify the person responsible to complete the prior project activity or activities, as well as noting what the next activity or activities will be. The task force leader who selected the members of the task force used the major sections listing of the project to assign responsibilities, as noted below:

MAJOR PROJECT SECTION	RESPONSIBILITY
Plan of action	Task force leader
Energy audit	Mechanical engineers, electrical engineers
Feasibility report	Task force leader, mechanical engineers, electrical engineers
Management approvals	Task force leader
Implementation planning and scheduling	Task force leader
Equipment procurement, installation, and tryout	Mechanical engineers, electrical engineers
Site design and construction	Project engineers
System tryout and launch	Task force (task force leader, mechanical engineers, electrical engineers, project engineers)

There will be occasions when members of the task force will need to call upon various department heads for assistance. They will use the network plan as a sup-

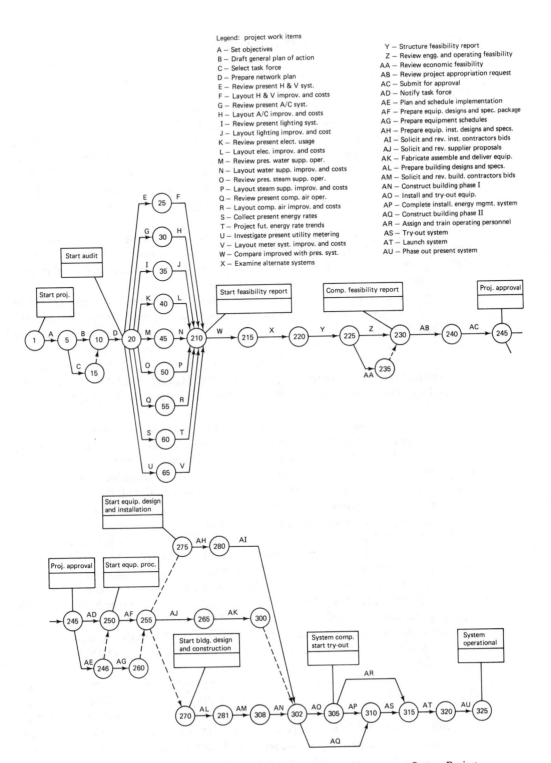

Legend: project work items

A — Set objectives
B — Draft general plan of action
C — Select task force
D — Prepare network plan
E — Review present H & V syst.
F — Layout H & V improv. and costs
G — Review present A/C syst.
H — Layout A/C improv. and costs
I — Review present lighting syst.
J — Layout lighting improv. and cost
K — Review present elect. usage
L — Layout elec. improv. and costs
M — Review pres. water supp. oper.
N — Layout water supp. improv. and costs
O — Review pres. steam supp. oper.
P — Layout steam supp. improv. and costs
Q — Review present comp. air oper.
R — Layout comp. air improv. and costs
S — Collect present energy rates
T — Project fut. energy rate trends
U — Investigate present utility metering
V — Layout meter syst. improv. and costs
W — Compare improved with pres. syst.
X — Examine alternate systems

Y — Structure feasibility report
Z — Review engg. and operating feasibility
AA — Review economic feasibility
AB — Review project appropriation request
AC — Submit for approval
AD — Notify task force
AE — Plan and schedule implementation
AF — Prepare equip. designs and spec. package
AG — Prepare equipment schedules
AH — Prepare equip. inst. designs and specs.
AI — Solicit and rev. inst. contractors bids
AJ — Solicit and rev. supplier proposals
AK — Fabricate assemble and deliver equip.
AL — Prepare building designs and specs.
AM — Solicit and rev. build. contractors bids
AN — Construct building phase I
AO — Install and try-out equip.
AP — Complete install. energy mgmt. system
AQ — Construct building phase II
AR — Assign and train operating personnel
AS — Try-out system
AT — Launch system
AU — Phase out present system

FIGURE 9-7 Planning diagram for the Energy Management System Project.

porting display to explain their need for help so that the project can be completed as planned.

After the network plan is completed and assignments made, the task force develops the time estimates for each project item. The best estimates come from those who specialize in the specific phases of the project work items. However, obtaining estimates from the best source may not always be possible (and there may be a lack of credibility associated with obtaining estimates from even the best source). There is a common tendency for those responsible for completing a specific project item to include various degrees of contingencies in the estimates they provide.

These types of estimates can quickly be uncovered by making a manual early start calculation of the project that will determine the project duration. "Overblown" estimates will show up on the critical items if the calculated project duration date extends beyond the planned completion date.

After the task force has completed the estimating and has developed a credible project completion date, the data are entered into the computer program. The plan and schedule will be broken out into the major project sections for use in carrying out the feasibility report, and implementing the project after approval mandates that the task force leader have additional personnel assigned to the project during the *investigate (or review) present systems* activity. Having the additional personnel assigned for other concurrent activities will depend on the progress of the investigation.

When management offers their support and encourages the work required to develop a plan of action for this project, all personnel associated with this project will have good reason to become dedicated and involved in the technique that is used. The personnel will go through a formal training program in order to understand the major elements of project management associated with the technique. An example of a typical training program outline is shown in Figure 9–8.

In the workshop sessions the project *installing an energy management system* will be used as a practical application of the planning, scheduling, and controlling methods presented in the seminar sessions. The task force team, under the guidance of the seminar leader, starts an exchange of ideas among the team members, and a project report will be completed later which will be a valuable reference document.

The length of the program is 24 hours of lectures and workshop sessions. This type of program is most effective when presented in three 8-hour segments over a three-week period. As participants will be applying this technique to a project with which they are involved, there is an added meaning to learning and to understanding the technique.

There are advantages to offering a training program to major equipment suppliers who will be submitting proposals. They may be able to reduce added costs due to uncertainties, as a plan of action showing major event timing and the overall plan will, to a great extent, clarify what is expected of them. A supplier who sees clearly his role in the plan will be the successful supplier. In this respect any expenses incurred for training may produce a good return.

SEMINAR OUTLINE

Seminar procedure, objectives, and scopes of course; project management introduction: definitions, applications, advantages.

Planning Network development: Set objectives, determine project work items; determine relationships among items; develop network diagram.

Workshop: Apply planning techniques to assigned project. Prepare input data for computer-calculated schedule for assigned project.

Scheduling Establish time estimates, calculate schedule, determine optional starting and finishing times of project work items; bar chart time schedules; computer-calculated schedules—business computers and fixed-frame computers.

Workshop: Calculate schedules (manual and computer) for assigned projects; construct bar charts (computer and manual).

Control Status of operations and management status reports; evaluating status, investigating "what if" situations, management reporting techniques.

Workshop: Develop sample status report for assigned project; evaluate computer graphic progress charts.

Project costs Procedures for establishing cost schedule, analyzing project cost distribution; monitoring costs through the indicated cost outcome method; analyzing actual with authorized costs; effect on timing schedule.

Planning personnel/labor Apply manual and computer approach for efficient utilization; effect on timing schedule.

Critique Comments and evaluation on managing projects with project management techniques.

FIGURE 9-8 Project management training program.

The majority of energy management system suppliers are hardware distributors or equipment manufacturers. They normally approach a system design assignment by selecting equipment that is available from their existing product line. And the supplier's salespeople will commit to delivery dates that are reasonable at the time of submitting proposals. Providing those who submit proposals with a detailed plan of action that they can forward to their manufacturing management will be an important communication expedient. Their understanding of the plan through their sales representatives is a major step leading to a successful project.

The merits and benefits of computer application for scheduling were discussed previously. Also discussed at length were the benefits of a network plan. As the energy management project evolves and becomes more involved, the value of the network plan and the computer-calculated schedule become more evident, and the use of the computer for progress reporting and rescheduling will become invaluable to the task force. Although the task force personnel understand that the success of the project is not completely dependent on the network plan and the computer as a tool, they know that this technique forms an excellent framework around which successful implementation of the project can evolve.

CONDUCTING THE AUDIT

Conducting the audit is the most extensive part of an energy management system study. The information gathered will not only determine whether an energy management system is an improvement in the operations but will also provide much other valuable information. It may even serve as a means to suggest a substitute or show that an energy management system would not contribute to any improvement. A thorough audit may take a relatively long time to complete unless an adequate number of qualified personnel are available to take part in the audit. In summary, there are four phases to an audit:

1. Develop an understanding of the present use of energy.
2. Establish cost of present energy use.
3. Establish requirements of new and improved system.
4. Compare operating costs of present with new and improved system.

From the computer printout of the network plan, shown in Figure 9–9, the task force leader can expand on his plan of action for this major section. The audit

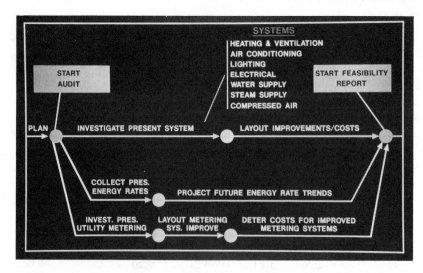

(a)

FIGURE 9–9 Audit phase: (a) planning diagram; (b) computer-generated schedule; (c) bar chart.

PROJECT MANAGEMENT	ENERGY MANAGEMENT SYSTEM				SOUTHEAST UNITED STATES
REPORT TYPE :STANDARD LISTING			PRINTING SEQUENCE :Earliest Activities First		
			SELECTION CRITERIA ::EA		
PLAN I.D. :IEMS VERSION 26			TIME NOW DATE :12/MAR/84		

ACTIVITY DESCRIPTION	EARLIEST START	EARLIEST FINISH	LATEST START	LATEST FINISH	DURATION	FLOAT
:EA REVIEW PRESENT H&V SYS	16/APR/84	4/MAY/84	16/APR/84	4/MAY/84	15	0 *
:EA REVIEW PRESENT ELECTRICAL SYS	16/APR/84	27/APR/84	23/APR/84	4/MAY/84	10	5
:EA REVIEW PRESENT A/C SYS	16/APR/84	27/APR/84	30/APR/84	11/MAY/84	10	10
:EA INVESTIGATE PRES UTILITY METERING	16/APR/84	27/APR/84	30/APR/84	11/MAY/84	10	10
:EA REVIEW PRESENT STEAM SUPPLY SYS	16/APR/84	20/APR/84	7/MAY/84	11/MAY/84	5	15
:EA REVIEW PRESENT COMP AIR SYS	16/APR/84	20/APR/84	14/MAY/84	18/MAY/84	5	20
:EA COL PRES ENERGY RATES	16/APR/84	20/APR/84	14/MAY/84	18/MAY/84	5	20
:EA REVIEW PRESENT WATER SUPPLY SYS	16/APR/84	20/APR/84	14/MAY/84	18/MAY/84	5	20
:EA REVIEW PRESENT LIGHTING SYS	16/APR/84	20/APR/84	14/MAY/84	18/MAY/84	5	20
:EA LAYOUT STEAM SUPPLY IMP & COSTS	23/APR/84	4/MAY/84	14/MAY/84	25/MAY/84	10	15
:EA PROJ FUT ENERGY RATE TRENDS	23/APR/84	27/APR/84	21/MAY/84	25/MAY/84	5	20
:EA LAYOUT LIGHTING IMP & COSTS	23/APR/84	27/APR/84	21/MAY/84	25/MAY/84	5	20
:EA LAYOUT COMP AIR IMP & COSTS	23/APR/84	27/APR/84	21/MAY/84	25/MAY/84	5	20
:EA LAYOUT WATER SUPPLY IMP & COSTS	23/APR/84	27/APR/84	21/MAY/84	25/MAY/84	5	20
:EA LAYOUT ELECTRICAL IMP & COSTS	30/APR/84	18/MAY/84	7/MAY/84	25/MAY/84	15	5
:EA LAYOUT A/C IMP & COSTS	30/APR/84	11/MAY/84	14/MAY/84	25/MAY/84	10	10
:EA LAYOUT METERING SYS & COSTS	30/APR/84	11/MAY/84	14/MAY/84	25/MAY/84	10	10
:EA LAYOUT H&V IMP & COSTS	7/MAY/84	25/MAY/84	7/MAY/84	25/MAY/84	15	0 *

(b)

PROJECT MANAGEMENT	ENERGY MANAGEMENT SYSTEM	SOUTHEAST UNITED STATES
REPORT TYPE :COMPRESSED PERIOD BARCHART		PRINTING SEQUENCE :Earliest Activities First
		SELECTION CRITERIA ::EA
PLAN I.D. :IEMS VERSION 24		TIME NOW DATE :12/MAR/84

```
=======================================1984================================================1985=================================
PERIOD COMMENCING DATE       11212   17    14  12    16  13    11   15  13    17    14  14  11    16  13  11    15   1
MONTH                        1MAR    1MAY 1JUN 1JUL 1AUG 1SEP  1OCT 1NOV 1DEC 1JAN 1FEB 1MAR 1APR 1MAY 1JUN 1JUL 1AUG  1
PERIOD COMMENCING TIME UNIT  18 123  148   168 188  11131133 1153 11781198 1223 12431263 1283 1308 1328 1348 1373  1
==================================================================================================================================
:EA REVIEW PRESENT H&V SYS            l  l  CC 1C     l    l     l    l    l     l    l    l    l    l    l    l    l
:EA REVIEW PRESENT ELECTRICAL SYS     l  l  ==1.      l    l     l    l    l     l    l    l    l    l    l    l    l
:EA REVIEW PRESENT REVIEW PRESENT A/C l  l  ==1..     l    l     l    l    l     l    l    l    l    l    l    l    l
:EA INVESTIGATE PRES UTILITY METERING l  l  ==1.      l    l     l    l    l     l    l    l    l    l    l    l    l

:EA REVIEW PRESENT STEAM SUPPLY SYS   l  l  =.1..     l    l     l    l    l     l    l    l    l    l    l    l    l
:EA REVIEW PRESENT COMP AIR SYS       l  l  =.1...    l    l     l    l    l     l    l    l    l    l    l    l    l
:EA COL PRES ENERGY RATES             l  l  =.1...    l    l     l    l    l     l    l    l    l    l    l    l    l
:EA REVIEW PRESENT WATER SUPPLY SYS   l  l  =.1...    l    l     l    l    l     l    l    l    l    l    l    l    l

:EA REVIEW PRESENT LIGHTING SYS       l  l  =.1...    l    l     l    l    l     l    l    l    l    l    l    l    l
:EA LAYOUT STEAM SUPPLY IMP & COSTS   l  l  =1=...1   l    l     l    l    l     l    l    l    l    l    l    l    l
:EA PROJ FUT ENERGY RATE TRENDS       l  l  =1....1   l    l     l    l    l     l    l    l    l    l    l    l    l
:EA LAYOUT LIGHTING IMP & COSTS       l  l  =1....1   l    l     l    l    l     l    l    l    l    l    l    l    l

:EA LAYOUT COMP AIR IMP & COSTS       l  l  =1....1   l    l     l    l    l     l    l    l    l    l    l    l    l
:EA LAYOUT WATER SUPPLY IMP & COSTS   l  l  =1....1   l    l     l    l    l     l    l    l    l    l    l    l    l
:EA LAYOUT ELECTRICAL IMP & COSTS     l  l  =1===.1   l    l     l    l    l     l    l    l    l    l    l    l    l
:EA LAYOUT A/C IMP & COSTS            l  l  =1==..1   l    l     l    l    l     l    l    l    l    l    l    l    l

:EA LAYOUT METERING SYS & COSTS       l  l  =1==..1   l    l     l    l    l     l    l    l    l    l    l    l    l
:EA LAYOUT H&V IMP & COSTS            l  l  1CCCC1    l    l     l    l    l     l    l    l    l    l    l    l    l
==================================================================================================================================
```

Barchart Key:- CCC :Critical Activities   === :Non Critical Activities   NNN :Activity with neg float   ... :Float

(c)

FIGURE 9-9 (*Continued*)

will start on April 16 and is scheduled to be completed by May 18. During this four-week period, added personnel are required. The task force leader recruited the needed personnel for the *investigate (or review) present systems* activity. Whether additional personnel to be assigned to other phases are needed will depend on the progress of the investigation.

The task force leader outlined the form in which the investigation of each subsystem would be handled. This outline was given to the audit team members to use as a guide:

1. Gather and review available data:
   - Description of system.
   - Procedures for operating system.
   - Diagrams.

2. Techniques:
   - Interview supervisory and operating personnel.
   - Obtain or prepare charts and diagrams.
   - Tabulate information.

3. Analyze present system:
   - Develop understanding of the present system.
   - Analyze the potential for proposed automatic controls.
   - Establish present costs for the system.
   - Prepare operations data:
     - Actual requirements.
     - Define responsibilities.
   - Prepare charts and diagrams.
   - Validate facts.
   - Review with operating personnel.

Although the task force will direct the effort, there will be a need to recruit personnel from other departments in order to satisfy the timing objectives. At MAS Products there are seven energy subsystems that need to be audited. These can essentially be done concurrently, as shown in the plan. Completing the audit is dependent on recruiting qualified persons to assist in completing these subsystems. They will be contributing to the project's success.

The task force leader will select additional personnel on their knowledge of the subsystems to be audited: heating and ventilation, air conditioning, lighting, electrical, water supply, steam supply, and compressed air. The task force leader prepared a descriptive summary of each subsystem, determining the scope of work for distribution.

Heating, Ventilation, and Air Conditioning

The heating, ventilating, and air-conditioning systems are usually the major users of building energy. Considering operating costs as well as scheduled maintenance and repair costs, these systems make up an appreciable expense item. Although costs are important, a great deal of attention should be devoted to the physiological and psychological efforts of a *controlled environment* among the people working in the facility. The effect of the controlled environment on the quality of the product produced must also be considered.

A controlled environment may not only mean simply controlling temperature, but also coordinating control of humidity and ventilation. Cleanliness of the surrounding air is another major consideration.

Investigating the existing heating, ventilating, and air-conditioning systems requires a systematic and logical procedure. There are many formats on energy conservation available from vendors, such as handbooks on conducting surveys for conservation purposes, which will also cover such items as operation and maintenance, and potential energy conservation projects requiring facility expenditures.

One of the more popular facility projects is an energy management system that can place the heating, ventilating, and air-conditioning systems in an automatic mode that will provide operational efficiencies and lower operating costs. The computer memory will contain building occupancy data, such as production startup and shutdown times, janitorial schedules, and weekends and holiday dates. Instructions to the computer will shut down and start up heating, ventilating, and air-conditioning equipment in line with production hours. Considerable energy can be saved through automatic operation.

Lighting

Lighting may be one of the largest wasters of energy in a building, and from an energy conservation viewpoint, represents potential savings. Electrical use for lighting can be reduced from 5 to 15% with improved maintenance and good operating practice. Conservation savings dollars cannot be gained at the expense of human safety and efficiency. There is a fundamental need for the people in a facility to be able to see without eye strain, and this can be done by providing good illumination. There are decided advantages to providing good illumination, and it is important that energy conservation methods introduced to save lighting costs do not interfere with safe, efficient operation.

Good illumination can work together with lighting conservation. Recent improvements in the use of high-pressure sodium lighting has not only realized appreciable savings but provides more intense illumination. Proper illumination allows for decided productivity improvements.

- Greater accuracy, which means improved product quality (greater accuracy means less scrap)
- More easily maintained cleanliness and neatness
- Less eye strain

- Fewer accidents
- Better utilization of floor space

All of these improvements lead to increased production and lower costs.

Lighting is so people-oriented that investigation of this subsystem carries an additional factor when advising lighting control improvements. The member of the task force who will investigate the lighting subsystem will use the format shown in Figure 9-10 to tabulate the present lighting system.

The energy management system can provide automatic lighting control by setting up various schedules that are stored in the computer's memory. When occupancy times, weekend and holiday data, and offshift data with janitorial schedules are entered into memory, the lighting zones can be turned on and off according to production and administrative office area schedules.

Another feature to be investigated for any appreciable savings is shutting off a selected number of lighting fixtures in storage areas, administrative hallways and corridors, and all other areas where there is little production activity. In these areas the lighting levels should be suitable only for persons to move about from one location to another.

Electrical Energy Consumption

The electrical *energy consumption* is only one of the elements that affect electrical costs. In addition to energy consumption changes, demand changes and power factor penalty changes account for most of the cost, and there is an opportunity here to maintain some control with energy conservation measures.

Electrical usage, when being investigated with the other subsystems, has a great deal of energy conservation potential in controlling overall plant power demand. The most effective action that can be taken is to reduce the peak power usage periods. By studying the daily plant demand profile of power usage, it is possible to identify major loads that contribute to high equipment and lighting demands. Demand is defined as the load in kilowatts during any 15- or 30-minute interval.

Schedule			Bays			Lamps		Light fixtures	
Shifts/ day	Days/ week	Hours/ day	Size	No.	Truss ht.	Type	Rate	Per bay	Total

FIGURE 9-10   Suggested format for tabulating present lighting.

Controlling the peak kilowatt demand is accomplished by the energy management system's computer control of "sheddable" noncritical loads, which can be turned off when the upward trend shows that the peak period will soon be reached.

The energy management system can also monitor the operation of critical electrically powered equipment so that maintenance personnel are alerted when a malfunction occurs. The system can monitor electrical substation circuit breakers located in roof penthouses, and the ability to pinpoint the problem in this area for maintenance personnel can minimize production downtime.

Electrical operation improvements by demand control offers a unique opportunity for reducing electrical costs without making too many building environmental changes. Demand control is essentially the scheduling of the operational time of controllable electrical loads, allowing each its appropriate amount of time but in some sort of sequencing arrangement. One procedure to follow to effect such control is as follows:

1. Identify last year's maximum monthly billing demand.
2. Identify all variable loads and prioritize these loads with their size.
3. Subtract the kilowatt total of all variable loads from the maximum monthly billing demand to obtain a base load.
4. Determine the approximate hours of operation of each of the variable loads and calculate the kilowatt-hours of energy required to support its operation. Total the kilowatt-hours.
5. Divide the total kilowatt-hours of operation of all variable loads by the operating hours to arrive at the total effective variable load.
6. The total effective variable load will be added to the base load to obtain the theoretical maximum demand load, which will be the setting of the demand controller.
7. By calculating the theoretical maximum demand each month, a new demand load setting is made on the demand controller.

Utilities demand changes vary from location to location, as they are designed to reimburse utilities for the capital investment needed to maintain and increase power plant capacity. There are other electrical changes, such as fuel adjustments, surcharges, primary discounts, and taxes. These are affected by demand and energy use. A good example of the control of demand is load "shedding." A schematic of how such load shedding action takes place is shown in Figure 9–11.

Water Supply

In some operations, water costs can comprise as much as 10 to 15% of total utility costs. Accompanying sewage costs that are related directly to the water bill have increased appreciably over the years to cover the high cost of municipal treatment facility and operating costs.

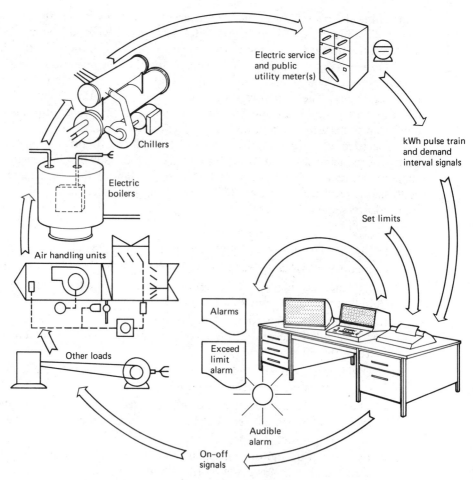

Electric service
and public
utility meter(s)

Chillers

Electric
boilers

kWh pulse train
and demand
interval signals

Set limits

Air handling units

Alarms

Exceed
limit
alarm

Other loads

Audible
alarm

On–off
signals

FIGURE 9-11   Schematic of a typical demand monitor and control program.

Savings can be realized by improving operation of the hot and cold water supply system. One of the first things to be investigated is the thermostat settings, to see that they are set at the lowest acceptable temperature. This will not only help in reducing steam use but will lessen the amount of water used.

Communication is also considered a conservation expedient. Publish water costs figures in the company paper, together with explanations of ways in which people can contribute to a reduction in water costs. The company paper is also used to request people to contribute additional suggestions.

Steam Supply

The boilers providing the steam supply for the plant are important to the production operations. While their uninterrupted operation is absolutely necessary, steam boilers can become inefficient and wasteful in energy consumption primarily because of inefficient combustion.

Steam leaks in piping, fittings, valves, and traps could add up to an impressive and wasteful amount of energy. A detailed survey of the total steam supply system, including leaks, needs to be made on a periodic basis. There could be a potential 10 to 25% energy savings that can be realized through proper operating and maintenance improvements in the steam boilers and steam supply system.

As the fuel burns, it is converted into heat energy in the boiler. There are three items that are heated:

1. Water, which is converted into steam, needs to be utilized efficiently.
2. Boiler walls (shell) and the surroundings, through which heat energy is lost.
3. Products of combustion that pass through the stack, through which heat energy is also lost.

Boilers that generate the steam supply are 75 to 85% efficient. Manufacturers usually rate boilers on a fuel-to-steam efficiency basis. Stack losses are 18%, and radiation, convection, and miscellaneous heat losses through the shell account for the remaining 2%.

Heat carried away by the hot flue gases generated during combustion accounts for the loss, with higher stack gas temperatures and larger amounts of excess air increasing this loss. Other items causing losses are heat of unburned fuel and products of incomplete combustion with improperly adjusted burners or insufficient combustion air.

Perfect combustion is the product of precisely controlled amounts of air and fuel. Yet because of mixing and mechanical problems, this level of efficiency is impracticable in plant operations. Even with excess air being supplied, perfect combustion is impossible in today's modern boilers. Efficient operation depends on providing enough excess air to burn as much fuel as possible, while minimizing heat losses through the stack.

In addition to the boiler inefficiencies, there are potential steam losses in the distribution system. Steam leaks and improperly maintained insulation placed over the steam lines as well as steam traps are the main contributors to losses. At 100 psi, a common steam pressure used in plants, one leak $\frac{3}{16}$ inch in diameter at prevailing steam generation costs of $6 per 1000 lb will cost $12,000 per year. A process plant containing several thousand feet of steam piping could suffer thousands of dollars in losses from steam leaks if not properly inspected. Insulation is another example of how steam losses can accumulate. One 10-foot section of pipe that has its insulation removed results in a heat loss of $1500 per year.

One approach to promoting steam conservation is to communicate to the operating people in the plant the importance of boilers and the steam supply system.

- Illustrate the cost of waste steam due to leaks and unnecessary venting.
- Publicize the cost of steam and its sensitivity to added costs through additional wasteful measures.

Compressed Air

Compressed air is vital to the operation of a plant and is used extensively in almost every production and service department. The compressors are usually the reciprocating type that supply air in the plant to operate equipment at a pressure of 90 psi. To provide this amount of pressure, the compressors discharge at 110 to 125 psi. Compressors of the size used in this facility are water cooled, the water carrying away the heat generated from the air compression.

An appreciable amount of energy is expended in the operation of the compressor's electrical energy not only for generating the compressed air, but for the cooling water requirements. In a plant the size of MAS Industries, using 2 million gallons of water per day for this purpose is common.

The present compressed air usage can be reduced as much as 15% through the adoption of certain improved operational procedures and maintenance practices. For example, an air compressor operating at 100 psi requires approximately 1 hp for every 5 cfm. Reducing air pressure from 100 psi to 80 psi reduces power usage by 12%.

An energy management system will permit monitoring the use of compressed air on weekends and off-shifts to detect waste. There are many other operating and maintenance improvements, such as shutting down idle compressors, and use of small auxiliary compressors for local use to replace main compressors at the powerhouse on weekends or during low production periods.

Facility Costs

The preceding descriptions of the present subsystems were presented in summary form to lay the groundwork for the development of a detailed investigation. Supplier guides and various energy handbooks can provide the task force with the detailed formats to use for developing existing operating requirements and costs.

From the operating data and costs, the task force can lay out an energy management system with facility costs and the improved operating procedure. The procedure outline followed by the task force to lay out the improved system is as follows:

1. Identify major features.
   a. Weaknesses in the present system.
   b. Opportunities for improvements.
   c. Requirements of the new system.
2. Outline requirements of the improved system.
   a. Prepare layouts.
   b. Consider exception reporting.
   c. Prepare flowcharts.
   d. Establish operations.
   e. Outline alternative systems.

- Prepare data of alternative systems comparable to base system.
- Consider ideas of others.
3. Prepare cost estimates:
   a. Facility costs.
   b. Operating costs.
      - Personnel.
      - Obtain current labor, materials rates.

Typical energy savings, which range from 6 to 38% for natural gas and 5 to 16% for electricity when installing an energy management system will justify an installation of this type. In determining these savings, it will be necessary to measure energy use at strategic areas, including major building and production equipment and processes, building lighting zones, building heating and ventilating zones, and the powerhouse. The task force must now consider a metering system for the facility.

Meters

Metering is essential in determining costs and overall system efficiency, and is an integral part of an effective energy control strategy. Proper metering is a diagnostic tool, enabling users to detect discrepancies before waste becomes a major issue. Although important to any conservation strategy, precise measurement of most of the utilities has proved difficult, and there are many who consider metering to be an inexact science. However, tremendous strides have been made in developing meters with improved performance, capable of more accurate measurements.

Despite concerns by some regarding their accuracy, meters are absolutely necessary if we are to know precisely where energy is being used. The areas in which meters are generally used for monitoring purposes (and are eventually phased into the control mode) include air-conditioning systems, heating and ventilating, exhaust systems, electrical substations, lighting, compressed air, water supply, and steam supply (boilers). Meters are a high-tech construction with continual improvements. New claims of improved meters by manufacturers are noted in every issue of trade periodicals.

Coinciding with meter measurements are monitors used to maintain checks on temperatures, flows, and pressures. On the market today is a portable, noncontact infrared thermometer for temperature measurements that will save energy when used to adjust the operating temperature of equipment. It senses infrared radiation from the target, and an electronic circuit converts this radiation to a heat readout in degrees. The thermometer can be used in energy conservation for making steam trap inspections, monitoring heat exchangers and steam lines for leaks, and locating heat losses through insulation. The instrument can also be used to monitor temperatures of products in manufacturing processes such as food, pharmaceuticals, rubber, and textiles. By taking frequent accurate readings of product temperatures, process temperatures can be optimized to reduce energy waste.

How a monitor conserves energy as well as realizing savings can be illustrated as follows. The infrared thermometer was used to determine that the conditioned room used to process material was running 5°F colder than the operating temperature specified. This information allowed the 5-hp motor that runs the compressor to be cycled off more often:

Savings: 90 kW day per compressor
90 at $0.06/kWh = $5.40 per day

Although the savings amount does not suggest a significant conservation effort, these types of ongoing plant conservation programs can accumulate into an impressive savings record. The plan of action on determining the need of a metering system includes these major steps:

1. Investigate metering for each utility.
2. Lay out new and improved metering for each utility.
3. Determine facility costs and operational savings.
4. Identify the rate of return (payout) of each facility.

To implement the foregoing plan of action, these detailed steps should be followed:

1. Bring up to date the "as-built" drawings of the distribution piping: compressed air, natural gas, steam, water. Also bring the electrical supply and distribution layouts up to date.
2. Locate meters within the distribution network and the major user locations. (One purpose of these meters will be accountability. Profit centers will measure energy use along with other operating costs.
3. Investigate state-of-the-art meters so that the meters that are procured will not only be adequate for accounting purposes but can interface with a monitoring and control system (energy management system) for energy conservation purposes.

After laying out the meters and determining the types of meters to be used, the task force will ask for proposals to furnish and install meters, and after installation adjust and calibrate them for accurate measurement. Costs for a complete metering system can become expensive, so there may be a decision to install in phases. After one area is completed and there is enough evidence to show justification to continue the metering installations, funding will be provided for the next area.

Energy Rates

Until 1985, governmental regulatory commissions maintained utility rate control through utility firms' operating and cost information. When energy was cheap and abundant, utilities and regulatory commissions structured rates to encourage use. As fuel costs soared in the 1970s, however, political pressures distorted utility rate structures, and industry was made to subsidize other classes of users. Where industry has intervened, there has been some control on the rates imposed on industry.

There are ways to control rates other than rate intervention. Switching fuels where plants have alternate fuel capability is also effective. A typical example is shown in Figure 9–12, where the price of fuel oil shows a downward trend starting in 1981, and in one year the price dropped below the price of natural gas. In 1982, when these projections were made, fuel oil was expected to remain cheaper indefinitely. Where operations had alternate natural gas/fuel oil capability, plant energy costs can be reduced by developing a procedure that can switch gas and oil expeditiously as rates vary.

In addition to rate intervention and switching fuels, rates can be controlled by negotiation. "Self-help" gas has received considerable attention since 1985. Changes in federal regulations allow users to seek lower gas prices at the well and by negotiating with pipeline companies to transport the gas. As a result, lower gas prices are competing with the fuel oil rates.

Coinciding with reviewing the overall utility rate structure are other reviews associated with the rates that may reduce the utility bill. A checklist covering operations and administrative expedients will be helpful in controlling the utility bill. Day-by-day *operations* should check the following:

- Inaccurate meters
- Improper metering methods
- Wrong meter constant
- Improper load arrangements, combination of loads
- Peak shaving not applied
- Poor efficiency factor

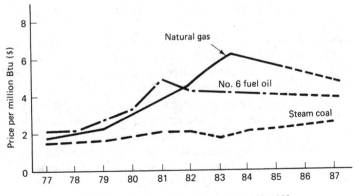

FIGURE 9–12   Trends in fuel prices, 1972–1982.

Administrative checks on the utility bill may be even more effective. For example, there are items that may not be correctly shown on the bill that can cause higher billings, such as:

- Favorable rates not being used
- Erroneous demand; wrong utilization of estimated and/or measured demand
- Appropriate discount
- Fuel clause adjustments
- Improper prorating
- Current regulations not applied
- Rate not granted on effective date
- Improper service equipment costs
- Improper ratchet application
- Tariff supplement not applied

Other areas that need to be explained with the utility forms are:

- Any special rates given competitors
- Methods to qualify for cheaper rates
- Policies of utility firm for recovering overpayments

To justify expenditures for improved energy management systems, the task force plans to show, through the energy rate structure, the savings that can be realized. At today's rates the savings can be a direct calculation; however, the problem begins when savings in future years are to be considered. Normally, average savings over 5 or, in many cases, 10 years are used for considering the return.

Forecasting rates is indeed an art. Sam Goldwin, a movie mogul of the past, was quoted as saying: "Forecasting is *very* difficult, especially when you have to look in the future." Rate projections become a part of a business plan of any firm that is energy intensive. What is used is what a firm considers to be the best available source. One of the better sources of energy forecasts is the Energy Information Administration Annual Report to Congress, published yearly.

Local utility firms also offer projections for the areas they service and probably provide a more accurate appraisal of a localized area. Consideration should also be given the vast number of editorials and trade articles. Finally, your own judgments should be entered into the forecasting formula.

To show the dilemma in forecasting, the following tabulation shows how forecasts from the same source several years apart will differ.

	NATURAL GAS ($/Mcf)*	
	June 30, 1983	August 1, 1986
1983	5.79	5.43 (A)
1984	6.66	5.34 (A)
1985	7.12	5.55 (A)
1986	7.55	5.34 (A)
1987	8.23	5.09
1988	8.97	4.97

*(A), actual.

In 1983, planners using natural gas projection for feasibility studies could be recommending energy saving equipment using natural gas as fuel that, once installed, say in a two-year period, would offer no actual savings. The funds expended could probably have been used for some cost-saving facility that showed a good return, but did not two years ago when the savings were calculated. Note the same type of tabulation for electricity using the same forecasts.

	ELECTRICITY CENTS/kWh)*	
	June 30, 1983	August 1, 1986
1983	4.33	5.40 (A)
1984	4.94	5.56 (A)
1985	5.54	6.34 (A)
1986	6.04	6.00 (A)
1987	6.59	6.35
1988	7.18	6.72

*(A), actual.

In contrast to lowered projections for natural gas rates, electricity rate projections are accelerating upward. What energy-saving equipment might now be installed realizing appreciable savings had the forecasts been more accurate?

When the task force completes the audit phase, they assemble all the data for use in preparing the feasibility report. (Admittedly, considerably more detail is needed, but the intent in this chapter is primarily to emphasize and discuss the sequential procedure to be used in accordance with project management practices.

PREPARING THE FEASIBILITY REPORT

The expedient in selling the proposal is the feasibility report (Figure 9–13). It should have the same degree of importance as any other phase because this document will be seen by those who will approve the funds for installing the energy management system. There may be persons with authority to approve who may have little knowledge of energy systems and energy costs. They may even have little knowledge of the plant where the system is to be installed, or they may have just been appointed to a new management position. Therefore, in structuring the feasibility report, it will be necessary to know who the readers will be. If there has been involvement throughout the program by those who will also approve it, the degree of detail may be less than if there are members of management less familiar with the project.

The feasibility report will follow a specific pattern that leads to obtaining management approval: (1) compare improved with present system, (2) examine alternative systems, (3) structure feasibility report, (4) review economic feasibility, (5) review engineering and operating feasibility, and (6) prepare project appropriation request.

Comparing the Improved and Present Systems

The first job in developing the feasibility report is to compare the merits of the proposed system with the present method of operation. Comparing alternative methods of operation that were investigated during the course of the study may be part of this exercise.

The savings to be realized may concern reduction in personnel, less material usage, and minimizing equipment operation (as much as an elimination of a complete shift). The savings may be in the form of cost avoidance. Equipment may not have to be modified for added production, or the savings may be intangible (i.e., they cannot be quantified). A good example is that morale may increase when a more efficient operation is installed that lightens the load of the operator.

The improved system needs to be analyzed for its facility cost, which will include the engineering, equipment procurement, (any) site construction, equipment installation, and tryout.

Examining Alternative Systems

Looking at other improved systems is a necessary part of the feasibility study. This adds credibility to the selection of the favorite system, as the comparison should clearly show it as the most desirable system.

Reviewing Economic Feasibility

All proposed energy-savings projects must compete with other cost-savings projects, such as automating a production area or changing the newer equipment, for ap-

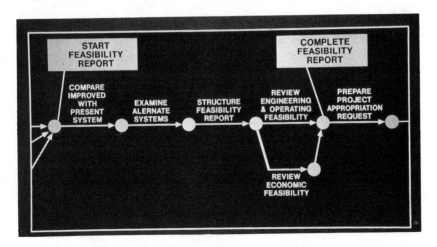

(a)

```
PROJECT MANAGEMENT                          ENERGY MANAGEMENT SYSTEM                              SOUTHEAST UNITED STATES
       REPORT TYPE :STANDARD LISTING                                 PRINTING SEQUENCE  :Earliest Activities First
                                                                     SELECTION CRITERIA ::FR
       PLAN I.D.   :IEMS      VERSION  24                            TIME NOW DATE      :12/MAR/84
========================================================================================================================
       ACTIVITY DESCRIPTION                 EARLIEST      EARLIEST      LATEST       LATEST       DURATION  FLOAT
                                            START         FINISH        START        FINISH
========================================================================================================================
:FR COMPARE IMP WITH PRESENT SYS            28/MAY/84      8/JUN/84     28/MAY/84     8/JUN/84        10      0 *
:FR EXAMINE ALTERNATE SYS                   11/JUN/84     22/JUN/84     11/JUN/84    22/JUN/84        10      0 *
:FR STRUCTURE FEASIBILITY REPORT            25/JUN/84      6/JUL/84     25/JUN/84     6/JUL/84        10      0 *
:FR REVIEW ENG & OPERATING FEASIBILITY       9/JUL/84     13/JUL/84      9/JUL/84    13/JUL/84         5      0 *
------------------------------------------------------------------------------------------------------------------------
:FR REVIEW ECONOMIC FEASIBILITY              9/JUL/84     13/JUL/84      9/JUL/84    13/JUL/84         5      0 *
========================================================================================================================
```

(b)

```
PROJECT MANAGEMENT                          ENERGY MANAGEMENT SYSTEM                              SOUTHEAST UNITED STATES
       REPORT TYPE :COMPRESSED PERIOD BARCHART                       PRINTING SEQUENCE  :Earliest Activities First
                                                                     SELECTION CRITERIA ::FR
       PLAN I.D.   :IEMS      VERSION  24                            TIME NOW DATE      :12/MAR/84
                                 =1984===                                              ===1985==
       PERIOD COMMENCING DATE    11212    17   14   12    16  13   11   15  13   17    14  14  11    16  13  11   15   1
       MONTH                     1MAR     1MAY 1JUN 1JUL  1AUG 1SEP 1OCT 1NOV 1DEC 1JAN 1FEB 1MAR 1APR  1MAY 1JUN 1JUL  1AUG  1
       PERIOD COMMENCING TIME UNIT 18 123  148  168  188   11131133 1153 11781198 1223 124312631283  130813281348  1373  1
========================================================================================================================
:FR COMPARE IMP WITH PRESENT SYS    1  1    1   C1C  1    1    1    1    1    1    1    1   1   1    1    1   1    1    1
:FR EXAMINE ALTERNATE SYS           1  1    1   1CCC1     1    1    1    1    1    1    1   1   1    1    1   1    1    1
:FR STRUCTURE FEASIBILITY REPORT    1  1    1    1  C1CC  1    1    1    1    1    1    1   1   1    1    1   1    1    1
:FR REVIEW ENG & OPERATING FEASIBILITY 1 1  1    1   1 C  1    1    1    1    1    1    1   1   1    1    1   1    1    1
------------------------------------------------------------------------------------------------------------------------
:FR REVIEW ECONOMIC FEASIBILITY     1  1    1    1   1 C  1    1    1    1    1    1    1   1   1    1    1   1    1    1
========================================================================================================================
Barchart Key:-  CCC :Critical Activities   === :Non Critical Activities   NNN :Activity with neg float   ... :Float
```

(c)

FIGURE 9-13 *Feasibility report* phase: (a) planning diagram; (b) computer-generated schedule; (c) bar chart.

proved funding. Economic feasibility is basically the amount of savings that can be realized, and thus compared with the facility costs to determine whether there is a desirable financial return. Financial procedures dictate the elements used in this calculation. It can become quite complex and should be completed by the finance group with members of the task force to assist in providing data.

Initial proposals from equipment suppliers will be the basis for selecting the best system. At first it will be desirable to receive a written proposal. After comparing these proposals, meetings should be arranged at which to meet those suppliers who have prepared the top proposals. Meanwhile, the task force has become familiar with the contents of the proposal and will be able to formulate intelligent questions. This type of preparation minimizes the need for follow-up meetings to clarify issues raised in the proposals.

The two most promising proposals should then be selected for final consideration. At this time the areas in which there was not too much detail consideration will bring out the best proposal. These areas include such items as the complete training package, applications support, the extent of the warranties, and the warranty times.

The chief responsibility of the task force is to provide reliable data that have been collected and received from experienced personnel. Firm quotations in written proposals are important to submitting credible data. These are some cost items that should be considered in the economic feasibility study:

- Total installed cost of the system to be supplied
- Detailed listing of what is included in the system to be supplied
- Added costs to make up the total system, including site work, utility connections
- Comparison of a leasing arrangement with the purchase price, and the disposition of the investment tax credit

Determining Engineering and Operating Feasibility

At times too much emphasis is placed on the monetary value of a project. Savings compared to costs appear so attractive that the question "Will it work?" may be overlooked. The task force, who will have to be responsible to "make it work," needs to be assured that there is compatibility in the engineering and design of the system with its operating capability, and maintenance of the equipment will be handled within the operating capability. A representative of the plant engineering or maintenance activity needs to participate, and his or her concerns will include the following:

- Preventive maintenance schedules
- Recommended spare parts

- Location of service office and number of technicians who work out of office
- Training and experience of technicians compatible with the equipment that is being considered
- Maintenance training

Operating reliability must also be considered. The proposed energy management system should also be reviewed with the skilled operating personnel and supervision. Questions that will be asked include the following:

- Where have other like systems been installed? (Visits to several locations may be helpful.)
- How long have these systems been in operation?
- Will the manufacturer set up tests for critical equipment components at the manufacturing plant?
- What are the warranty terms? What does the warranty cover? What is the length of the warranty?
- What is the uptime record, and will a specific uptime be guaranteed?

Specific training details should be covered in the supplier's proposal. The length of training, the location, and the amount of time spent training operators after the system is in the launching phase are all part of a complete proposal.

Structure of the Feasibility Report

A standard report outline should allow for all the essential information to be included in the report. The major sections of the report are outlined as follows:

- Introduction
  - Objectives
  - How study is carried out
- Summary
  - Findings
  - Conclusions and recommendations
- Costs/savings
- Other benefits
- Installation data
- Operating data
- Appendix

A feasibility report will also refer to collecting the data and assembling it in a form that can be used for portraying all aspects of feasibility: economic, engineering, and operating, The advantages of an energy management system will be summarized with both tangible and intangible benefits:

- *Timely implementation of conservation measures.* More efficient operation will reduce utility costs by load "shedding," load duty cycling, and startup and shutdown optimization.
- *Improved personnel utilization.* Control functions will be handled quickly and conveniently from a central point. Personnel who previously were required to tour the plant to start and stop equipment and to make routine inspections will now be made available for other specific duties.
- *More efficient operation.* Preprogramming to control and reset equipment to suit prevailing conditions will permit smooth operations.
- *Effective preventive maintenance.* Periodic analysis of equipment operation at the control center will provide more accurate preventive maintenance scheduling and inspections.
- *Increased operating uptime.* Detecting irregularities at the control center can reduce the overall time necessary to make corrections.
- *Improved safety and good housekeeping.* Detecting troublesome and unsafe conditions at the control center allows for instant correction. Maintaining a building pressure balance will help prevent undesirable air movements.

When done thoroughly, the feasibility report will ease the approval process, for the simple reason that much effort will be spent by the qualified task force in the preparation of the report. There is confidence that it will be a feasible project and there is enough creditability within the group that if there are distinct signs of an inadequate return, the project will be aborted. Yet the confidence of the task force in the feasibility is not enough to obtain approval by management. The danger is that the fate of the project is in the hands of persons whose background is remote to the nature of the project.

OBTAINING MANAGEMENT APPROVAL

There are two important steps to complete in this section (Figure 9–14): (1) preparing and reviewing the project appropriation request, and (2) submitting the project appropriation request for approval.

Preparing the Project Appropriation Request

A project appropriation request is generally the vehicle used to obtain approval of the concept of the program and to commit and spend funds to accomplish the program. There will usually be a format that provides specific instructions regarding preparation of the request. Usually, a representative of the finance section will prepare the request format, which will contain these sections:

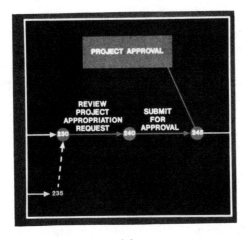

(a)

PROJECT MANAGEMENT ENERGY MANAGEMENT SYSTEM SOUTHEAST UNITED STATES
 REPORT TYPE :STANDARD LISTING PRINTING SEQUENCE :Earliest Activities First
 SELECTION CRITERIA ::MA
 PLAN I.D. :IEMS VERSION 24 TIME NOW DATE :12/MAR/84

ACTIVITY DESCRIPTION	EARLIEST START	EARLIEST FINISH	LATEST START	LATEST FINISH	DURATION	FLOAT
:MA REVIEW PROJECT APPROP REQUEST	16/JUL/84	27/JUL/84	16/JUL/84	27/JUL/84	10	0 *
:MA SUBMIT FOR APPROVAL	30/JUL/84	17/AUG/84	30/JUL/84	17/AUG/84	15	0 *

(b)

PROJECT MANAGEMENT ENERGY MANAGEMENT SYSTEM SOUTHEAST UNITED STATES
 REPORT TYPE :COMPRESSED PERIOD BARCHART PRINTING SEQUENCE :Earliest Activities First
 SELECTION CRITERIA ::MA
 PLAN I.D. :IEMS VERSION 24 TIME NOW DATE :12/MAR/84

	=1984=										=1985=							
PERIOD COMMENCING DATE	11212	17	14 12	16 13	11	15 13	17	14 14 11	16 13 11	15 1
MONTH	1MAR	1MAY 1JUN 1JUL	1AUG 1SEP	1OCT 1NOV 1DEC	1JAN 1FEB 1MAR 1APR	1MAY 1JUN 1JUL 1AUG 1
PERIOD COMMENCING TIME UNIT	18 123	148	168 188	11131133	1153	11781198	1223	12431263 1283	130813281348	1373 1

:MA REVIEW PROJECT APPROP REQUEST	1 1	1	1	1	1 CC1	1	1	1	1	1	1	1 1	1	1 1	1	1	1
:MA SUBMIT FOR APPROVAL	1 1	1	1	1	C 1CCC 1	1	1	1	1	1	1	1 1	1	1 1	1	1	1

Barchart Key:- CCC :Critical Activities   === :Non Critical Activities   NNN :Activity with neg float   ... :Float

(c)

FIGURE 9-14 *Obtain management approval* phase: (a) planning diagram; (b) computer-generated schedule; (c) bar chart.

- A *"face" sheet* that describes the project, summarizes the costs and financial justification, and suggests a completion date. The program description, which needs to be completed in sufficient detail to explain thoroughly the need for the proposed expenditure, should include the following:
  - An explanation of the particular actions that are planned
  - The factors that created the need for the action
  - The basis for estimating the project amounts

- A description of the other alternatives that were considered and why they were rejected
- Critical timing requirements
- The effect of any previously planned programs
- Savings expected to be realized; payback expected
- Authorized management signature approvals

- A *profit and cash flow analysis sheet* will show all the factors that relate to variable costs and nonvariable and fixed costs, as well as the items associated with cash flow. A typical cost-savings project may have the data shown in Figure 9-15.

- A *project detail sheet* includes the work items that need to be done, with their respective costs to complete. Whenever possible the project item costs need to be supported by firm supplier quotations, contractor bids, and completed engineering drawings for construction and installation. There should be a separate cost tabulation for each work item for freight, auxilliaries, and controls, and for any physical rearrangement that is not associated with new construction or installation of new equipment (see Figure 9-16).

Submitting the Request for Approval

When the project appropriation request is essentially complete, the task force should conduct reviews with operation management to obtain their support before reviewing the project with top management. The task force should reveal any limitations that can be expected with the proposal system, but provide assurance of the practicality of what is being proposed. There may be some controversial areas and they should be brought out for discussion. These types of discussions may show that more supporting data are required.

A successful study will convince the operating management first that improvements are needed. The system needs to be sold in such a manner that the operating personnel shall be considered the final authority. Top management in most cases supports the operation management. Presentation of the proposal to top management should be a planned affair.

- Provide the documentary material at least three weeks before the meeting so that it can be reviewed by top management and the top financial staff.
- Structure the format of the meeting. Time, place, and expected length of meeting need to be conveyed to the offices of top management as early as possible.
- Follow the format of the meeting. If it becomes disjointed, management members may associate this as a weakness of the project.

A carefully planned project request will usually get management approval. Once management approves the project concept and expenditures, the task force faces the remaining steps to be taken to implement and complete the project.

	1985	1986	1987	1988	1989
Variable costs					
Direct materials and incoming transportation					
Direct labor and fringe					
Indirect labor and fringe					
Other overhead					
Variable cost contingency					
Total variable costs					
Fixed and nonvariable costs					
Indirect labor and fringe					
Other overhead					
Taxes and insurance					
Preproduction and launching expense					
Project expense					
Administrative and selling					
Depreciation					
Amortization					
Other					
Total fixed and nonvariable costs					
Profits before taxes					
Cash flow					
Income taxes					
Investment tax credits					
Energy tax credits					
Amortization					
Capitalized tooling					
Inventories					
Other working capital					
Other cash charges					
Annual cash flow					

FIGURE 9-15 Example of a project cash flow analysis sheet.

- Plan and schedule project implementation.
- Procure, install, and try out equipment.
- Design and construct site.
- Try out and launch system.

Item no.	Description	No. of units	Total cost	Basic equipment item	Auxiliaries and controls	Installation	Freight

Project title

Prepared by

Approved by

(a)

Item no.	Description	Physical quantity	Unit of measure	Total estimated cost	Cost of materials	Cost of labor	Other costs	Total cost

Project title

Prepared by

Approved by

(b)

FIGURE 9-16 Example of a project detail sheet for (a) equipment and (b) building (or site) construction.

PLANNING AND SCHEDULING PROJECT IMPLEMENTATION

Once management approves funds and the concept for this project, there becomes a sense of urgency to begin implementation. Two major efforts begin now: (1) notifying and mobilizing the task force, and (2) planning and scheduling the implementation of the project (Figure 9–17).

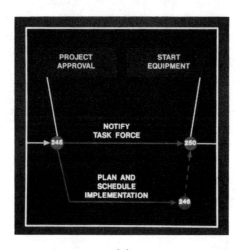

(a)

PROJECT MANAGEMENT   ENERGY MANAGEMENT SYSTEM   SOUTHEAST UNITED STATES
      REPORT TYPE :STANDARD LISTING   PRINTING SEQUENCE :Earliest Activities First
                                                                                        SELECTION CRITERIA ::PI
      PLAN I.D.   :IEMS   VERSION 24   TIME NOW DATE   :12/MAR/84

ACTIVITY DESCRIPTION	EARLIEST START	EARLIEST FINISH	LATEST START	LATEST FINISH	DURATION	FLOAT
:PI PLAN & SCHEDULE IMPLEMENTATION	20/AUG/84	7/SEP/84	20/AUG/84	7/SEP/84	15	0 *
:PI NOTIFY TASK FORCE	20/AUG/84	24/AUG/84	3/SEP/84	7/SEP/84	5	10

(b)

PROJECT MANAGEMENT   ENERGY MANAGEMENT SYSTEM   SOUTHEAST UNITED STATES
      REPORT TYPE :COMPRESSED PERIOD BARCHART   PRINTING SEQUENCE :Earliest Activities First
                                                                                        SELECTION CRITERIA ::PI
      PLAN I.D.   :IEMS   VERSION 24   TIME NOW DATE   :12/MAR/84

```
                                  ===1984===                                      ====1985====
    PERIOD COMMENCING DATE        |1212   17   14  12   16  13    11   15  13  17   14  14  11    16  13  11   15   1
    MONTH                         1MAR   1MAY 1JUN 1JUL 1AUG 1SEP 1OCT 1NOV 1DEC 1JAN 1FEB 1MAR 1APR 1MAY 1JUN 1JUL 1AUG 1
    PERIOD COMMENCING TIME UNIT   18 123  148  168 188  11131133 1153 11781198 1223 124312631283 130813281348 1373 1
    =================================================================================================================
    :PI PLAN & SCHEDULE IMPLEMENTATION   |  |    |    |    |    |  CICC |    |    |    |    |    |    |    |    |    |    |
    :PI NOTIFY TASK FORCE                |  |    |    |    |    |  =1.. |    |    |    |    |    |    |    |    |    |    |
```

Barchart Key:- CCC :Critical Activities   === :Non Critical Activities   NNN :Activity with neg float   ... :Float

(c)

FIGURE 9–17 *Plan and schedule project implementation* phase: (a) planning diagram; (b) computer-generated schedule; (c) bar chart.

Notifying the Task Force

During the feasibility study and the management approval process, members of the task force may be assigned to other projects waiting for approval of this project. While their efforts were necessary during the audit phase (to develop feasibility and secure approval), they would be "on hold" until there is official notice to proceed. Any efforts until project approval could produce wasted effort if there is outright disapproval of the project or management may want to change the concept.

There is then another scenario that may develop. A completely different concept concerning the direction the energy conservation programs should follow may have to be considered after higher management had reviewed the project and the various options that are normally listed in the project detail. A completely different task force or a partially different group may have to be used depending on the type of program being considered. In this particular case, the project as originally submitted was approved, and the same task force that developed the feasibility study was called back to begin the implementation.

Reviewing and Implementing the Plan and Schedule

Once the task force is again mobilized, each member will update the work under his or her responsibility. There will be a review of the plan and schedule developed previously for the approval process. As the technique used for the preliminary plan of developing the feasibility report was effective in obtaining project approval for the energy management system, the task force expanded on the planning diagram (Figure 9-6) to prepare the computerized schedule. From this schedule, shown in Figure 9-18, the project is expected to be completed in one year from the start of implementation.

The task force will review their work load through the project implementation portion of the project. Although there will be outside contractors and suppliers used for all the work, the task force will need to provide equipment specifications, process equipment orders, and follow through as project managers for the equipment procurement.

Once the planning diagram and the corresponding schedule have been completed, the task force will be able to develop a personnel loading analysis. Personnel requirements for every activity will be inputted into the resource allocation feature of the project management software package, resulting in computer reports of the weekly work load of each engineering skill. Resource summaries using both the early start and late start schedules are shown in Figure 9-19a and b, respectively.

Members of the task force will also be involved in developing the site "user requirements" and process site improvement orders for design and construction.

PROJECT MANAGEMENT   ENERGY MANAGEMENT SYSTEM   SOUTHEAST UNITED STATES
    REPORT TYPE :STANDARD LISTING   PRINTING SEQUENCE :Earliest Activities First
                                                       SELECTION CRITERIA :ALL
    PLAN I.D.   :IEMS   VERSION 26   TIME NOW DATE   :12/MAR/84

ACTIVITY DESCRIPTION	EARLIEST START	EARLIEST FINISH	LATEST START	LATEST FINISH	DURATION	FLOAT
:PA SET OBJECTIVES	12/MAR/84	16/MAR/84	12/MAR/84	16/MAR/84	5	0 *
:PA SELECT TASK FORCE	19/MAR/84	23/MAR/84	19/MAR/84	23/MAR/84	5	0 *
:PA DRAFT GENERAL PLAN OF ACTION	19/MAR/84	23/MAR/84	19/MAR/84	23/MAR/84	5	0 *
:PA PREPARE NETWORK PLAN	26/MAR/84	13/APR/84	26/MAR/84	13/APR/84	15	0 *
:EA REVIEW PRESENT H&V SYS	16/APR/84	4/MAY/84	16/APR/84	4/MAY/84	15	0 *
:EA REVIEW PRESENT ELECTRICAL SYS	16/APR/84	27/APR/84	23/APR/84	4/MAY/84	10	5
:EA REVIEW PRESENT A/C SYS	16/APR/84	27/APR/84	30/APR/84	11/MAY/84	10	10
:EA INVESTIGATE PRES UTILITY METERING	16/APR/84	27/APR/84	30/APR/84	11/MAY/84	10	10
:EA REVIEW PRESENT STEAM SUPPLY SYS	16/APR/84	20/APR/84	7/MAY/84	11/MAY/84	5	15
:EA REVIEW PRESENT COMP AIR SYS	16/APR/84	20/APR/84	14/MAY/84	18/MAY/84	5	20
:EA COL PRES ENERGY RATES	16/APR/84	20/APR/84	14/MAY/84	18/MAY/84	5	20
:EA REVIEW PRESENT WATER SUPPLY SYS	16/APR/84	20/APR/84	14/MAY/84	18/MAY/84	5	20
:EA REVIEW PRESENT LIGHTING SYS	16/APR/84	20/APR/84	14/MAY/84	18/MAY/84	5	20
:EA LAYOUT STEAM SUPPLY IMP & COSTS	23/APR/84	4/MAY/84	14/MAY/84	25/MAY/84	10	15
:EA PROJ FUT ENERGY RATE TRENDS	23/APR/84	27/APR/84	21/MAY/84	25/MAY/84	5	20
:EA LAYOUT LIGHTING IMP & COSTS	23/APR/84	27/APR/84	21/MAY/84	25/MAY/84	5	20
:EA LAYOUT COMP AIR IMP & COSTS	23/APR/84	27/APR/84	21/MAY/84	25/MAY/84	5	20
:EA LAYOUT WATER SUPPLY IMP & COSTS	23/APR/84	27/APR/84	21/MAY/84	25/MAY/84	5	20
:EA LAYOUT ELECTRICAL IMP & COSTS	30/APR/84	18/MAY/84	7/MAY/84	25/MAY/84	15	5
:EA LAYOUT A/C IMP & COSTS	30/APR/84	11/MAY/84	14/MAY/84	25/MAY/84	10	10
:EA LAYOUT METERING SYS & COSTS	30/APR/84	11/MAY/84	14/MAY/84	25/MAY/84	10	10
:EA LAYOUT H&V IMP & COSTS	7/MAY/84	25/MAY/84	7/MAY/84	25/MAY/84	15	0 *
:FR COMPARE IMP WITH PRESENT SYS	28/MAY/84	8/JUN/84	28/MAY/84	8/JUN/84	10	0 *
:FR EXAMINE ALTERNATE SYS	11/JUN/84	22/JUN/84	11/JUN/84	22/JUN/84	10	0 *
:FR STRUCTURE FEASIBILITY REPORT	25/JUN/84	6/JUL/84	25/JUN/84	6/JUL/84	10	0 *
:FR REVIEW ENG & OPERATING FEASIBILITY	9/JUL/84	13/JUL/84	9/JUL/84	13/JUL/84	5	0 *
:FR REVIEW ECONOMIC FEASIBILITY	9/JUL/84	13/JUL/84	9/JUL/84	13/JUL/84	5	0 *
:MA REVIEW PROJECT APPROP REQUEST	16/JUL/84	27/JUL/84	16/JUL/84	27/JUL/84	10	0 *
:MA SUBMIT FOR APPROVAL	30/JUL/84	17/AUG/84	30/JUL/84	17/AUG/84	15	0 *
:PI PLAN & SCHEDULE IMPLEMENTATION	20/AUG/84	7/SEP/84	20/AUG/84	7/SEP/84	15	0 *
:PI NOTIFY TASK FORCE	20/AUG/84	24/AUG/84	3/SEP/84	7/SEP/84	5	10
:EP PREPARE EQUIP DES & SPECS	10/SEP/84	5/OCT/84	10/SEP/84	5/OCT/84	20	0 *
:EP PREPARE EQUIP SCHEDULE	10/SEP/84	21/SEP/84	24/SEP/84	5/OCT/84	10	10
:CS PREPARE SITE DES & SPECS	8/OCT/84	30/NOV/84	8/OCT/84	30/NOV/84	40	0 *
:EP SOL & REV SUPPLIER PROPSAL	8/OCT/84	2/NOV/84	8/OCT/84	2/NOV/84	20	0 *
:EP PREPARE EQUIP INST DES & SPECS	8/OCT/84	26/OCT/84	7/JAN/85	25/JAN/85	15	65
:EP SOL & REV INST CONT BIDS	29/OCT/84	23/NOV/84	28/JAN/85	22/FEB/85	20	65
:EP FAB & ASS & DELIVER EQUIPMENT	5/NOV/84	22/FEB/85	5/NOV/84	22/FEB/85	80	0 *
:CS SOL & REV SITE CONT BIDS	3/DEC/84	28/DEC/84	3/DEC/84	28/DEC/84	20	0 *
:CS CONST SITE-PHASE 1	31/DEC/84	22/FEB/85	31/DEC/84	22/FEB/85	40	0 *
:EP INST & TRYOUT EQUIPMENT	25/FEB/85	19/APR/85	25/FEB/85	19/APR/85	40	0 *
:LS COMPLETE INST EMS	22/APR/85	17/MAY/85	22/APR/85	17/MAY/85	20	0 *
:LS ASSIGN & TRAIN OPERATING PERSONNEL	22/APR/85	17/MAY/85	20/MAY/85	14/JUN/85	20	20
:LS TRYOUT SYSTEM	20/MAY/85	14/JUN/85	20/MAY/85	14/JUN/85	20	0 *
:LS LAUNCH SYSTEM	17/JUN/85	12/JUL/85	17/JUN/85	12/JUL/85	20	0 *
:LS PHASE OUT PRESENT SYSTEM	15/JUL/85	9/AUG/85	15/JUL/85	9/AUG/85	20	0 *

FIGURE 9-18 Computerized schedule for the energy management system project.

Finally, the task force will direct the construction of the site, installation of the equipment, equipment tryout, and system tryout and launch.

Since the distribution of engineers on the early start schedule is not too uniform and more engineering hours for each skill are required than available (which means a great deal of overtime), the late start schedule was reviewed for comparison.

As both schedules show about the same work load, it is advisable to use the

PROJECT MANAGEMENT ENERGY MANAGEMENT SYSTEM SOUTHEAST UNITED STATES
    REPORT TYPE :COMPLETE RESOURCES REPORT REPORT BASIS :ACTIVITIES AT EARLY START
    START DATE :13/APR/84 SELECTION CRITERIA :ALL
    PLAN I.D. :IEMS VERSION 26 TIME NOW DATE :12/MAR/84

PE=PROJECT ENGINEER   ME=MECHANICAL ENGINEER   EE=ELECTRICAL ENGINEER   TE=TASK FORCE LEADER
EL=EL (NO CODE)

	PE	ME	EE	TE	EL			PE	ME	EE	TE	EL	
13/APR/84	2	4	3				24/DEC/84	1	2	1	1	
23/APR/84	2	5	3				31/DEC/84	2	2	2		
30/APR/84	1	3	2				7/JAN/85	2	2	2		
7/MAY/84	1	2	3				14/JAN/85	2	2	2		
14/MAY/84		1	2				21/JAN/85	2	2	2		
21/MAY/84		1	1				28/JAN/85	2	2	2		
28/MAY/84							4/FEB/85	2	2	2		
4/JUN/84							11/FEB/85	2	2	2		
11/JUN/84							18/FEB/85	2	2	2		
18/JUN/84							25/FEB/85	1	4	4		
25/JUN/84							4/MAR/85	1	4	4		
2/JUL/84							11/MAR/85	1	4	4		
9/JUL/84							18/MAR/85	1	4	4		
16/JUL/84							25/MAR/85	1	4	4		
23/JUL/84							1/APR/85	1	4	4		
30/JUL/84							8/APR/85	1	4	4		
6/AUG/84							15/APR/85	1	4	4		
13/AUG/84							22/APR/85	1	4	6		
20/AUG/84							29/APR/85	1	4	6		
27/AUG/84							6/MAY/85	1	4	6		
3/SEP/84							13/MAY/85	1	4	6		
10/SEP/84		3	5	1			20/MAY/85	1	2	4		
17/SEP/84		3	5	1			27/MAY/85	1	2	4		
24/SEP/84		2	3				3/JUN/85	1	2	4		
1/OCT/84		2	3				10/JUN/85	1	2	4		
8/OCT/84		6	3	1			17/JUN/85		4	4		
15/OCT/84		6	3	1			24/JUN/85		4	4		
22/OCT/84		6	3	1			1/JUL/85		4	4		
29/OCT/84		5	2	1			8/JUL/85		4	4		
5/NOV/84	1	5	2				15/JUL/85		2		1	2
12/NOV/84	1	5	2				22/JUL/85		2		1	2
19/NOV/84	1	5	2				29/JUL/85		2		1	2
26/NOV/84	1	4	1				5/AUG/85		2		1	2
3/DEC/84	1	2	1	1			12/AUG/85					
10/DEC/84	1	2	1	1			19/AUG/85					
17/DEC/84	1	2	1	1			26/AUG/85					
24/DEC/84	1	2	1	1								

- From 13/Apr/84 to the end of the project (week of 5/Aug/85) a wide range of engineering skills is required:

SKILL	RANGE
Project engineer	1–2
Mechanical engineer	1–6
Electrical engineer	1–6

- There was a four-month period when no engineers were required (during the feasibility and project approval phases). During this time the engineers assigned to the task force were returned to their own organization.

FIGURE 9-19a   Engineering work load: early start schedule.

```
PROJECT MANAGEMENT                              ENERGY MANAGEMENT SYSTEM                        SOUTHEAST UNITED STATES
    REPORT TYPE  :COMPLETE RESOURCES REPORT                              REPORT BASIS      :ACTIVITIES AT EARLY START
    START DATE   :13/APR/84                                             SELECTION CRITERIA :ALL
    PLAN I.D.    :IEMS     VERSION  26                                   TIME NOW DATE     :12/MAR/84
```

PE=PROJECT ENGINEER   ME=MECHANICAL ENGINEER   EE=ELECTRICAL ENGINEER   TE=TASK FORCE LEADER
EL=EL (NO CODE)

Date	PE	ME	EE	TE	EL		Date	PE	ME	EE	TE	EL
13/APR/84	2	4	3				24/DEC/84	1	2	1	1	
23/APR/84	2	5	3				31/DEC/84	2	2	2		
30/APR/84	1	3	2				7/JAN/85	2	2	2		
7/MAY/84	1	2	3				14/JAN/85	2	2	2		
14/MAY/84		1	2				21/JAN/85	2	2	2		
21/MAY/84		1	1				28/JAN/85	2	2	2		
28/MAY/84							4/FEB/85	2	2	2		
4/JUN/84							11/FEB/85	2	2	2		
11/JUN/84							18/FEB/85	2	2	2		
18/JUN/84							25/FEB/85	1	4	4		
25/JUN/84							4/MAR/85	1	4	4		
2/JUL/84							11/MAR/85	1	4	4		
9/JUL/84							18/MAR/85	1	4	4		
16/JUL/84							25/MAR/85	1	4	4		
23/JUL/84							1/APR/85	1	4	4		
30/JUL/84							8/APR/85	1	4	4		
6/AUG/84							15/APR/85	1	4	4		
13/AUG/84							22/APR/85	1	4	6		
20/AUG/84							29/APR/85	1	4	6		
27/AUG/84							6/MAY/85	1	4	6		
3/SEP/84							13/MAY/85	1	4	6		
10/SEP/84		3	5	1			20/MAY/85	1	2	4		
17/SEP/84		3	5	1			27/MAY/85	1	2	4		
24/SEP/84		2	3				3/JUN/85	1	2	4		
1/OCT/84		2	3				10/JUN/85	1	2	4		
8/OCT/84		6	3	1			17/JUN/85		4	4		
15/OCT/84		6	3	1			24/JUN/85		4	4		
22/OCT/84		6	3	1			1/JUL/85		4	4		
29/OCT/84		5	2	1			8/JUL/85		4	4		
5/NOV/84	1	5	2				15/JUL/85		2		1	2
12/NOV/84	1	5	2				22/JUL/85		2		1	2
19/NOV/84	1	5	2				29/JUL/85		2		1	2
26/NOV/84	1	4	1				5/AUG/85		2		1	2
3/DEC/84	1	2	1	1			12/AUG/85					
10/DEC/84	1	2	1	1			19/AUG/85					
17/DEC/84	1	2	1	1			26/AUG/85					
24/DEC/84	1	2	1	1								

- From 13/Apr/84 to the end of the project, a wide range of engineering skills is required:

SKILL	RANGE
Project engineer	1-2
Mechanical engineer	1-5
Electrical engineer	1-6

- Depending on the availability of engineers from other locations, overtime for those assigned to this project will be excessive.

FIGURE 9-19b   Engineering work load: late start schedule.

early start schedule. Supplementing the overtime can be temporary hiring of engineers from outside engineering firms who specialize in facility programs.

Utilizing outside engineering firms to obtain selective engineering skills is done often. Since these engineers will not be familiar with the project, the task force leader needs to have a thorough lineup developed to sustain an efficient and productive arrangement with the existing personnel. An astute task force leader will use the planning diagram as an orientation tool to familiarize the new engineers on the project.

PROCURING, INSTALLING, AND TRYING OUT THE EQUIPMENT

The work associated with this section includes the following (Figure 9-20): (1) preparing equipment designs and a specification package, (2) soliciting and reviewing supplier proposals, (3) preparing equipment schedules, (4) preparing equipment installation designs and specifications, (5) fabricating, assembling, and delivering equipment, (6) soliciting and reviewing installation contractor's bids, and (7) installing and trying out equipment. During this period there are a great number of meetings with engineering and operating personnel, who, although they may not be directly involved with the project, will nevertheless be helpful in selection of the equipment through their knowledge of the operation. Contacts with suppliers on an informal basis will also be helpful. While time consuming, meetings with all knowledgeable persons is worthwhile. These experiences provide the impetus to start the equipment procurement phases with some confidence. It is important to make allowances in the timing and work load analysis to perform this necessary function.

Preparing the Equipment Design and Specification Package

The major theme in the preparation of the package is to establish a high standard of quality for the equipment to be furnished. First, there needs to be a systematic approach to developing the process so that the functions and operations of the system can be realized. For this systematic approach to start in the right direction, it is absolutely necessary to prepare a detailed layout of the equipment to show how it will be positioned on the plant floor. Once completed, this plant equipment layout serves as a valuable tool and guide in the preparation of the equipment design and specification.

In today's engineering climate of specialization, the owner will first prepare a set of specifications relating to what the equipment is expected to do so that it will perform satisfactorily. Second, the specific engineering and design details for fabrication and assembly will usually be delegated to a specialized engineering firm. Or the owner may select another alternative that is also popular—having the equipment supplier also provide the equipment design and details required for fabrication and

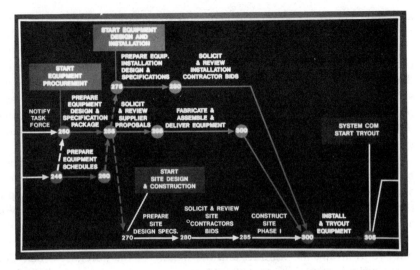

(a)

PROJECT MANAGEMENT   ENERGY MANAGEMENT SYSTEM   SOUTHEAST UNITED STATES
      REPORT TYPE :STANDARD LISTING   PRINTING SEQUENCE :Earliest Activities First
                                                                          SELECTION CRITERIA ::EP
      PLAN I.D.   :IEMS   VERSION 24   TIME NOW DATE   :12/MAR/84

ACTIVITY DESCRIPTION	EARLIEST START	EARLIEST FINISH	LATEST START	LATEST FINISH	DURATION	FLOAT
:EP PREPARE EQUIP DES & SPECS	10/SEP/84	5/OCT/84	10/SEP/84	5/OCT/84	20	0 *
:EP PREPARE EQUIP SCHEDULE	10/SEP/84	21/SEP/84	24/SEP/84	5/OCT/84	10	10
:EP SOL & REV SUPPLIER PROPSAL	8/OCT/84	2/NOV/84	8/OCT/84	2/NOV/84	20	0 *
:EP PREPARE EQUIP INST DES & SPECS	8/OCT/84	26/OCT/84	7/JAN/85	25/JAN/85	15	65
:EP SOL & REV INST CONT BIDS	29/OCT/84	23/NOV/84	28/JAN/85	22/FEB/85	20	65
:EP FAB & ASS & DELIVER EQUIPMENT	5/NOV/84	22/FEB/85	5/NOV/84	22/FEB/85	80	0 *
:EP INST & TRYOUT EQUIPMENT	25/FEB/85	19/APR/85	25/FEB/85	19/APR/85	40	0 *

(b)

PROJECT MANAGEMENT   ENERGY MANAGEMENT SYSTEM   SOUTHEAST UNITED STATES
      REPORT TYPE :COMPRESSED PERIOD BARCHART   PRINTING SEQUENCE :Earliest Activities First
                                                                          SELECTION CRITERIA ::EP
      PLAN I.D.   :IEMS   VERSION 24   TIME NOW DATE   :12/MAR/84

```
============1984=============================================1985==========
PERIOD COMMENCING DATE       11212   17   14   12    16  13   11   15  13   17   14  14   11    16  13  11   15   1
MONTH                        1MAR    1MAY 1JUN 1JUL  1AUG 1SEP 1OCT 1NOV 1DEC 1JAN 1FEB 1MAR 1APR  1MAY 1JUN 1JUL 1AUG 1
PERIOD COMMENCING TIME UNIT  18 123  148  168  188   1131133 1153 11781198 1223 12431263 1283   13081328 1348 1373 1

:EP PREPARE EQUIP DES & SPECS    1   1    1    1    1    1    1 CCC 1C  1    1    1    1    1      1    1   1    1    1
:EP PREPARE EQUIP SCHEDULE       1   1    1    1    1    1    1 ===1.   1    1    1    1    1      1    1   1    1    1
:EP SOL & REV SUPPLIER PROPSAL   1   1    1    1    1    1    1 CCC 1C  1    1    1    1    1      1    1   1    1    1
:EP PREPARE EQUIP INST DES & SPECS 1 1    1    1    1    1    1 ===1....1....1....1    1    1      1    1   1    1    1

:EP SOL & REV INST CONT BIDS     1   1    1    1    1    1    1   =1===1....1....1....1....1      1    1   1    1    1
:EP FAB & ASS & DELIVER EQUIPMENT 1  1    1    1    1    1    1   1CCC 1CCCC 1CCCC 1CCC 1  1      1    1   1    1    1
:EP INST & TRYOUT EQUIPMENT      1   1    1    1    1    1    1   1    1    1 C 1CCC 1CCCC 1      1    1   1    1    1
```
Barchart Key:- CCC :Critical Activities === :Non Critical Activities NNN :Activity with neg float ... :Float

(c)

FIGURE 9-20 *Procure, install, and tryout equipment* phase: (a) planning diagram; (b) computer-generated schedule; (c) bar chart.

assembly. The owner will review and approve the designs prior to the start of fabrication and assembly.

If the owner has elected to have the designs, or simply the design requirements, prepared separately, the specifications are then sent to a list of invited bidders. The document used is known as a request for quotation. Between five and eight bidders submitting their proposals should provide adequate review for a satisfactory proposal that the owner will finally select. The owner cannot minimize the importance of the selection process, as the bidders will usually supplement the content of the specifications with improvements.

Control systems have become complex, and selection of price alone may not be the correct approach. How each supplier's equipment will function to solve the application needs to be analyzed, and the evaluation may be a lengthy process. In the final evaluation it may be necessary for the original specification to be altered and bidding started all over again. There may be an occasion when only one supplier is close enough to the owner's specifications, and the differences may be negotiated prior to awarding the contract and the signing of the purchase order. Complexity of the order is something that should be recognized at the beginning of this phase. In the planning of this phase, allowing adequate time to process such an order will help toward the timeliness of the completion of the total energy management system.

Soliciting and Reviewing the Supplier Proposals

In most firms there is a purchasing activity that administers the contacts with suppliers for equipment procurement and with contractors for equipment installation and, if necessary, contractors for site construction. The purchasing activity serves an important function, and thoroughness in this performance can be a virtue.

Allowance for adequate time to solicit and review proposals needs to be incorporated in the schedule. Depending on the magnitude of the request, a range of two to eight weeks can cover the duration of this activity. Specifically, for the energy management system equipment, a supplier should be given at least two to three weeks for preparing a proposal. Review time is dependent on complexity—in this instance, two to three weeks would be required for review by the engineers. Purchasing will also be involved in checking legal aspects of the proposal, investigating the credibility of the supplier to deliver and comparing the overall bid process.

Limiting the list of potential bidders makes sense when there has been prior evaluation of the available equipment suppliers. Especially when the specifications are complex, reviewing the proposals can become a large task, requiring time that can be more valuably spent in another phase. About five bidders are adequate for proposal comparison.

At times there may be suppliers' proposals with very few differences, requiring meetings with them at the same time to explain or clarify parts of the specifications.

Resubmittal of their proposals should then provide the best proposal on which a purchase order can be written.

Preparing the Equipment Schedules

Scheduling equipment procurement, while discussed previously, bears further and repeated review. From the author's experience suppliers *are not* disciplined in the project management sense of scheduling delivery of their product. Therefore, it is incumbent on the owner to direct and guide the delivery. Provision for owner direction starts with including this item in the specifications. With few exceptions, the supplier will submit a delivery date in his proposal. *This is not enough* when deliveries of equipment extend beyond three or four weeks. For these situations, the supplier needs to provide important events, or milestones, that lead up to the delivery date. (And incidentally, observe carefully that the proposal specifically states delivery at the owner's receiving area. In many cases the interpretation could be delivery at the supplier's shipping area. Shipping time, depending on the mode of travel, can appreciably change a planned start of the installation milestone.)

The owner may provide in the specifications for the supplier to furnish a milestone schedule, or if the need exists, a planning diagram with a computerized schedule based on the planning diagram. Although additional effort may be required for the detail, the task force most certainly would have an excellent control expedient. And the chances are quite high that the equipment will arrive at the owner's site on time.

Why is there such a positive attitude? Because the element of awareness is distributed among the persons involved. Its communication feature is excellent.

Preparing the Equipment Installation Designs and Specifications

This particular part of the equipment design and procurement phase is the least understood and consequently is not given the proper attention. The scope of work can become a "bouncing ball"—the equipment designer believes these items should be handled by the owner, and the owner will often assume the equipment supplier includes this work with the equipment design and specifications. Clarification is essential.

Equipment installation designs and specifications are essentially the foundation requirements (pits, anchors, trenches, etc.), utility connections (electrical distribution, water piping, drainage system, natural gas, compressed air), and the equipment that generates the utility services. Preparation of these drawings and specifications starts after the equipment designs are far enough along so that foundations and services can be determined. It is important that the supplier proposal include when foundation and utility information will be furnished, and in what detail.

Preparation of installation designs requires use of the plant layout drawings to show the routing of the distribution of the utility piping and the exact location for the foundations. These drawings provide the dimensions that the installation contractor will use.

Preventing physical interferences within the plant is one of many reasons for preparing installation drawings. Good installation designs will also provide proper pipe sizing and adequate electrical conduit and wiring arrangements that help maintain production operations.

The task force needs to stay involved, overseeing the exchange of information between the equipment designer and the equipment installation designer. Changes made during the equipment design stage may affect utility services to the equipment, and the foundation design changes of this nature must be "fed" to the equipment installation designer as soon as the changes are noted and have been approved by the owner.

On occasion the equipment installation designer may inform the equipment designer of discrepancies of information he had received which may relate to a design concern. Communication need not be through the owner at all times; however, confirmation of changes and related matters should be part of the agenda of owner-sponsored meetings held at regular intervals.

Installation drawings and specifications are prepared so that the contractor who is bidding on them will be able to separate the mechanical and electrical sections to have the special subcontractors bid on their respective sections. Preparing thorough installation drawings and specifications will allow bidders to prepare accurate quotations, and the task force will find it easier to evaluate the bids.

Fabricating, Assembling, and Delivering the Equipment

This task usually starts with preliminary discussions with equipment suppliers, including delivery schedules. The most critical equipment deliveries become the basis for the scheduling of this item. It is important to provide equipment suppliers with *only* the *early start* and *finish times* to use in developing their schedules. Equipment suppliers are notoriously late in delivering equipment. Most owners contribute unknowingly to this situation. Equipment suppliers emphasize quality and cost when selling equipment. These firms are made up of highly qualified engineers skilled in specific disciplines with a combined talent to produce a competitive salable product. What most lack are project management skills. The initial reason the author selected this text subject was the number of equipment suppliers who provided technical proposals but did not include comprehensive schedules. Their lack of knowledge of project management detracted from the description of the equipment to be provided.

Soliciting and Reviewing the Installation Contractor's Bids

The procedures for obtaining bids and the subsequent reviews are similar to the equipment supplier bid process. Any changes would relate to the personnel involved, who specialize primarily in building construction and are more familiar with building service equipment installations.

As building services equipment may not be as complex and sophisticated as the hardware and controls equipment of an energy management system, searching for qualified bidders may require more time than ordinarily required by other projects. A good source of qualified bidders may be the equipment suppliers, who probably have experienced the performance of several contractors who have installed their equipment.

When there is still doubt that the management of the installation firms could supervise a technically oriented installation of this type, even though the skilled trades would be qualified, the owner has other alternatives to ensure quality installation. In many instances, the owner provides for the installation contractors to obtain the services of a qualified supervisor or engineer from the equipment supplier to be the field supervisor for the installation work or to act as an adviser to the contractor. In the second arrangement, the contractor is still responsible for all the supervising activities: assigning skilled trades personnel, ordering the material, and handling all administrative requirements.

The matter of payment for these services is stated in the specifications. If the owner provides for the compensation, the specifications for this provision need not be as detailed as when the contractor is required to pay for these services. In the latter, specifications will detail the scope of assignments of the equipment supplier's representative.

This detail serves two purposes: First, the owner will be satisfied that the work will be completed in accordance with the supplier's designs, and second, all the bidders will be aware of the scope of services the supplier's representative will provide. Consequently, the costing of this item should be consistent among the bidders.

Installing and Trying Out Equipment

Installation can start when two major actions are complete. The site (or building) is essentially completed, permitting installation to start, and adequate equipment has been delivered to permit installation to start. The task force, having "tracked" both of these "paths" (site and equipment procurement), have reassured themselves as to the installation start date. The installation contractor may already have mobilized on the site (as his contract may include receiving delivery of the equipment prior to the start of installation).

The installation contractor should be completing or have completed by this time a detailed plan and schedule of the equipment installation work. This is to be reviewed by the owner, who will approve if it is shown to be in accordance with the objectives of the project. This schedule should be monitored at least monthly, the critical items assessed on its impact on the completion date and, depending on its seriousness, resolution of the problem. The task force, based on this information, should prepare a progress report summarized in such a manner that management can review and understand it. Acceptable status reports have been illustrated in previous chapters.

Knowledge of progress must be known in shorter periods by the persons directly involved with the installation. There should be weekly meetings with the contractor and subcontractor personnel and key equipment supplier personnel (when equipment deliveries have become critical, if they are arriving "piecemeal," or if there are complexity concerns during installation). At these meetings the quality of both material and installation performance can be discussed in addition to timing review and concerns.

Another expedient for control is the use of a daily format to record pertinent data relating to contractor activities during installation. A typical format is shown in Figure 9–21.

This record can have future use in the event of differences between the contractor and the owner. (In fact, the knowledge that the owner is keeping such a record can possibly prevent undue claims against the owner.) Most contractors and subcontractors operate with integrity; however, if difficulty appears, contractors and subcontractors will search for any "avenue" to avoid losses. Thorough understanding of owner and contractor positions can prevent difficult situations.) Consistency of job performance with quality awareness will provide a timely and successful completion of the installation.

Equipment tryout can start upon the completion of two major "paths": utility service facilities and individual equipment or process components. This individual tryout is required before total system tryout to minimize and isolate the problems that will occur when the entire system is started. It will make for an earlier launching of the total process system.

At tryout, electricians will do such tasks as starting motors for proper rotation, and check balancing and vibrations. Mechanical personnel will check valves for control of water, natural gas, and compressed air supply to equipment. Electrical technicians will check individual electronic controls, computer programming, and sensors for adequate performance.

It is advisable to have plant personnel perform the tryout tasks. If, by contract, contractor personnel are responsible for the equipment to operate satisfactorily in this tryout period, the owner should still authorize his skilled personnel and selected supervision to observe. Persons being trained to operate the equipment should also be present. At this time, potential equipment malfunctions will appear and may possibly become a chronic problem.

Observation and note taking (a diary of experiences) will be invaluable during

DAILY REPORT ON EQUIPMENT INSTALLATION

_____ PLANT

PROJECT & ITEM NO. _____

LOCATION _____

PURCHASE ORDER _____

GENERAL CONTRACTOR _____

DATE _____

TEMP. _____

WEATHER _____

DAILY MANPOWER BREAKDOWN

CONTRACTOR & SUB-CONTRACTORS	TRADES												TOTAL
	BRICK LAYERS	CARP.	ELECT.	IRON WORKERS	LAB.	MILL-WRIGHTS	PIPE-FITTERS	RIGGERS	SHEET METAL				
_____													
_____													
_____													
_____													
_____													
_____													
_____													
_____													

WORK PROGRESS (EQUIPMENT OR PROCESS BEING INSTALLED, % COMPLETE, SPECIFIC PROBLEM, ETC.)

_____

_____

_____

_____

_____

_____

_____

_____

_____

_____

_____

_____

AUTHORIZED ADDITIONAL WORK (NOTICE TO PROCEED, MANPOWER, STATUS, ETC.)

_____

_____

_____

EQUIPMENT RECEIVED (MANUFACTURER, SCHEDULED DELIVERY DATE, CONDITION AT ARRIVAL, ETC.)

_____

_____

_____

SIGNED _____

FIGURE 9-21 Sample format for daily report on equipment installation.

system tryout, launching, and finally, during production. Plant personnel will start developing punch lists of individual equipment items during equipment tryout, and this task will continue through system tryout and launch.

DESIGNING AND CONSTRUCTING THE SITE

The work included in this section is as follows (Figure 9–22): (1) preparing site construction design and specifications, (2) soliciting and reviewing site contractors, and (3) constructing the site, phases I and II.

Preparing the Site Construction Designs and Specifications

In many cases where there is a building, a building addition, or building modifications are required, the services of an architect-engineer may be necessary. The work may either be too large or too complex to be handled within the owner's engineering group (if there is one). To avoid misunderstanding with the architect-engineering firm that is to be retained, the owner should provide a list of guidelines, or instructions, to be used by the architect-engineer to submit his proposal. These guidelines should include the owner's concepts of the design and specification work that is to be provided:

- *Owner's representative.* All building construction and/or equipment installation work under contract will be handled for and on behalf of the owner by a representative designated by the owner. (Where the construction manager concept is considered, the representative may be the contracting firm that has been awarded the order. In this event a separate set of instructions will be required on the construction manager's duties and responsibilities.)
- *Scope of services.* The services expected of the architect-engineer shall include:
  - Preparing preliminary designs and layouts (based on owner requirements obtained through provided data and meetings).
  - Preparing the working drawings and specifications.
  - Preparing and issuing proposal forms (with drawings and specifications).
  - Writing and issuing bulletins for added and deleted work.
  - Preparing estimates of cost of construction and for bulletin work.
  - Rendering assistance to contractors and equipment suppliers during the proposal preparation period.
  - Reviewing all shop and detail drawings to determine their compliance with the contract drawings and specifications.
  - Maintaining tracings of the construction drawings to reflect the as-built condition of the work.
  - Rendering assistance to the contractor and equipment supplier during the course of construction by furnishing sketches.

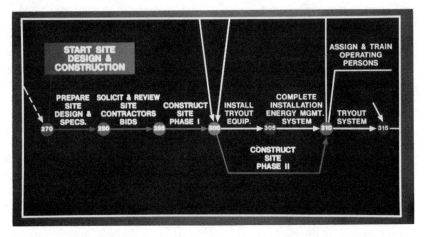

(a)

PROJECT MANAGEMENT   ENERGY MANAGEMENT SYSTEM   SOUTHEAST UNITED STATES
        REPORT TYPE :STANDARD LISTING   PRINTING SEQUENCE :Earliest Activities First
                                                                                                SELECTION CRITERIA ::CS
        PLAN I.D.   :IEMS   VERSION 24   TIME NOW DATE   :12/MAR/84

ACTIVITY DESCRIPTION	EARLIEST START	EARLIEST FINISH	LATEST START	LATEST FINISH	DURATION	FLOAT
:CS PREPARE SITE DES & SPECS	8/OCT/84	30/NOV/84	8/OCT/84	30/NOV/84	40	0 *
:CS SOL & REV SITE CONT BIDS	3/DEC/84	28/DEC/84	3/DEC/84	28/DEC/84	20	0 *
:CS CONST SITE-PHASE 1	31/DEC/84	22/FEB/85	31/DEC/84	22/FEB/85	40	0 *

(b)

PROJECT MANAGEMENT   ENERGY MANAGEMENT SYSTEM   SOUTHEAST UNITED STATES
        REPORT TYPE :COMPRESSED PERIOD BARCHART   PRINTING SEQUENCE :Earliest Activities First
                                                                                                SELECTION CRITERIA ::CS
        PLAN I.D.   :IEMS   VERSION 24   TIME NOW DATE   :12/MAR/84

```
==========================1984=============================1985=====
PERIOD COMMENCING DATE    11212  17  14  12  16  13  11  15  13  17  14  14  11  16  13  11  15   1
MONTH                     1MAR   1MAY 1JUN1JUL 1AUG1SEP 1OCT 1NOV1DEC 1JAN 1FEB1MAR1APR 1MAY1JUN1JUL 1AUG 1
PERIOD COMMENCING TIME UNIT 18 123  148  168 188  11131133 1153 11781198 1223 124312631283 130813281348 1373 1
==================================================================
:CS PREPARE SITE DES & SPECS  1  1   1   1   1   1   1   1  CCC 1CCC 1C   1   1   1   1   1   1   1   1   1
:CS SOL & REV SITE CONT BIDS  1  1   1   1   1   1   1   1   1   1CCCC 1   1   1   1   1   1   1   1   1
:CS CONST SITE-PHASE 1        1  1   1   1   1   1   1   1   1   1CCCC 1CCC 1   1   1   1   1   1   1   1
```

Barchart Key:- CCC :Critical Activities   === :Non Critical Activities   NNN :Activity with neg float ... :Float

(c)

FIGURE 9-22 *Design and construct site* phase: (a) planning diagram; (b) computer-generated schedule; (c) bar chart.

- *Codes and regulations.* The architect-engineer needs to be specifically instructed to prepare the designs, plans, and specifications in accordance with all federal, state, county, and local building and environmental regulations.
- The fee for engineering services is usually based on a percentage of the cost of construction.

Once the architect-engineer's work begins, it should proceed in a sequence that can be defined in these phases:

- *Phase 1:* preliminary engineering
- *Phase 2:* development engineering
- *Phase 3:* follow-up engineering
- *Phase 4:* record engineering

Preliminary engineering represents the data that the architect-engineer will use to substantiate the completed designs and specifications. It will include the owner's design requirements (sometimes referred to as user requirements) that have either been prepared by the owner or developed by the architect-engineer after meetings and discussions with the owner's representatives; specific citing of standard specifications, codes, and other generally accepted regulations that will be used in the development of the designs and specifications; basic assumptions that will be used in preparing designs of specific elements of the project; and rationale for the proper selection of the equipment.

The owner should expect the architect-engineer to provide all the preliminary engineering data in an organized fashion, divided into the various sections of an engineering project: architectural, civil, structural, mechanical, and electrical.

After preliminary engineering has been completed, the *developmental engineering* phase, a continuation of the design analysis that evolves into a set of contract documents, produces a clearly defined package of drawings and specifications that allows for accurate cost estimating and facilitates construction. The contract documents should consist of these sections:

- Proposal form
- General conditions for building construction
- Special requirements
- Construction specifications
- Construction drawings

The proposal form will refer to the work authorized by the contract and for which the funds have been approved. A proposal form will usually include a unit price schedule to be used for additions and deductions from the base bid proposal; alternative proposals from the base proposal; major subcontractors; and cost breakdowns of major sections of the work included in the project. A sample proposal form is shown in Figure 9–23.

The general conditions for building construction include restrictions that the contractor must comply with so that the owner is protected. Pertinent items that are listed in the general conditions are shown in Figure 9–24.

Special requirements supplement the general conditions by including information pertaining to the specific project. A sample of the items included in special requirements is shown in Figure 9–25.

Central Utilities Control System

PF-1
FORM OF PROPOSAL

NAME OF BIDDER _____

ADDRESS_____PHONE_____

DATE _____

PF.01   PROPOSAL:

The Undersigned, hereinafter referred to as the Contractor, proposes to
provide the complete design and furnish all labor, materials, tools,
equipment, and supervision required and to perform all work required for
materials and equipment procurement and installation in connection with
the Central Utilities Control System at the   Plant,
                for the   Company,   ,
hereinafter referred to as the Owner, in strict accordance with the
Owner's General Conditions (for Lump Sum Equipment Installation Contracts, January 19), Drawings, and Specifications as prepared by the
Systems Department and Plant Engineering Department,   Division,
for the lump sum firm price of _____
_____Dollars ($_____).

PF.01A   SCHEDULE OF ALTERNATES:

The Undersigned submits the following alternate prices, giving the
amounts to be added or deducted from the base lump sum proposal amount.
The alternate prices shall include all charges for incidental expenses,
supervision, taxes, insurance, overhead, and profit.

Alternate No. 1

Add to the base proposal all costs associated with the complete design
and installation of the Steam Supply System, including all the required
labor, materials, tools, equipment, and supervision.

                                    Add   _____

PF.02   TIME FOR COMPLETION:

The Undersigned agrees to begin work immediately after notice of award
of contract and to complete all work shown on the Drawings in _____
consecutive calendar days, Sundays and Holidays included, after date
of notice of award of contract.

All engineering and fabrication work, including procurement of pur-
chased components and subcontractor work, if applicable, shall be
scheduled so as to complete installation on or before the completion
date noted below:

    Installation Completion - 4/19/85

FIGURE 9-23 Sample proposal form included in the contract documents.

1. Definitions
2. Examination of premises
3. Surveys
4. Laws, ordinances, and regulations
5. Building permits
6. Taxes
7. Taxes: assigned orders or contracts
8. Alternate, separate, and unit prices
9. Acceptance and rejection of proposals
10. Specifications
11. Specifications and drawings to be cooperative
12. Signed plans and specifications
13. Number of working drawings and specifications
14. Assignment and subletting of contract
15. Review of contractor's drawings
16. Owner's options
17. Approval of equipment and material manufacturers
18. Samples to be submitted
19. Tests
20. Measurement and fitting of parts
21. Inspection of work away from premises
22. Quality of materials and workmanship
23. Delivery of materials
24. Removal of unfit units
25. Moving materials
26. Accident prevention
27. Explosives
28. Fire precautions and protection
29. Liability insurance
30. Owner's and contractor's responsibilities: fire and certain other risks
31. Contractor's responsibility for personal injuries and property damage
32. Contractor's responsibility: other risks
33. Progress schedule and time of completion
34. Contractor responsible for coordination and quality of work
35. Priority of items of work
36. Delays and extensions of time
37. Acceleration of work
38. Contractor's superintendent
39. Assistance by resident engineer or architect-engineer
40. Cooperation
41. Contractor to assist owner
42. Contractor's meetings
43. Installation of owner's equipment and machines
44. Alterations and additions
45. Patents
46. Performance bond
47. Liens
48. Schedule of prices and allocation of owner's cost
49. Contractor's payment requests
50. Payments to contractor
51. Patching and replacing of damaged work
52. Glass damage
53. Contractor's default
54. Suspension of operations
55. Termination by owner
56. Cleaning of premises
57. Guarantee

FIGURE 9-24 General conditions/items included in the contract documents.

Central Utilities Control System

100.00-1
SPECIAL REQUIREMENTS

100.01   GENERAL NOTE:

The provisions of the   Company "General Conditions for Lump Sum
Equipment Installation Contracts" bound herewith form a part of the following Specifications, and the Contractor shall consult them in detail for
instructions pertaining to the work.

In the event of a conflict between provisions of the ■General Conditions■
and provisions of the "Special Requirements," those of the "Special
Requirements" will take precedence.

100.02   DRAWINGS AND DATA SHEETS:

The accompanying drawings and the attached data sheets form a part of these
Specifications and all work mentioned or indicated thereon in any manner
shall be performed as though it were written out and described under the
various headings of this Specification.

100.03   SCOPE OF WORK:

The work contemplated by these Specifications consists of furnishing all
labor, material, equipment, and services required for providing a complete
system of central utilities control for the   Plant,
           for the   Company,   . The control
system shall provide monitoring, indication, and operation of equipment and
systems as hereinafter specified and scheduled and shall include all acces-
sories, appurtenances, and incidental items required for the completion of
same, even though such items are not specifically shown or mentioned herein.
It is the intent of these Specifications to provide a central utilities
control system that will accomplish not only those functions required at
this time, but shall also permit future additions.

Contractor shall be responsible for, but not limited to, the following:

1. The furnishing of all materials, equipment, and labor of every kind
    required to carry out the intent of the Drawings, Data Sheets, and
    Specifications. Where it is not specifically indicated, materials
    and equipment are to be furnished by this Contractor.

2. The quality and sufficiency of all materials so furnished.

3. All mechanical and control piping, conduit, wire and cable, panels,
    etc., necessary to provide a completed installation.

4. Preparation of all drawings, details, and specifications necessary for
    the installation and connection of all equipment.

5. Central Utilities Control System engineering as required to insure
    successful completion of the project.

FIGURE 9-25 Sample page of special requirements items included in the contract
documents.

The *follow-up engineering* phase is especially important for the architect-engineer, as he now has the opportunity to review and check the contract documents as they are being released to contractors for bidding purposes. During bidding the architect-engineer can issue *addenda,* which are formal notifications to the bidders that the plans and specifications have been revised (additions or deletions have been made) and the bidders must reflect these in their proposals.

Once the contract has been awarded and work has begun, the architect-engineer will notify the contractor of additions, deletions, or revisions to the work through the issuance of bulletins. A bulletin is not an order to proceed with the revised work, but the beginning of the procedure for the work to be done. As every construction job inevitably requires some changes, usually more than expected, the bulletin procedure provides a means of maintaining control of the timing and costs of the added or revised work. Preparing bulletins to the contract documents should follow this procedure:

1. State very briefly the subject or title.
2. Describe the changes in the work to be done.
3. State the reason for the changes to the work. (The reason "required by owner" is not adequate.)
4. Include supplementary material and equipment specifications as required.
5. Specify when changes to drawings do not change the scope of work.
6. Identify each drawing to be released as part of the bulletin.
7. Identify the changes on a drawing in some fashion, such as a heavy ring around the changed sections drawn on the reverse side of the drawing.
8. Request the contractor to submit a proposal to perform the work.

The *record engineering* phase is the final place where the architect-engineer documents the project. Submitted to the owner, the document will contain statistics of the facility, such as square-foot area of manufacturing and administration.

Soliciting and Reviewing the Site Contractors' Bids

The procedure followed is essentially the same as soliciting and reviewing equipment suppliers' proposals as well as proposals received from the equipment installation contractors.

Proposals for construction contracts will usually contain a lump sum amount for the total project, with added detail of each subcontractor's proposal. It is most interesting to observe, on many occasions, that the same subcontractor will provide different bids to the respective contractors, suggesting they play favorites. When the range of bids that are submitted are close, each contractor is invited to review his proposal so that any disparity of thought among the contractors can be known, in order to provide a proposal of common understanding. Contractors who may have provided proposals based on a misunderstanding may be asked to resubmit their proposal.

Constructing the Site

Many textbooks on construction are available that outline procedures the contractors follow to ensure that construction work progresses in an orderly fashion. This section concentrates more on the owner/contractor relationship. The owner is interested in project status, and the contractor will usually report monthly. (Reporting of this type has been discussed in previous sections.) Daily progress reports allow the owner to follow the contractors' work on a more current basis; consequently, the monthly report places the daily progress reports in the proper perspective: contractors with their work force, descriptions of work under way, and problems being encountered on the job. A sample progress report is shown in Figure 9–26.

Although contractors may be diligent and efficient on the construction site, actual progress may depend on the timely delivery of material and equipment. In previous sections of the book we sounded a note of caution regarding suppliers' weaknesses and methods used to control their delivery promises. Now it is up to the contractor and the owner's representative to ensure timely deliveries. One expedient is to prepare and maintain an up-to-date material and equipment status report. Figure 9–27 illustrates a typical report that the owner can use.

Extra work is a reality on construction projects. Changes in field conditions, discrepancies in the engineering drawings, and modified equipment details can create additional work for which the contractor will require funds over the stated contract lump sum figure. An astute owner will maintain a procedure to control disbursement of these kinds of extra costs. This same owner will have forecast added funds, and a specific amount will be included in the authorized project spending amount. The owner needs to set up a cost procedure so that all funds spent are within the authorized project amount. Some control expedients are as follows:

- The contractor must make a written notice of a claim for increased compensation for alterations or additions to the original order before there will be any consideration by the owner.
- The contractor must show all additions or deletions from the contracted work through the use of bulletins and field authorities.
- Before beginning any alteration or additional work on the original order, the contractor must receive a written order to proceed from the owner in the form of a purchase order amendment.

The contractor will submit to the owner a monthly status report of the additions and deletions that have been authorized. The status report should follow this format:

Daily Report on Progress of Building

Location_____   DATE_____
                                               WEATHER_____
Building_____Job No._____   TEMP._____

CONTRACTORS	NO. MEN	CONTRACTORS	NO. MEN

REMARKS—State in full progress of work.

_____
_____
_____
_____
_____
_____
_____
_____
_____
_____
_____
_____
_____
_____
_____
_____
_____
_____
_____
_____
_____
_____
_____
_____
_____

DELINQUENT CONTRACTORS—State in full when notified to be on job, etc.

_____
_____

DRAWINGS REQUIRED
_____

RECEIVED DRAWINGS | RECEIVED BULLETINS
_____

                              RES. ENGINEER_____

RES. ENGINEER TO HAND REPORT TO OFFICE EACH NIGHT.   KEEP CARBON COPY IN BOOK ON JOB.
TURN IN ON COMPLETION.   UNDER DELINQUENTS, MENTION IN ADVANCE WHEN CONTRACTOR AND
MATERIALS SHOULD ARRIVE AT JOB ACCORDING TO SCHEDULE.

FIGURE 9–26 Daily progress report: contractor status.

PROJECT MATERIAL AND EQUIPMENT STATUS REPORT

PROJECT TITLE _____ TRADE _____ DATE _____

| MATERIAL OR EQUIPMENT | VENDOR, P.O. NO. AND DATE | DATE REQUIRED | DRAWINGS TO A-E | | SCHEDULED DELIVERY DATE | DATE CHECKED* | % OF MATERIAL DELIVERED | REMARKS |
			SUBMITTED	APPROVED				

FIGURE 9-27   Project material and equipment report.

FIELD AUTHORITY/BULLETIN

No.	RECEIVED (DATE)	RETURNED (WITH QUOTE) (DATE)	APPROVED (DATE)

The most important ingredient in maintaining a report procedure is awareness. A contractor who becomes aware that the owner, through these reports, exerts such an effort to see that his project will be completed on time and within budget will make the necessary effort to fulfill the owner's wishes.

- The supplier will guarantee all work against defective material and workmanship for a specified period after completion of the work and acceptance by the owner.
- The supplier, at his own expense, will correct the defective material and workmanship.
- The supplier will submit a complete set of drawings, specifically fire protection details, to the owner for the necessary approval prior to the start of installation.

- The supplier will perform all fire protection work in compliance with the owner's fire underwriters.
- The supplier will include in his original proposal the cost of any premium or overtime that is required to meet the completion date.
- The supplier will provide unit prices for extra work that may be required.

TRYING OUT AND LAUNCHING THE SYSTEM

There are several important activities that contribute to the successful launching of an energy management system. Launching is the phase of the project that recognizes the need for a certain period of time to elapse before a system can be considered ready for successful operation. The activities associated with the tryout and launch are as follows (Figure 9-28): (1) assigning and training personnel, (2) completing installation of the energy management system, (3) trying out the system, (4) launching the system, and (5) phasing out the present system.

Tryout and launch can also be described as the *startup* of operation. Proper startup refers to the planned sequences of equipment testing, balancing of the systems, and their final acceptance, when applicable. The startup process will be completed in various stages over a period of time, the length of which is dependent on the complexity and the scope of the project.

As the startup is actually the first stage of operation, careful thought needs to be given to selecting a "team leader" to direct this process. For a successful operation there will need to be a plan and schedule for coordinating the people and equipment used for the startup. With startup being one of the last phases to be completed in a project, its plan and schedule become all the more important, to be certain that, due to delays of prior phases, there will be no imposed "shortcuts" in the startup process that may create problems when operations begin.

Assigning and Training Personnel

The plan needs to provide timely selection and training of personnel, who are essential to startup as well as through the launching period. For training, substantial completion of the startup manuals is necessary. Startup manuals are essentially a tool to familiarize operating and maintenance personnel with the new system and represent the communication link with the persons who have designed and installed the system.

Assigning qualified personnel for the operation of an energy management system begins the preparation of operating and maintenance manuals as early as possible to allow as much time as necessary for adequate training. This is a valuable form of documentation that becomes used not only for training but also as a reference for operators and maintenance personnel when operations are under way. The manuals will be organized in such a manner that there will be separate volumes for each

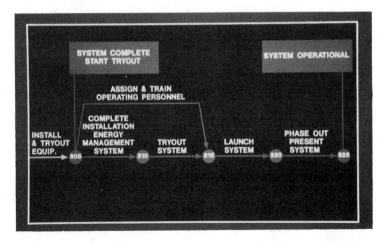

(a)

PROJECT MANAGEMENT		ENERGY MANAGEMENT SYSTEM			SOUTHEAST UNITED STATES		
REPORT TYPE :STANDARD LISTING				PRINTING SEQUENCE :Earliest Activities First			
				SELECTION CRITERIA ::LS			
PLAN I.D. :IEMS VERSION 24				TIME NOW DATE :12/MAR/84			
ACTIVITY DESCRIPTION	EARLIEST START	EARLIEST FINISH	LATEST START	LATEST FINISH	DURATION	FLOAT	
:LS COMPLETE INST EMS	22/APR/85	17/MAY/85	22/APR/85	17/MAY/85	20	0 *	
:LS ASSIGN & TRAIN OPERATING PERSONNEL	22/APR/85	17/MAY/85	20/MAY/85	14/JUN/85	20	20	
:LS TRYOUT SYSTEM	20/MAY/85	14/JUN/85	20/MAY/85	14/JUN/85	20	0 *	
:LS LAUNCH SYSTEM	17/JUN/85	12/JUL/85	17/JUN/85	12/JUL/85	20	0 *	
:LS PHASE OUT PRESENT SYSTEM	15/JUL/85	9/AUG/85	15/JUL/85	9/AUG/85	20	0 *	

(b)

```
PROJECT MANAGEMENT                     ENERGY MANAGEMENT SYSTEM                        SOUTHEAST UNITED STATES
     REPORT TYPE :COMPRESSED PERIOD BARCHART                   PRINTING SEQUENCE  :Earliest Activities First
                                                               SELECTION CRITERIA ::LS
     PLAN I.D.   :IEMS     VERSION 24                          TIME NOW DATE     :12/MAR/84
=======================================1984==================================1985====================================
                                  11212   17  14  12   16  13   11   15  13   17   14  14  11    16  13  11    15   1
PERIOD COMMENCING DATE
MONTH                             1MAR   1MAY 1JUN 1JUL 1AUG 1SEP 1OCT 1NOV 1DEC 1JAN 1FEB 1MAR 1APR  1MAY 1JUN 1JUL 1AUG 1
PERIOD COMMENCING TIME UNIT       18 123  148  168 188  11131133 1153 11781198 1223 12431263 1283  130813281348 1373 1
=====================================================================================================================
:LS COMPLETE INST EMS             1  1   1    1   1    1   1    1    1   1    1    1    1   1     CCICC 1   1    1    1
:LS ASSIGN & TRAIN OPERATING PERSONNEL 1  1   1   1   1    1   1    1    1   1    1    1    1   1    ==1==.1.. 1   1    1
:LS TRYOUT SYSTEM                 1  1   1    1   1    1   1    1    1   1    1    1    1   1     1 CCICC 1   1    1
:LS LAUNCH SYSTEM                 1  1   1    1   1    1   1    1    1   1    1    1    1   1     1   1 C1CCC 1    1
:LS PHASE OUT PRESENT SYSTEM      1  1   1    1   1    1   1    1    1   1    1    1    1   1     1   1   1 CCICC  1
=====================================================================================================================
Barchart Key:- CCC :Critical Activities  === :Non Critical Activities  NNN :Activity with neg float  ... :Float
```

(c)

FIGURE 9-28 *Tryout and launch system* phase: (a) planning diagram; (b) computer-generated schedule; (c) bar chart.

major energy subsystem, and separate sections within each volume for the equipment used in operating the system.

- Use three ring binders that allow for insertion of added material or removal of outdated data or data not usable because of changes.
- As this material will be used over a number of years and by a number of people, use good quality binders and paper. Consider the use of plastic protection sheets for information that is expected to be referred to frequently.
- In the instruction portion of the manuals, use clear, short, directive sentences. Leave no room for misinterpretation, and tailor the instructions to the education and skills of the staff.
- As technical specifications are complex, deriving the basic instructions for the manual must follow these steps:
  - What to do
  - When to do it
  - How to do it
  - Why to do it

There are several types of manuals to be developed to satisfy the various phases of the project and operation as well as the various disciplines that will use these manuals. There are startup manuals, operations manuals, and maintenance manuals.

Startup procedures that are carefully prepared and used will be of great benefit, as the time between completion of the tryout period and actual operation (completion of the launch period) will be reduced. Startups using adequate startup manuals for training personnel with well-planned sequences of system tryout, including balancing and testing of components, will accrue definite savings. An organized approach to beginning the system on-line is documented in the startup manual.

The first part of startup manuals, which contains the startup plan of action, provides the reader with some assurance that the startup was thought through (similar to the theme set up for the total project). Startup manuals supplement the design drawings and specifications and complement the operating and maintenance manuals. They are especially important to prepare for automated (computer-controlled) energy management systems.

Operating and maintenance manuals will include a separate section (chapter) for each energy system. Each chapter describing the energy system will include these subsections:

- Introduction
- Table of contents
- Description of the system
  - Engineering data
  - Flow diagrams
- Startup procedures

- Operational procedures
  - Operation sequences
  - Emergency procedures
- Maintenance
  - Preventive maintenance
  - Corrective maintenance
  - Troubleshooting procedures
  - Special maintenance requirements
  - Manufacturers' literature
  - Shop drawings
  - Spare parts list
- Record filing system

Important for the use of the manual is a final and complete set of "as-built" drawings that show all construction, fixed equipment, and mechanical and electrical supply and distribution systems.

To ensure that these manuals are practical and will be used (as they can readily become too complex and difficult to use), there needs to be understanding that they serve two distinct functions:

1. Instruction manual
2. Technical reference

The instruction manual outlines the specific work efforts: *what* to do, *when* to do it, *how* to do it, and *why* to do it. The technical reference includes equipment and systems, description, design criteria, operation and maintenance sequences, major maintenance overhaul details, parts lists, and equipment repair history.

The manuals need to emphasize the importance of the business of record keeping, specifically the equipment repair history. Important to maintaining a high rate of "uptime" of the system is the knowledge gained of the dates and times, past records of inspection (including the lubrication); dates and times (including costs) of maintenance and repairs; and visits by manufacturer representatives concerning equipment problems. All information needs to be recorded in a well-organized and readily usable format. Verbal transmittal of operating and maintenance events is of little value and is an ineffective way of communicating with management and other plant personnel.

Completing Installation of the Energy Management System

When the installation and tryout of the equipment are essentially completed, there will be certain parts of the system that may not be complete. There may be additional sensors required, there may be some redundancy in the functions of certain equipment, or there may be specific equipment components that are not functioning as expected. A specific length of time is allotted in the plan for procurement as well as installation and subsequent tryout of the new components. Starting up before the revisions are made (and there may be pressures to do so) will cause eventual problems. It could be as serious as causing a shutdown of the operation, even though it is understood that this may eventually occur. An even more serious situation is that the system will be operating inefficiently, with frequent shutdowns to make maintenance corrections.

It may be beneficial to assign the persons who will be operating and maintaining the system during the final stages of this activity. If there appear to be specific problem areas where new components are being ordered and installed, and there is a chance that the problems will recur, worthwhile experience may be gained during the equipment procurement and installation phase when equipment tryout was completed.

The basic difference is the timing associated with monitoring progress. Arrangements should be made to monitor progress and compare it to the plan on a daily basis. To effect such an arrangement requires considerable planning. All persons associated with the project need to be informed, from plant management to the maintenance and operating personnel. Plant management should be informed weekly of the present status and the major problems. These problems may concern personnel. Informing personnel who may feel that their jobs may be in peril is important. This may actually determine the eventual successful operation of the system. An actual experience of the author when installing a utilities monitoring and control system (years before the term *energy management system* was used to describe the system) demonstrates the consequences very vividly. The plant service personnel were not told that there would be a reduction in force once the control system became operable. Deliberate "slowdowns" during tryout and during operations resulted in the entire system not achieving all the savings that were expected.

Meetings need to be held daily. Separate meetings with specific personnel are preferable to a group meeting that encompasses all personnel involved in launching objectives.

Activity	Participants
Discuss status of jobs and work to be performed	Maintenance and operating personnel
Discuss status of total project and specific jobs; set plans for the jobs of the immediate future	Maintenance and operating supervisors, technical staff (task force), contractors
Lay out work plan, identify personnel needs for next three days, resolve safety concerns	Technical staff, plant supervision, contractors

At this time the leadership may change from the startup leader to the person who will be responsible for operating the system. In most instances this person may be responsible for both activities. In any event, the person responsible must also have the authority to keep the work on schedule in accordance with the plan, so as to avoid outside pressures and interferences relating to the operation of the system.

Phasing Out the Present System

The most effective way to get the energy management system into a routine operation (i.e., it becomes part of the plant's daily operation) is to successfully phase in specific sections. To determine what section to phase in initially can be based on several considerations: ease of phasing in the operation, amount of savings to be realized, and importance to overall performance of plant.

A specific plan for the phase-in should be developed and be implemented by the technical specialists together with any of the supplier experts who will devote full time in the plant to making the system operable.

The system becomes operable by gradually shifting responsibility to plant personnel by initiating them with the preparation of routine daily logs, routine inspections, and preventive maintenance programs. Outstanding problem lists will also be turned over.

At the conclusion of the project the task force should prepare a summary report that can be used as a reference for similar projects that may be planned in the future for other locations. The report should list recommendations, contain suggestions for improvement over the present system, and identify the performance of the equipment and controls. It is most important to prepare the report immediately after completing the project (or each phase), while the details are still vivid in the minds of the task force.

EXERCISES

1. Name the six general steps in the development of the feasibility report.
2. Once project approval for a facility program is obtained, what major phases of the work are yet to be completed?
3. The present network plan for the energy management system shows a description of the milestones but does not include dates for the start or completion of the milestones. From the computer reports already developed, complete the following tabulation of milestones and dates:

MILESTONE	DATE
Start plan of action	March 13, 1989
Start audit	April 17, 1989

(cont.)

MILESTONE	DATE
————	——
————	——
————	——
.	.
.	.
.	.
System operational	——

4. It may be necessary to develop a complete timing schedule before Exercise 3 can be completed. *Note:* The bar charts that are shown in this chapter may not be accurate enough to use. If this situation exists, prepare the necessary computer reports showing earliest and latest start times, and earliest and latest finish times for this program.

5. One of the major concerns that the task force leader will encounter is the number of skilled personnel available to conduct the audit phase. Assume that you take the role of the task force leader in this situation:
   - There are *three* mechanical engineers and *two* electrical engineers available for the audit phase.
   - You have to accept the durations shown in this chapter for each of the activities that make up the audit phase.
   - The established start date of the audit phase is April 17, 1989; the completion date is May 26, 1989.

   (a) You are to develop a personnel loading schedule in accordance with the foregoing parameters. Your instructions are to minimize overtime requirements. *Hint:* Prepare personnel/labor histograms and resource summaries from the computer software package to support your answer.

   (b) Since management absolutely forbids overtime, develop your options and supporting documents to arrive at the best solution.

Appendix A
Critique

The Waste Heat Recovery Project presents itself as being successfully completed as far as the project personnel who participated in its implementation are concerned. The lessons learned from a successful project should be communicated to persons, for various reasons, through documentation.

PROJECT DOCUMENTATION

A project report as outlined in Chapter 1 is considered an important communication expedient. It can also be a good method for those associated with the project to document the project and its accomplishments. Documentation should cover these features:

- Summary
- Project plan (with a planned schedule and an organization)
- Project control
- Project costs
- Labor utilization

Documentation of the Waste Heat Recovery Project can be of value for several reasons:

- It can serve as a training guide for other personnel who are to be oriented in project management techniques.

- It can be used discretely as a vehicle for "self-promotion"—not necessarily to diminish anyone else's contribution, just not to minimize yours.

The desire to get on with the next project is usually uppermost on the minds of project personnel, and the need to document the previous project may not seem that important. However, there could be any number of reasons to document other than those that preserve the reputation of the project personnel:

- Time delays that are attributed to suppliers, weather conditions, and so on.
- Cost overruns caused by initial financial decisions, or changes made during the project through added requirements

Waste Heat Recovery Project. To test whether this project was successful, these rules need to be followed:

1. *The basis for this project is sound.* The feasibility report proved that substantial energy savings can be realized through the installation of a waste heat recovery system.

2. *There is a clear plan with objectives to terminate the project.* Each of the major completion milestones—researching various systems, design and procure equipment, installation—were established with a practical schedule based on previous experience and suppliers' delivery dates.

3. *The project organization with its project manager are qualified.* The project manager, with his appointed engineers and members of the management team, developed the detailed plan and schedule at the start of the project which provided for selection and training of operating personnel early in the project and were considered important activities of the project.

4. *Definition of project items are adequate.* The discipline used by the project personnel to document a description of all project items allowed for a check for adequacy, duplicity, and redundancy. Estimated costs for each item were based on these descriptions.

5. *Management techniques that are applied are appropriate.* Network analysis was used for planning and scheduling; management by objectives and management by exception were applied for project control; cost analysis techniques included the indicated cost outcome method for project cost control; and computer analysis was used in the resource-leveling process.

6. *There is more than "lip service" support required from company management.* Patience practiced by management at the start of the project while the planning process was being developed helped a great deal in achieving the success of the project—its objectives in time, cost, and resources were met. Financial support was provided when project control improvements required added software effort.

PROJECT PLAN

The first step in planning a project is to state the objectives clearly so that the project can start off on the right track.

- Define the purpose for pursuing the project.
- Define the scope of the project.
- State the expected results of the project.

Waste Heat Recovery Project. The main intent of this project is to reduce the energy costs in operating this manufacturing plant. Through a feasibility study, a project was formulated to design and install a waste heat recovery system that redirects the flue gases from the furnace stack to operate a steam boiler. The engineers and assigned members of a management team will, in addition to developing this project, study this application for future installations.

The project start for the Phase II Waste Heat Recovery Project is scheduled for October 3, 1988, and the system would be ready to begin operations on April 24, 1989. After a one-month launching period, this system is expected to save fuel costs at a yearly rate of $200,000.

The project required these major tasks: researching various heat recovery systems; designing and installing the system; procuring equipment; and selecting and training operating supervision and personnel. In addition, this project was assigned the task of initiating the implementation of the phase II system.

The following planned schedule was implemented:

Activity	Scheduled Date
Complete organization	November 14, 1988
Complete researching systems	January 30, 1989
Complete equipment procurement	March 13, 1989
Complete installation	April 25, 1989

There are several points to remember when preparing a plan:

- Early planning is the key to a successful project. It is advantageous to assign a full-time manager to projects early, to develop procedures and plan the required tools, facilities, and equipment; develop the site and home office organization; develop a personnel and labor plan; review designs; estimate the project budget; and prepare the master project schedule and the detail schedule.

- Plan the project so that there is a balance between cost and time, and avoid excesses in labor, equipment, and any other required resources.
- A graphical portrayal of the plans for carrying out the work has proved to be the most effective planning expedient.
- Plan and schedule on the basis of past experience on similar projects. It will be necessary to replan and reschedule continually because of unexpected delays or progress.
- Develop a *workable plan* of the project work items that make up the project, including a description of their interrelationships; *schedule* these activities in an acceptable time span; and *control* the conduct of the scheduled work.
- One should *first plan* the work and *then work* the plan.

PROJECT ORGANIZATION

As soon as management has approved the project, a task force or project organization should be formed to implement the project. The first step is to select a project manager (or leader) and define his or her responsibilities. As is the case in many projects, this project manager may initially be the task force leader who had directed the project feasibility study to completion, then the project to completion, and finally will assume responsibility as the operating manager, as is the situation in the Waste Heat Recovery Project. As project manager, this person will be required to form an organization that will assist him or her in fulfilling these responsibilities:

- Formulating the plan.
- Designing and installing the system.
- Reviewing progress against schedule.
- Monitoring project cost performance. (Normally, project costs were developed during the feasibility phase, and since these costs were the basis of establishing feasibility, they will be considered the project budget.)

Waste Heat Recovery Project. The project manager, who would also become the operating manager, was advised that four engineers and six members of a special management team would be assigned to his task force. For other projects, the project manager may assume the responsibility of determining the number and types of skills required based on the project needs; however, for this project, prior investigation by those who conducted the feasibility study recommended this task force. (It should be pointed out that had the project plan for the Waste Heat Recovery Project been completed concurrent with the feasibility report, more consideration would probably have been given to the task force requirements.) The weaknesses of not having completed a thorough project plan will be evident when reviewing the personnel allocation for the Waste Heat Recovery Project.

PROJECT TIME AND COST CONTROL

From the time objectives and from determining the tasks needed to complete the project, members of the task force established estimates for each of the project items. The most effective method to establish time (as well as cost) is to receive commitments from each of those persons (or departments) that have been assigned responsibility for the completion of their respective tasks. There must be a commitment from those participating in this project.

Once the overall schedule was established, there are review meetings to check progress against schedule. Control must be firm, especially at the beginning of a project, when the tone of the entire project is invariably set. The "early warning system" of the network planning technique allows for immediate corrective action as delays become evident.

Providing status reports that document the review meeting are an absolute necessity to inform all the participants, the owners, and/or management of the project progress. The report needs to be clear and concise, highlighting the problem areas and what is being done to correct the problem. Placing too much detail in the management summary report defeats the purpose of providing the necessary information.

Project Time for the Waste Heat Recovery Project. The project team published a status report that consisted of a cover letter, executive highlights, and a status summary.

- *Cover letter.* Addressed to participants and other interested persons, the letter briefly states the purpose of the report. Overall project status and a summary of key concerns with recommendations are also included.
- *Highlights.* Accompanying the cover letter is a list of the key items that affect the progress of the project. The highlights (one page) are listed in bullet (•) form.
- *Status summary.* Half of this page is a graphic portrayal (bar chart) of the progress; the bottom half explains the "exception" items and itemizes the key milestones.

The status review at the end of week 20 revealed that the Waste Heat Recovery Project was 2 weeks behind its planned schedule of 29 weeks. Immediate corrective measures were implemented that permitted the project to be completed on schedule. The status report was a useful "tool" as management was informed through the report of the proposed corrective measures, and approved them as they affected the operating procedures of various departments, all in adequate time for implementation.

Project cost control follows the same pattern as the techniques that were applied in controlling time. Setting costs became the responsibility of the department that established the timing. In similar fashion, keeping within the budgeted costs requires as much attention whether it is an entire department budget or individual project items. Periodic cost reviews are held at the same frequency as project timing reviews and are frequently held at the same session.

Cost Control for the Waste Heat Recovery Project. The project team prepared an Indicated Cost Outcome Report that compares the budgeted costs of the project with potential costs (or indicated costs). At the end of week 15, the accounting department provided a record of the committed expenditures-to-date to the project team, who added the projected costs to arrive at the indicated cost. The week 15 review showed a potential cost overrun of $12,500. The project team evaluated the overrun in the following manner:

- Week 15 is about halfway through the project
- The overrun trend suggests an overrun of over 10% by the end of the project.
- As a 10% overrun is the limit imposed on project costs, the project team recommended immediate changes in the project to reduce the overrun appreciably.

Continued periodic cost reviews kept those responsible cognizant of the project cost implications. The disciplines installed permitted the authorized (or budgeted) costs to be met at the completion of the project.

LABOR UTILIZATION

Although the implementation of the Waste Heat Recovery Project is, for the most part, to be completed by suppliers and outside contractors, there appeared to be a lack of personnel, engineers, and members of the management team to supervise and coordinate the project. Using the resource-leveling computer programs during the planning process, the engineer and management team requirements were determined and compared using the following representative schedules:

- Early start
- Late start

As the early and late start schedules revealed greater personnel requirements than were available, the planned duration was allowed to extend to the date when *available* personnel met the number of *required* personnel. After reviewing the options, it was decided that the planned project completion date would be held. This date could be held by having the available personnel work additional hours when necessary.

Gilmore Equipment Installation Project

Gilmore Industries' Board of Directors approved a program in the amount of $483,200 to expand the paint finishing line of their fabricating plant. The expansion will also require a building addition to accommodate added storage requirements. The board directed Gilmore management to complete this program by March 15, 1983, contingent on the engineers starting the design of the equipment on October 4, 1982.

Production will need to resume again on March 15, 1983, and to help ensure this completion date, Gilmore has requested M&A, an industrial engineering and contracting firm, to prepare a plan of action as quickly as possible. (Subsequently, M&A was awarded a contract to design, construct, and install this facility.)

In the plan of action, M&A recommended that the critical equipment items requiring a longer delivery time (or long lead) be placed on order prior to completion of all the design and the associated details. Although M&A explained that placing orders for the long-lead equipment without a complete specification package may incur added procurement costs, there is a good chance that this approach will help in completing the project as planned.

M&A also recommended that the building addition be given special attention and that its design and construction be so arranged that the installation of equipment can start before the building is completed. They recommended further that the building construction contractor "close in" the building as the first priority to allow installation to start as early as possible.

The plan of action, as submitted by M&A, convinced Gilmore management that if the plan is followed, this project can be completed on time and within budget. M&A was instructed to proceed.

PLANNING THE INSTALLATION

M&A provided a detailed plan of action to satisfy Gilmore Industries that the completion date of this project would be met. For the planning and scheduling of the project to proceed in proper sequence, M&A developed the following steps for the planning phase:

1. *Establish objectives.* The requirements that motivated the project will determine the objectives. Interim objectives are significant in meeting the main objectives. These interim objectives are established after a preliminary plan has been developed.

2. *Develop a plan.* M&A will list all the jobs (or activities) that have to be done to complete the job. These jobs are then delineated after the jobs necessary to complete the project were decided upon and the relations between them are determined. As this involves an analysis of each job, it will be necessary to determine which jobs precede and succeed the other jobs in the project, and which jobs can be accomplished concurrently.

3. *Prepare a planning diagram.* This is the final step in the planning phase when the work sequence is portrayed in a network (or planning) diagram. The portrayal will reflect the planning work that has listed the jobs to be done, divided them into groups representing major sections of the project, and then determined their interrelationships.

There are computer software programs that will graphically portray the planning phase after all of the foregoing work has been completed. However, these computer graphics are not too effective for use as a planning tool for the project planner at the present time, but it is only a matter of time when computer graphics can replace the "hand-drawn" diagrams that tend to customize the project plan in graphic form.

Although the procedure summarized may vary to some degree, M&A provided instructions to their personnel to detail the job as follows:

1. *Establish objectives.* As the initial effort, M&A concentrates on establishing the major objectives of this project. Then objectives are documented as shown in Figure B–1 and become the basis for developing the work that needs to be done to complete the project. After preparing these objectives, M&A will contact those within Gilmore Industries and their firm to review and approve these objectives before proceeding to the next step in the planning process.

2. *Identify project jobs (or activities).* Proper listing of all the work required to accomplish the project is very important to the success of the plans and the planning diagram. For successful implementation of the project, M&A knows that it is vital that the jobs that contribute to the completion of this project are accounted for, and encompass all phases of the work. Major

Activity	Date
Start project: start equipment design	October 4, 1982
Complete "close in" of building: phase I	December 31, 1982
Complete initial deliveries at building site	January 14, 1983

Start production on new line:
  contain program within authorized
  budget of $483,200
	March 25, 1983

FIGURE B-1 Major objectives for the Gilmore Equipment Installation Project.

omissions will cause inaccuracies in scheduling and could possibly result in failure to complete the project on time. When M&A personnel completed the job description list of the major phases of the Gilmore Installation Project, they also included a summary description to facilitate review and approvals by all those involved in this project. The list with the accompanying descriptions is developed by those personnel who are knowledgeable and who will be actively engaged in this project. The jobs and the accompanying descriptions are shown in Figure B-2.

Work Item	Description
Design production equipment	Design equipment based on process parameters, production rates
Prepare equipment detail drawings	From designs, prepare component and assembly drawings, bills of materials
Prepare equipment installation drawings	Prepare drawings for foundations, anchoring, mechanical and electrical systems
Remove existing equipment	Disconnect electrical and mechanical services, remove equipment from site
Prepare site	Make necessary site improvements including excavation, grading, roadways, underground piping

FIGURE B-2 Major activities with descriptions for the Gilmore Equipment Installation Project.

Design building	Prepare construction drawings for building structure, mechanical and electrical services
Construct building: phase I	Erect building structure to accept equipment installation
Construct building: phase II	Install mechanical and electrical services to complete equipment installation
Fabricate equipment (in shop)	Perform tooling, machining of equipment components in accordance with detail drawings
Procure long-lead equipment items	Place advance orders for equipment with long delivery dates, fabricate and deliver to site
Procure ancillary equipment	Place orders for equipment conveyors and motors, fabricate and deliver to site.
Assemble equipment (in shop)	Assemble components and deliver to site
Install equipment: phase I	Place new equipment on location, anchor, and set in place; install ancillary equipment
Install equipment: phase II	Connect mechanical and electrical services, install controls, install long-lead equipment
Develop operating procedures	Prepare operating schedules, production rates
Select and train personnel	Review personnel résumés, organize training classes for equipment operation
Debug equipment	Test equipment performance, tolerances
Develop and design automatic controls	Select desired operational sequence and design control system
Select controls supplier	Receive suppliers proposals, evaluate, and award contract
Fabricate and assemble controls package	Build components, assemble, and ship controls package to site

FIGURE B-2 (*Continued*)

3. *Group jobs into major sections of work.* To assist in establishing the relations between jobs, M&A divided the project into groups of closely related functions under the categories of work to be performed. (This is an optional expedient that can be helpful when the project is complex and lengthy. It is also helpful to break up the major sections for implementing the cost

control procedures.) The major sections of work in the Gilmore Installation Project are shown in Figure B–3.

4. *Determine relations between activities.* Establishing the relations for the project activities generally involves a substantial amount of discussion with the responsible parties. The success of these discussions becomes evident

---

Major Sections of Work

Equipment

- Design production equipment
- Prepare design details.
- Fabricate equipment (in shop).
- Assemble equipment (in shop).
- Install equipment: phase I.
- Install equipment: phase II.
- Debug equipment.
- Procure long-lead equipment.
- Procure ancillary equipment.

Building

- Design building.
- Construct building: phase I.
- Construct building: phase II.

Site

- Prepare equipment installation drawings.
- Remove existing equipment.
- Prepare site.

Controls

- Develop and design automatic controls.
- Select controls supplier.
- Fabricate and assemble controls.

Personnel

- Develop operating procedures.
- Select and train personnel.

FIGURE B–3 Major sections of work in the Gilmore Equipment Installation Project.

when the activities are connected in the planning diagram. The resulting agreement on the flow of work should promote understanding of how various efforts and responsibilities tie together in the overall project.

5. *Draw subdiagrams and prepare planning diagram.* At the same time that M&A are determining the relations between the project jobs, they are preparing a number of subdiagrams of the major work sections. They have found from experience that combining the relationships of the project activities with the subdiagrams, through a step-by-step procedure, becomes useful in forming the complete planning diagram. This procedure is illustrated by displaying the first and the final subdiagrams as shown in Figure B–4.

M&A prepared several diagrams, one shown in Figure B–5a, before completing the final planning diagram (Figure B–5b), and after reviews among the various supervisory personnel, who then approved the final plan, submitted the equipment installation planning diagram to Gilmore Industries for their use in reviewing the project as it progresses.

For projects that may not be complex, there may be fewer steps in the preparation of the planning diagram. Complexibility arises when there are several areas of responsibilities by different departments in the implementation of a project. M&A is now ready to begin the scheduling phase of the Gilmore Installation Project.

USING THE PERSONAL COMPUTER

M&A is using a software package, designed especially for project management, that they plan to use in the field. Although not as complete as the project management package now being used with the mainframe computer, this package does provide a fairly complete timing schedule, an adequate bar chart schedule, and resource allocation for late start and early start schedules. In addition, the timing schedules can be sorted by the responsible subcontractors and suppliers. Milestones show the major events and interim milestones show those events that need to be completed on a timely basis to ensure a timely project completion date. Figures B–6 to B–8 show some of the reports that M&A can get from using a personal computer such as the IBM PC, HP–150, Victor, or Apple.

Using the Computer Printout Reports

The reports that M&A selected paralleled the information that they now develop by the manual approach. M&A also recognized the weakness by using the manual approach for analyzing the personnel/labor requirements, which were not conclusive. M&A would soon realize the superiority of the computer system in the analysis of personnel/labor requirements. The types of reports produced for M&A to use in planning the Gilmore Equipment Project included the following:

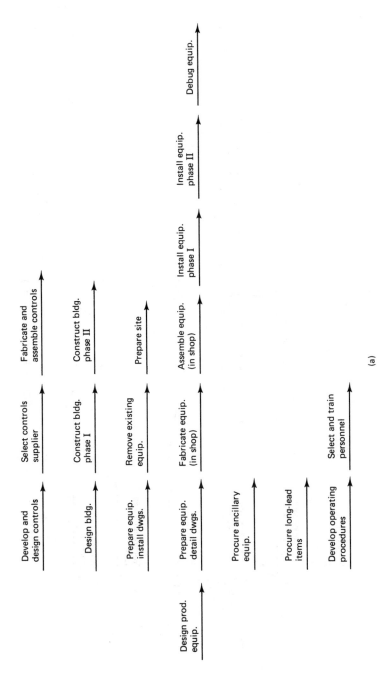

FIGURE B-4 Subdiagrams for the Gilmore Equipment Installation Project: (a) first step; (b) final step.

(a)

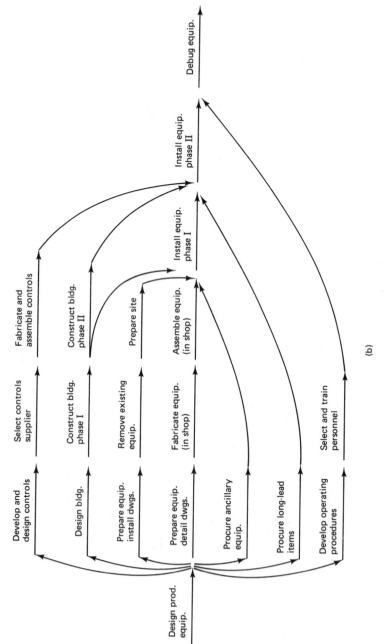

FIGURE B-4 *(Continued)*

(b)

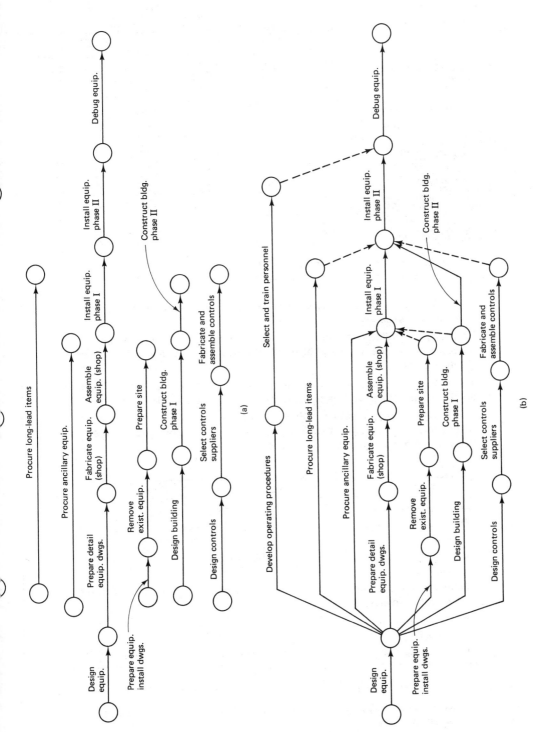

FIGURE B-5 Planning diagrams for the Gilmore Equipment Installation Project: (a) first step; (b) final step.

285

REPORT TYPE :STANDARD LISTING   PRINTING SEQUENCE :Earliest Activities First

SELECTION CRITERIA :ALL

PLAN I.D.   :GEI   VERSION 3   TIME NOW DATE   : 4/OCT/82

ACTIVITY DESCRIPTION	EARLIEST START	EARLIEST FINISH	LATEST START	LATEST FINISH	DURATION	FLOAT
1– 2 DESIGN EQUIPMENT	4/OCT/82	15/OCT/82	4/OCT/82	15/OCT/82	10	0 *
2– 5 DEVELOP & DESIGN AUTO CONTROLS	18/OCT/82	12/NOV/82	18/OCT/82	12/NOV/82	20	0 *
2– 9 DESIGN BUILDING	18/OCT/82	12/NOV/82	25/OCT/82	19/NOV/82	20	5
2– 15 PROCURE ANCILLARY EQUIPMENT	18/OCT/82	17/DEC/82	22/NOV/82	21/JAN/83	45	25
2– 12 PREPARE EQUIPMENT DETAIL DRAWINGS	18/OCT/82	5/NOV/82	6/DEC/82	24/DEC/82	15	35
2– 8 PROCURE LONG LEAD EQUIPMENT	18/OCT/82	24/DEC/82	6/DEC/82	11/FEB/83	50	35
2– 11 PREPARE EQUIPMENT INSTALLATION DRAWI	18/OCT/82	29/OCT/82	13/DEC/82	24/DEC/82	10	40
2– 3 DEVELOP OPERATING PROCEDURES	18/OCT/82	29/OCT/82	24/JAN/83	4/FEB/83	10	70
11– 16 REMOVE EXISTING EQUIPMENT	1/NOV/82	12/NOV/82	27/DEC/82	7/JAN/83	10	40
3– 4 SELECT & TRAIN PERSONNEL	1/NOV/82	19/NOV/82	7/FEB/83	25/FEB/83	15	70
12– 13 FABRICATE EQUIPMENT	8/NOV/82	26/NOV/82	27/DEC/82	14/JAN/83	15	35
5– 6 SELECT CONTROLS SUPPLIER	15/NOV/82	3/DEC/82	15/NOV/82	3/DEC/82	15	0 *
9– 18 CONSTRUCT BUILDING PHASE I	15/NOV/82	24/DEC/82	22/NOV/82	31/DEC/82	30	5
16– 17 PREPARE SITE	15/NOV/82	26/NOV/82	10/JAN/83	21/JAN/83	10	40
13– 15 ASSEMBLE EQUIPMENT(IN SHOP)	29/NOV/82	3/DEC/82	17/JAN/83	21/JAN/83	5	35
6– 7 FABRICATE & ASSEMBLE CONTROLS PACKAG	6/DEC/82	11/FEB/83	6/DEC/82	11/FEB/83	50	0 *
18– 19 CONSTRUCT BUILDING PHASE II	27/DEC/82	4/FEB/83	3/JAN/83	11/FEB/83	30	5
15– 19 INSTALL EQUIPMENT PHASE I	27/DEC/82	14/JAN/83	24/JAN/83	11/FEB/83	15	20
19– 20 INSTALL EQUIPMENT PHASE II	14/FEB/83	25/FEB/83	14/FEB/83	25/FEB/83	10	0 *
20– 21 DEBUG EQUIPMENT	28/FEB/83	4/MAR/83	28/FEB/83	4/MAR/83	5	0 *

- This schedule shows the project activities that can be started at their earliest times in that sequence.
- The critical activities can be seen in the *float* column. 0* float items are the most critical; at the other end of the float times are activities with as much as 70 days of float.
- This project fits the average ratio of critical activities to total 15%. (Of the 20 activities that comprise this project, six were most critical.)
- Using this schedule together with the listing schedule will determine what activities must be started at their earliest times without any variance to avoid a delay in the project duration.

ACTIVITY	"MUST" START	"MUST" COMPLETE
Design equipment	4/Oct/82	15/Oct/82
Develop and design automotive controls	18/Oct/82	12/Nov/82
Select controls supplier	15/Nov/82	3/Dec/82
Fabricate and assemble controls package	6/Dec/82	11/Feb/83
Install equipment: phase II	14/Feb/83	25/Feb/83
Debug equipment	28/Feb/83	4/Mar/83

FIGURE B-6 Project activities (by most critical activities first) for the Gilmore Equipment Installation Project.

```
PROJECT MANAGEMENT              GILMORE EQUIPMENT INSTALLATION        DETROIT MICHIGAN
        REPORT TYPE :MILESTONE                      PRINTING SEQUENCE  :Earliest Activities First
                                                    SELECTION CRITERIA :MILESTONE
        PLAN I.D.   :GEI    VERSION  3              TIME NOW DATE      : 4/OCT/82
================================================================================================
        MILESTONE                   EARLIEST EVENT          LATEST EVENT
        DESCRIPTION                      TIME                   TIME
================================================================================================
  1-   1 START PROJECT                 4/OCT/82              4/OCT/82
  2-   2 COMPLETE EQUIPMENT DESIGN    18/OCT/82             18/OCT/82
 15-  15 RECEIVE EQUIPMENT START PHASE I INST 27/DEC/82     24/JAN/83
 19-  19 START PHASE II INSTALLATION  14/FEB/83             14/FEB/83
 ------------------------------------------------------------------------------------------------
  7-   7 RECEIVE CONTROLS             14/FEB/83             14/FEB/83
 21-  21 START PRODUCTION              7/MAR/83              7/MAR/83
================================================================================================
```

- This report summarizes the major events, including interim milestones.
- Several of the milestones are designated as critical events.
- These are shown by the *earliest event time* and *latest event time* for each milestone having the same date.
- Milestones showing different dates for earliest event time and latest event time can either mean there is float available or that the milestone may be behind:
  - There is float available at a milestone when the latest event date is later than the earliest event date.
  - The milestone is projected to be behind planned schedule when the latest event date shows an earlier date than the earliest event date.

FIGURE B-7 Milestone report for the Gilmore Equipment Installation Project.

- Work schedule report (early start schedule)
  - Lists all the specified work items
  - Shows the early and late start and finish dates.
  - Lists total and free floats
- Weekly bar chart (early start schedule)
  - Represents graphically the duration and the relative time frame of all work items
  - Graphic representation placed on a weekly time scale
- Scheduled earnings report
  - Lists cost status of all specified work items
  - Shows current and projected cost performance
- Resource utilization reports represent graphically the utilization of designers, drafters, and engineers using the early start and late start schedules

The available number of designers and engineers, six and eight, respectively, are not exceeded on any given day.

```
PROJECT MANAGEMENT                              GILMORE EQUIPMENT INSTALLATION                                    DETROIT MICHIGAN
         REPORT TYPE :COMPRESSED PERIOD BARCHART                                  PRINTING SEQUENCE  :Earliest Activities First
                                                                                 SELECTION CRITERIA :ALL
         PLAN I.D.   :GEI      VERSION  3                                         TIME NOW DATE      : 4/OCT/82
================================================1982===========================================1983=====================================
    PERIOD COMMENCING DATE        14 I11 I18I25 I1 I8   I15I22 I29I6  I13I20  I27I3  I10I17 I24I31 I7 I14 I21I28 I7 I14 I
    MONTH                         IOCT I  I    INOV I  I   I IDEC I  I  IJANI  I  I  I  IFEB I  I  IMAR   I
    PERIOD COMMENCING TIME UNIT   I2 I7  I12I17 I22I27 I32I37 I42I47 I52I57 I62I67 I72I77 I82I87 I92I97 I102  I112   I
================================================================================================================================
 1-  2 DESIGN EQUIPMENT               ICC ICCC I  I   I   I  I    I   I    I    I    I    I    I    I    I   I    I
 2-  5 DEVELOP & DESIGN AUTO CONTROLS I   I    ICC ICCC ICC ICCC I    I    I    I    I    I    I    I    I    I   I
 2-  9 DESIGN BUILDING               I   I    I==I===I==I===I...I.  I    I    I    I    I    I    I    I    I   I
 2- 15 PROCURE ANCILLARY EQUIPMENT   I   I    I==I===I==I===I==I===I==I===I=..I..I.I..I.I..I.I..I.I...I  I    I    I   I

 2- 12 PREPARE EQUIPMENT DETAIL DRAWI I   I    I==I===I==I=..I.I..I.I..I.I..I.I..I.I...I    I    I    I    I    I   I
 2-  8 PROCURE LONG LEAD EQUIPMENT   I   I    I==I===I==I===I==I===I==I===I==I===I==I===I    I    I    I    I   I
 2- 11 PREPARE EQUIPMENT INSTALLATION I   I   I==I===I=..I.I..I.I..I.I..I.I..I.I..I.I.  I    I    I    I    I   I
 2-  3 DEVELOP OPERATING PROCEDURES   I   I    I==I===I=..I.I..I.I..I.I..I.I..I.I..I.I...I    I    I    I    I   I

11- 16 REMOVE EXISTING EQUIPMENT     I   I  I   I    I==I===I=..I.I..I.I..I.I..I.I..I.I...I    I    I    I    I   I
 3-  4 SELECT & TRAIN PERSONNEL      I   I  I   I    I==I===I==I=..I.I..I.I..I.I..I.I..I.I.  I    I    I    I   I
12- 13 FABRICATE EQUIPMENT           I   I  I   I    I==I===I==I===I==I===I==I===I==I===I.  I    I    I    I   I
 5-  6 SELECT CONTROLS SUPPLIER      I   I  I   I    I  I    ICC ICCC ICC IC  I    I    I    I    I    I    I   I

 9- 18 CONSTRUCT BUILDING PHASE I    I   I  I   I  I  I    I==I===I==I===I==I===I..I.   I    I    I    I    I   I
16- 17 PREPARE SITE                  I   I  I   I  I  I    I==I===I=..I.I..I.I..I.I..I.I..I.I...I   I    I    I   I
13- 15 ASSEMBLE EQUIPMENT(IN SHOP)   I   I  I   I  I  I    I   I==I=..I.I..I.I..I.I..I.I..I.I..I.I...I   I    I   I
 6-  7 FABRICATE & ASSEMBLE CONTROLS I   I  I   I  I  I  I  I   I    ICCC ICC ICCC ICC ICCC ICC ICCC ICC ICCC ICC IC  I    I   I

18- 19 CONSTRUCT BUILDING PHASE II   I   I  I  I  I  I  I  I  I  I    I  I    I==I===I==I===I==I===I..I..I.    I    I   I
15- 19 INSTALL EQUIPMENT PHASE I     I   I  I  I  I  I  I  I  I  I    I  I    I==I===I==I=..I.I..I.I..I.I.  I    I    I   I
19- 20 INSTALL EQUIPMENT PHASE II    I   I  I  I  I  I  I  I  I  I    I  I    I   I    I  I    I  ICCC ICC IC  I    I   I
20- 21 DEBUG EQUIPMENT               I   I  I  I  I  I  I  I  I  I    I  I    I   I    I  I    I   I   ICCC I   I   I
================================================================================================================================
Barchart Key:-  CCC :Critical Activities   ===:Non Critical Activities   NNN :Activity with neg float   ... :Float
```

- The project is planned to start with *design equipment* the first week in October 1982.

- The project is planned to complete with *debug equipment* the first week in March 1983.

- This bar chart provides weekly accuracy and can be used as a display for use by higher management levels.

- The chart offers the opportunity to view the overall project schedule showing the timing relationship of each activity's starting date, duration, finish date, and total and free floats.

FIGURE B-8 Weekly bar chart (early start schedule) for the Gilmore Equipment Installation Project.

M&A uses the bar chart printout for a display attachment in the status report to management. Although it does provide limited accuracy (depending on the total length of the project), the total project schedule can be reviewed on one sheet. The overall project schedule does show, in addition to a summary bar chart, the timing relationship of each project item's early start and finish dates, latest start, and total float.

Preparing Project Status Reports

After the timing schedules are developed, M&A can compare actual progress with the planned schedule. M&A project personnel communicate the project status to all levels of their management and to Gilmore Industries through a project status report. This status report contains the following documents: (1) cover letter, (2) executive highlights, and (3) summary progress schedule (including a bar chart). The basic differences between the bar chart used in the summary progress schedule and the one used in the progress schedule is that (1) the summary schedule uses the latest start–latest finish approach submitted to the higher levels of management, whereas (2) the progress schedule employs the early start–early finish schedule and is a working tool of the persons directly engaged in the implementation of the project.

Cover Letter. M&A will use this letter to communicate to Gilmore Industries a summary of the progress, anticipated completion dates of major events, brief statements concerning the status of critical items, and statements of resolutions to any potential project duration delays. The cover letter that summarized the status as of November 8, 1982, is shown in Figure B–9.

November 15, 1982

Gilmore Industries

Subject: November 8 Status
           Gilmore Equipment Installation Project

   Subject project at this time indicates the completion date to be March 21, 1983, 2 weeks beyond the planned completion date. The delay is caused by changes being made to the automatic controls design.
   It is anticipated that the changes will simplify the control systems and could shorten the fabrication time. We shall discuss this matter with the supplier who will fabricate the controls package in an attempt to shorten the fabrication time by at least 2 weeks.
   For further information on the status to date, we are attaching progress status highlights and a summary bar chart.

M&A Corporation

FIGURE B-9   Cover letter summarizing progress of the Gilmore Equipment Installation Project.

Executive Highlights. This feature used by M&A is an attachment to the cover letter that lists important happenings that will influence the project status. Important aspects of the project are structured in the listing in the form of bullets (•). Each point consists of a brief sentence or a maximum of two sentences. If the progress status report is to be brief, the highlights can be included with the cover letter. The highlights as of November 8, 1982, are shown in Figure B–10.

Summary Progress Schedule. The summary progress schedule depicting progress in a summary form allows M&A's client, Gilmore Industries, the ability to review the overall project progress on one attachment. The countless details associated with the day-to-day activities are summarized, and the management-by-exception technique of drawing most attention to critical items is applied. This summary schedule shows the following information:

- A graphic portrayal of the status, including changes to the planned completion date
- The actual progress status compared to the original plan

Calculating Designer Requirements

M&A is concerned over the availability of designers they will need for the Gilmore Installation Project and is using the resource utilization reports to select a schedule that will satisfy both the project timing requirements and the restriction on the number of designers available for this project, which is four. Using the early start schedule, the graph shown in Figure B–11 portrays the daily number of designers required weekly. Other schedules, late start and late finish (adjusted for float), were also used for comparison and to evaluate the schedule most appropriate to use.

- Building designs are 1 to 2 weeks behind the planned schedule, but with the available float time, this should cause no delays in having the building ready for starting the installation of the equipment.
- Preparation of equipment designs and details are on schedule.
- Procurement of the long-lead items and the ancillary equipment is proceeding as planned.
- Designers of the automatic controls have encountered problems that may result in a 2-week delay in the project.
- Project now expected to be completed March 21.

FIGURE B–10 Executive highlights of progress of the Gilmore Equipment Installation Project.

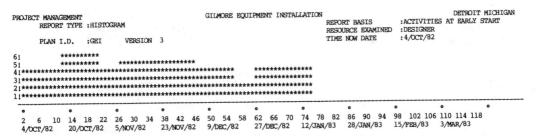

- With the early start schedule, designers are required from the week of October 4, 1982, to the week of January 10, 1983, a period of 15 weeks.
- The number of designers required daily varies from a maximum of six during the weeks of October 18 and 25 to a minimum of two during the week of December 2.
- There is a poor distribution of designers required during the period October 4 to January 10.
- A total of 330 designer days are required during this period.
- With five designers, the maximum available daily, the project duration during the week of February 29 does not have to be extended.

FIGURE B-11 Designer utilization (early start schedule) for the Gilmore Equipment Installation Project.

The early start schedule revealed a poor distribution of designers. The next schedule used was the late start schedule shown in Figure B-12. The project duration of this schedule remains the same as the early start schedule. The computer calculations present a display of all the project items that have float to be shown starting at this latest start. Total daily designer requirements are then totaled.

The late start schedule revealed just as poor a distribution of designers over the period of the project as noted in the early start schedule. Both these two schedules showed that more designers are required during specific periods than are available.

Calculating Draftperson Requirements

Following the same scheduling procedure as for designers, M&A completed the analysis of requirements compared with the availability of draftpersons. Figure B-13 shows the draftperson requirements using the early start schedule.

Although there is a good distribution of draftpersons in the early start sched-

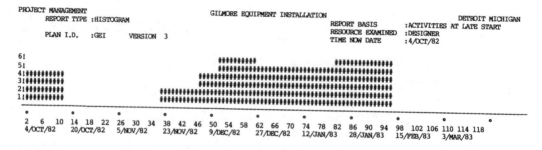

PROJECT MANAGEMENT
    REPORT TYPE : HISTOGRAM

    PLAN I.D.   :GEI   VERSION 3

GILMORE EQUIPMENT INSTALLATION   DETROIT MICHIGAN
              REPORT BASIS   :ACTIVITIES AT LATE START
              RESOURCE EXAMINED :DESIGNER
              TIME NOW DATE   :4/OCT/82

- With the late start schedule, designers are required from the week of October 4, 1982, to the week of February 7, 1983, with the exception of the period October 18 to November 15, when no designers will be required. There is a net total of 14 weeks when designers are required.

- The number of designers required daily varies from a maximum of five weeks during the weeks of December 6 and 13 to a minimum of none during the period October 18 to November 15.

- There is a poor distribution of designers required during period October 4 to February 28.

- A total of 330 designer days are required during this period.

FIGURE B-12   Designer utilization (late start schedule) for the Gilmore Equipment Installation Project.

ule, the number required far exceeds the number available. M&A now investigates the late start schedule, which is shown in Figure B–14.

Calculating Engineer Requirements

Following the same scheduling procedure as for draftsmen, M&A completed the analysis of requirements compared with the availability of engineers. Figure B–15 shows the engineer requirements using the early start schedule. Figure B–16 shows the engineer requirements using the late start schedule.

Preparing Resource Utilization Reports

Manual calculations used to determine personnel/labor requirements do not provide satisfactory planning information, so M&A used the computer calculations in arriv-

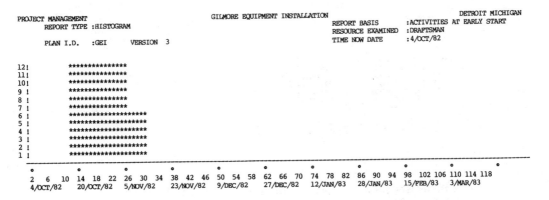

PROJECT MANAGEMENT · · · · · · · · · · · · · · · · · · GILMORE EQUIPMENT INSTALLATION · DETROIT MICHIGAN
   REPORT TYPE :HISTOGRAM · REPORT BASIS · · · · :ACTIVITIES AT EARLY START
· RESOURCE EXAMINED · :DRAFTSMAN
   PLAN I.D. · · :GEI · · · · VERSION 3 · TIME NOW DATE · · · · :4/OCT/82

- With the early start schedule, drafters are required from the week of October 18, 1982, to the week of November 8, 1982, a total of 4 weeks.
- During the foregoing period, the number of draftpersons required varies from a maximum of twelve for the weeks of October 18 to November 1, to a minimum of six for the week of November 8.
- There is a good distribution of draftpersons required during the period.
- A total of 210 draftperson days are required during this period.
- If six draftpersons are the maximum available daily and if the project completion during the week of February 28 needs to be maintained with the early start schedule, then overtime, added equipment, or expedited shipments are some items that need to be considered during the weeks of October 18 and 25 and November 1, when more than six draftpersons are needed.

FIGURE B-13 Drafter utilization (early start schedule) for the Gilmore Equipment Installation Project.

ing at decisions to develop a satisfactory labor/personnel schedule. The manual calculations did reveal two major concerns:

1. To achieve a uniform daily distribution of personnel/labor requirements will be difficult within the planned project duration.
2. The major personnel concerns are designers, drafters, and engineers. The number required daily exceeds the number that are available.

The computer software package that will be used will permit M&A to analyze the impact of the project duration by extending the completion date. By making use

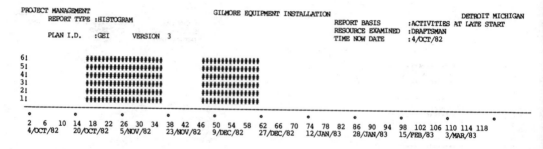

FIGURE B-14 Drafter utilization (late start schedule) for the Gilmore Equipment Installation Project.

of the float times of the noncritical project activities, the computer can apply rapid and accurate calculations in an attempt to achieve as uniform a distribution as possible for personnel requirements.

The resource summary data are shown in Figures B–17 and B–18. The early start schedule shown in Figure B–17 is a distribution summary on a weekly basis. The histogram allows for a daily count. The schedule shows:

- Average personnel per day on a weekly basis
- Total weekly costs

Similar data are shown in Figure B–18 on a latest start basis. A summary of the distribution is shown in Figure B–19.

Next, M&A used the comparison chart (Figure B–19) with the resource sum-

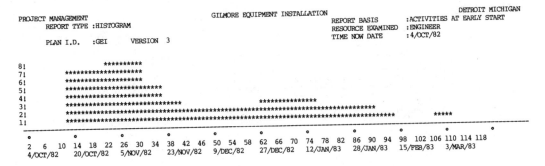

- With the early start schedule, engineers are required from the week of October 18, 1982 to February 28, 1983, a period of 20 weeks.
- The number of engineers required daily varies from a maximum of eight during the weeks of November 1 and 8 to a minimum of one during the weeks of February 7, 14, 21, and 28.
- There is a poor distribution of engineers during the period October 18 to February 28.
- A total of 325 engineer days are required during this period.
- If five engineers are the maximum available daily, and if the project duration cannot be extended and the early start schedule is to be maintained, then overtime, added equipment, or expedited shipments are some items that need to be considered during the weeks of November 1 and 8, when more than five engineers are needed.

FIGURE B-15   Engineer utilization (early start schedule) for the Gilmore Equipment Installation Project.

mary data (Figures B–17 and B–18) to determine whether the individual schedule revisions (including delaying the project) would justify the added overtime required to make for the deficiency in the number of personnel required. This comparison will show whether the added cost of overtime is worth requesting an extension of the project from Gilmore Industries.

In the final analysis, M&A decided that to sustain the good relationship of Gilmore Industries (as well as the building and equipment contractors who would need to change their scheduling), they would use the late start schedule as a guide and complete the project as planned.

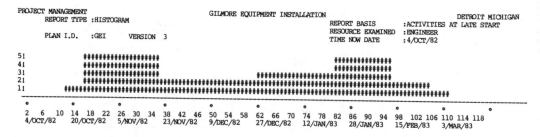

> - With the late start schedule, engineers are required from the week of October 18, 1982 to the week of February 28, 1982, a total of 20 weeks.
> - During this period the number of engineers varies from a maximum of five during the weeks of October 25, November 1, 8, and 15, January 24 and 31, and February 7 to a minimum of one during the weeks of October 18 and February 18.
> - There is a poor distribution of engineers required during the period October 18 to February 28.
> - A total of 325 engineer days are required during this period.

FIGURE B-16   Engineer utilization (late start schedule) for the Gilmore Equipment Installation Project.

The computer reports shown in Figures B–20 to B–23 relate to the costs of this project. As costs are also a resource, the reports are shown in the form of histograms, the same form in which the labor/personnel were shown. In another graphic form the costs are accumulated over the total project and depicted as a *cost flow curve*.

As the project gets under way, M&A will use these reports to compare the planned expenditures (shown on Figure B–21, if the early start schedule is being used; or Figure B–23, if the late start schedule is used) with the actual expenditures. Comparison of Figures B–21 and B–23 provides a good example of how costs are related to time.

When the early start schedule is used, by the third week in October, $22,700 will have been spent; with the late start schedule, it is late November before $20,760 will have been spent. Using the late start schedule may be significant if M&A receives monthly performance payments and would like to use these funds for their expenditures. A payment on November 1 would help toward the expenditure that will be incurred in the month of November. M&A would also use the cash flow curve to supplement the indicated cost outcome report by graphically depicting the comparison of planned versus actual expenditures.

```
PROJECT MANAGEMENT                  GILMORE EQUIPMENT INSTALLATION                       DETROIT MICHIGAN
     REPORT TYPE :COMPLETE RESOURCES REPORT              REPORT BASIS     :ACTIVITIES AT EARLY START
                 :AVERAGE DAILY DEMAND PER WEEK          SELECTION CRITERIA :ALL
     PLAN I.D.   :GEI    VERSION 3                       TIME NOW DATE     :4/OCT/82

   DE=DESIGNER              DP=DAILY COST IN HUNDREDS   $P=CASH FLOW IN HUNDREDS   EN=ENGINEER
   DR=DRAFTSMAN
```

	DE	DP	$P	EN	DR
4/OCT/82	4	2.00	2.00		
11/OCT/82	4	2.00	2.00		
18/OCT/82	6	41.40	41.40	7	12
25/OCT/82	6	41.40	41.40	7	12
1/NOV/82	4	45.40	45.40	8	12
8/NOV/82	5	51.80	51.80	8	6
15/NOV/82	5	106.80	106.80	5	
22/NOV/82	5	104.80	104.80	3	
29/NOV/82	5	94.80	94.80	2	
6/DEC/82	4	79.00	79.00	2	
13/DEC/82	4	79.00	79.00	2	
20/DEC/82	2	67.00	67.00	2	
27/DEC/82	4	41.33	41.33	3	
3/JAN/83	4	41.33	41.33	3	
10/JAN/83	4	41.33	41.33	3	
17/JAN/83		33.33	33.33	2	
24/JAN/83		33.33	33.33	2	
31/JAN/83		33.33	33.33	2	
7/FEB/83		5.00	5.00	1	
14/FEB/83		8.00	8.00		
21/FEB/83		8.00	8.00		
28/FEB/83		6.00	6.00	1	
7/MAR/83					
14/MAR/83					
21/MAR/83					
28/MAR/83					

FIGURE B-17 Weekly resource summary based on early start schedule for the Gilmore Equipment Installation Project.

```
PROJECT MANAGEMENT                  GILMORE EQUIPMENT INSTALLATION                       DETROIT MICHIGAN
     REPORT TYPE :COMPLETE RESOURCES REPORT              REPORT BASIS     :ACTIVITIES AT LATE START
                 :AVERAGE DAILY DEMAND PER WEEK          SELECTION CRITERIA :ALL
     PLAN I.D.   :GEI    VERSION 3                       TIME NOW DATE     :4/OCT/82

   DE=DESIGNER              DP=DAILY COST IN HUNDREDS   $P=CASH FLOW IN HUNDREDS   EN=ENGINEER
   DR=DRAFTSMAN
```

	DE	DP	$P	EN	DR
4/OCT/82	4	2.00	2.00		
11/OCT/82	4	2.00	2.00		
18/OCT/82		0.80	0.80	1	
25/OCT/82		10.80	10.80	5	6
1/NOV/82		10.80	10.80	5	6
8/NOV/82		10.80	10.80	5	6
15/NOV/82		10.80	10.80	5	6
22/NOV/82	2	62.80	62.80	2	
29/NOV/82	2	62.80	62.80	2	
6/DEC/82	4	82.60	82.60	2	6
13/DEC/82	6	83.60	83.60	2	6
20/DEC/82	6	83.60	83.60	2	6
27/DEC/82	5	94.00	94.00	3	
3/JAN/83	5	72.33	72.33	3	
10/JAN/83	5	87.33	87.33	3	
17/JAN/83	5	97.33	97.33	3	
24/JAN/83	6	55.33	55.33	5	
31/JAN/83	6	55.33	55.33	5	
7/FEB/83	6	55.33	55.33	5	
14/FEB/83		10.00	10.00	2	
21/FEB/83		10.00	10.00	2	
28/FEB/83		6.00	6.00	1	
7/MAR/83					
14/MAR/83					
21/MAR/83					
28/MAR/83					

FIGURE B-18 Weekly resource summary (latest start schedule) for the Gilmore Equipment Installation Project.

	Weeks Required	Personnel/Labor Distribution	Range Max.	Range Min.	Last Date Required (Week of)
Designers					Project start: October 4, 1982
Early start	15	Poor	6	2	1/10/83
Late start	14	Fair	5	0	2/7/83
Draftsmen					
Early start	4	Good	12	6	11/29/82
Late start	7	Good	6	6	12/20/82
Engineers					
Early start	20	Fair	8	1	2/28/83
Late start	20	Fair	5	1	2/28/83

FIGURE B-19 Personnel requirements comparison of early start and late start schedules for the Gilmore Equipment Installation Project.

```
PROJECT MANAGEMENT                              GILMORE EQUIPMENT INSTALLATION                          DETROIT MICHIGAN
       REPORT TYPE :HISTOGRAM                                              REPORT BASIS      :ACTIVITIES AT EARLY START
                                                                          RESOURCE EXAMINED :DAILY COST IN HUNDREDS
          PLAN I.D.   :GEI     VERSION 3                                   TIME NOW DATE     :4/OCT/82
200!
195!
190!
185!
180!
175!
170!
165!
160!
155!
150!
145!
140!
135!
130!
125!
120!
115!
110!                     *****
105!                     **********
100!                     **********
95 !                     ***************
90 !                     ****************
85 !                     ****************
80 !                     **************************
75 !                     **************************
70 !                     *********************************
65 !                     *********************************
60 !                     *********************************
55 !                 ************************************
50 !                 ************************************
45 !         *****************************************************
40 !         *****************************************************
35 !         ************************************************************
30 !         ************************************************************
25 !         ************************************************************
20 !         ************************************************************
15 !         ************************************************************
10 !         ********************************************************         ***************
5  !*****************************************************************************************
   --------------------------------------------------------------------------------------------------
    2   6   10  14  18  22  26  30  34  38  42  46  50  54  58  62  66  70  74  78  82  86  90  94  98  102 106 110 114 118
    4/OCT/82    20/OCT/82    5/NOV/82    23/NOV/82    9/DEC/82    27/DEC/82    12/JAN/83    28/JAN/83    15/FEB/83    3/MAR/83
```

FIGURE B-20 Daily cost (in hundreds of dollars) for the Gilmore Equipment Installation Project.

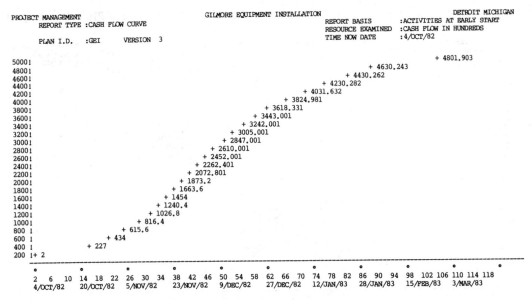

FIGURE B-21 Cumulative cost (in hundreds of dollars) for the Gilmore Equipment Installation Project.

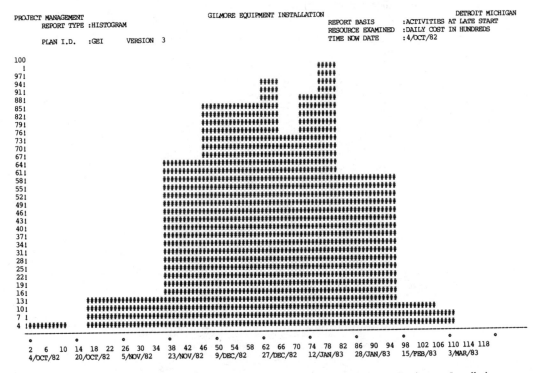

FIGURE B-22 Daily cost (in hundreds of dollars) for the Gilmore Equipment Installation Project (late start schedule).

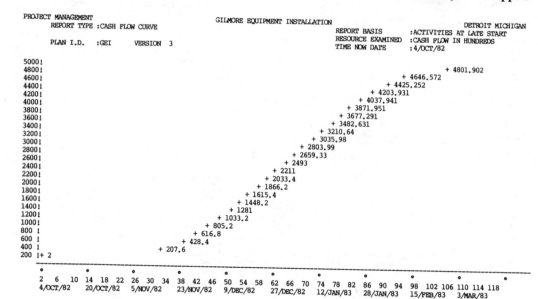

PROJECT MANAGEMENT
    REPORT TYPE :CASH FLOW CURVE   GILMORE EQUIPMENT INSTALLATION   DETROIT MICHIGAN
                                                                 REPORT BASIS   :ACTIVITIES AT LATE START
         PLAN I.D.   :GEI   VERSION 3   RESOURCE EXAMINED   :CASH FLOW IN HUNDREDS
                                                                 TIME NOW DATE   :4/OCT/82

```
5000!
4800!                                                                                    + 4801.902
4600!                                                                           + 4646.572
4400!                                                                      + 4425.252
4200!                                                                  + 4203.931
4000!                                                              + 4037.941
3800!                                                           + 3871.951
3600!                                                        + 3677.291
3400!                                                     + 3482.631
3200!                                                 + 3210.64
3000!                                              + 3035.98
2800!                                          + 2803.99
2600!                                       + 2659.33
2400!                                    + 2493
2200!                                 + 2211
2000!                              + 2033.4
1800!                           + 1866.2
1600!                        + 1615.4
1400!                     + 1448.2
1200!                  + 1281
1000!               + 1033.2
800 !            + 805.2
600 !         + 616.8
400 !      + 428.4
200 !+ 2 + 207.6
```

```
    2    6    10   14   18   22   26   30   34   38   42   46   50   54   58   62   66   70   74   78   82   86   90   94   98  102  106  110  114  118
  4/OCT/82      20/OCT/82      5/NOV/82       23/NOV/82      9/DEC/82      27/DEC/82      12/JAN/83      28/JAN/83      15/FEB/83      3/MAR/83
```

FIGURE B–23 Cumulative cost (in hundreds of dollars) for the Gilmore Equipment Installation Project (late start schedule).

Index